CYCLING
ORANGE COUNTY

58 Rides with Detailed Maps & Elevation Contours

BY DON AND SHARRON BRUNDIGE

SUNBELT PUBLICATIONS
San Diego, California

Cycling Orange County
Sunbelt Publications, Inc.
Copyright © 2007 by Don and Sharron Brundige
All rights reserved.
First edition 1988. Second edition 2007.

Edited by Jennifer Redmond
Cover design by Kathleen Wise
Composition by W.G. Hample and Associates
Project management by Jennifer Redmond
Photography by Don and Sharron Brundige, unless noted.
Printed in the United States of America

Sunbelt Publications, Inc.
P.O. Box 191126
San Diego, CA 92159-1126
(619) 258-4911, fax: (619) 258-4916
www.sunbeltbooks.com

10 09 08 07 06   5 4 3 2 1

"Adventures in the Natural History and Cultural Heritage of the Californias"
A Series Edited by Lowell Lindsay

Library of Congress Cataloging-in-Publication Data

Brundige, Don.
  Cycling Orange County / by Don and Sharron Brundige.
        p. cm.
  Includes index.
  ISBN-13: 978-0-932653-80-2
  ISBN-10: 0-932653-80-4
  1. Bicycle touring—California—Orange County—Guidebooks. 2. Orange County (Calif.)—Guidebooks. I. Brundige, Sharron. II. Title.

GV1045.5.C22O733 2006
796.6'40979496
                                                    2006030084

Cover Photograph by Linda McMillan Pyle: San Juan Creek from *Orange County Day Journeys and Picnics* by Linda McMillan Pyle. Used with permission.
Title page photograph: Irvine's South Lake

CONTENTS

51 Trips and 58 Rides

DEDICATION

To our family
....Who we love very much

George, Bernice, Don, Pat, Kathie, Jim, Stevie, Rich, Pon, Eric,
Astrid, Zoltan, Kyali, Greta, Sammie, Greg, Mark, Caitlyn, Mandy,
Pete, Diane, Bradley, Michelle, Vlad II, Ayana, and Vlad III.

ACKNOWLEDGMENTS

We offer our thanks to family, friends and bicycling acquaintances who gave us ideas, advice and plenty of encouragement while developing this biking book. This includes a "thank you" to the state, county and city agencies and individuals who offered their services and publications. Kudos to Sam Nunez, Robert Simms and the folks we met on the road, for sharing the tours. We also show particular gratitude to our venerable crew that was kind enough to review and comment on our original manuscript: Jill Morales, Al Hook and Walt Bond. We also thank Bernice Palmquist for her updates to our previously published book. Thank you Jacqui Broom and Alex Moi for helping us through so many computer crises.

We specifically wish to acknowledge the following individuals and/or organizations who provided some excellent ideas for bicycle trips in the original book: Donald K. Jensen and Toshio Kuba of the City of Buena Park; the Community Services Departments of Huntington Beach and Tustin; the Citizen's Advisory Committee of Newport Beach; the City of Costa Mesa; CALTRANS District 07: Public Transportation and Ridesharing Branch: Sherri Miller and Richard Sherry of the Orange County Environmental Management Agency: Transportation Planning; and Mary Shimono of the City of Rancho Santa Margarita.

Finally, we wish to thank our most recent contributors: Richard Sherry, Sherri Miller and Harry Persaud of the County of Orange Planning and Services Department; Will and Kathi Decker of the *Southern California Bicyclist* magazine for keeping us on our toes to update our tours; and Dick Farrar, Dave Monshaw, Mandie Loren, Bill Barr, Mary Beth Grigg, Gene Adler, Steven Izumi, Cheryl Denson, and Rod and Sandy Colianni, all local cycling enthusiasts, for providing corrections/updates to some of our previous ride descriptions.

INTRODUCTION

As with all our books, we wanted to provide a trip guide that concentrates on trip navigation, contains a large number of well-documented trips, provides the necessary trip maps and elevation contours, and is reasonably priced. Hopefully, we succeeded!

This guide was developed based on biking trips revisited in 2006 and corrections/ updates supplied by book users since the last printing. This is a new edition of our classic *Bicycle Rides: Orange County*, in a smaller, handier format, by Sunbelt Publications.

There are over 800 <u>one-way</u> bike miles and 51 on-road trips which blanket Orange County. Trips of exceptional length or complexity are broken down into segments or "rides." There are 58 rides included, and each ride is written to be as complete and self-standing as possible. The authors and riding buddies used 18-speed bicycles, although the vast majority of trips can be ridden with bikes having fewer gears. The few rides which are more amenable to hybrid and or fat-tire ("balloon-tire") bikes are noted. In no cases are mountain bikes required.

A cross section of trips is provided. There are some short-length family trips on separated bikepaths, many longer exploratory and workout trips for more experienced bikers on various quality bike routes, and a few "gut-buster" trips on open roadway for the most physically fit and motivated cyclists. The trip domains include cities, parks, beaches, harbors, rivers, lakes, valleys, canyons, and mountains. The trips vary from extremely scenic to somewhat monotonous (for example, certain stretches of the high-mileage concrete "wastelands" along the Class I river routes). There is a little something for everybody.

The strong emphasis in this book is "getting from here to there." This navigation is provided using detailed route descriptions in terms of landmarks, mileage, elevation contours, and a quality set of trip maps. Scenery, vistas, and scenic or historic landmarks and sightseeing attractions are regularly noted for each trip, although detailed information about these features must be sought out in other publications. Public restrooms and sources of water are identified on those few trips where these facilities are available. Pleasant rest spots are also pointed out. Finally, "wine and dine" spots are noted for two specific circumstances: 1) where places to eat along the route are scarce; and 2) where the establishment is too unique or exceptional not to mention.

HOW TO USE THIS BOOK

There are two ways to use this book: one way is for the person who wants to enjoy the research along with enjoying the bike ride, and another way for the biker who is just anxious to get out there "amongst em."

For the "anxious biker," follow Steps 1 through 5 below and split!

1. Check the "BEST RIDES BY CATEGORY" trip summary noted on the inside cover for candidate trips or use the "Master Trip Map" in the "TRIP ORGANIZA-TION" section to select areas of interest for the bike ride. Note the candidate trip numbers. (Another option is to select a trip by using the "INDEX TO LAND-MARKS AND ATTRACTIONS BY TRIP NUMBER," pages 203-205.)
2. Go to the "Master Trip Matrices" in the "TRIP ORGANIZATION" section and narrow down the number of candidate trips by reviewing their general features.
3. Read about the individual trips and select one. Make a photocopy of the trip(s) of interest subject to the copyright limitations noted on page ii.
4. Read and understand the safety rules described in the "GENERAL BIKING CON-SIDERATIONS" section and review the "CHECKLIST" section.
5. See you later. Enjoy the ride!

For the more methodical folks, continue reading the next chapter. By the time you're through, you'll understand the trip description and maps much better than the "anxious biker."

TRIP ORGANIZATION

This bike book is organized by trip number. Extended length trips are broken down into trip segments by ride number, which is the trip number plus a letter. Thus, Trip #17 is the "Santa Ana River Trail," while Ride #17A is the "Green River Road to Yorba Linda Park" segment. Trip numbers are in a general sequence governed by whether the tours are coastal, river, inland or special tours. Refer back to the "TABLE OF CON-TENTS" for the entire trip list.

The "Master Trip Maps" show the general trailhead location of trips using a circled reference number (i.e., ⑦ refers to Trip #7). Extended length trips are identified by circled numbers at both beginning and terminal points.

The "Master Trip Matrices" provide a quick reference for selecting candidate trips and for more detailed reading evaluation. The matrices are organized by trip number. The key trip descriptors provided in those matrices are briefly explained in the foot-notes at the below of the last matrix (page 8). A more detailed explanation of those descriptors is provided in the "TRIP DESCRIPTION/ TERMINOLOGY" section which follows.

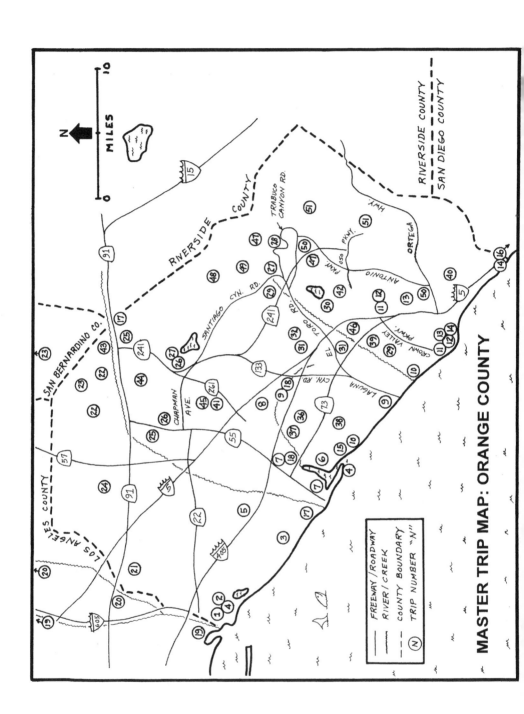

MASTER TRIP MAP: ORANGE COUNTY

FREEWAY / ROADWAY
RIVER / CREEK
COUNTY BOUNDARY
Ⓝ TRIP NUMBER "N"

MASTER TRIP MATRIX

| TRIP NO. | GENERAL LOCATION | LEVEL OF DIFFICULTY | | | ROUTE QUALITY | | | TRIP CHARACT.[2] | COMMENTS |
		L.O.D.[1]	MILES	ELEV.	BIKE TRAIL (%)	BIKE LANE (%)	OTHER (%)		
1	Seal Beach-Sunset Beach	E (r/t)	4.3 (1-w)	Flat	-	60	40	S, L, S/A	Seal Beach to Sunset Beach
2	Huntington Beach	E(1-w) M(r/t)	12.0 (r/t)	Flat	-	30	70	S, N, L, S/A	Sunset Aquatic Park/ Huntington Harbor
3	Huntington Beach	E	4.7	Flat	100	-	-	S, N, L, S/A	Huntington Central Park Loop
4	Sunset Beach-Newport Beach	E(1-w) M(r/t)	13.8	Flat	90	10	-	S, L, S/A	Sunset Beach to Newport Beach Strand
5	Fountain Valley	E	7.6	Flat	100	-	-	S, L, S/A	Mile Square Park Loop
6	Newport Beach	M	6.2	Mod.	-	90	10	S, N, S/A	Upper Newport Bay Loop
7	Newport Beach, Irvine	M	24.4	Mod.-Steep	15	80	5	S, N, L, S/A	Newport Beach/Irvine City Loop
8	Irvine, Tustin	M(r/t)	15.6	Flat	-	100	-	S, L	Irvine Bikeway (Loop) + Numerous Spur Trips
9	Irvine, Laguna Canyon, Laguna Beach	M(1-w) M-S(r/t)	10.6	Mod.	-	10	90	S, L, S/A,	Laguna Canyon Road
10	Corona Del Mar - Laguna Beach	M (1-w) M-S (r/t)	9.1 (1-w)	Mod.-Steep	-	70	30	S, L, E	Laguna Beach City Tour
11	Mission Viejo, Laguna Beach	M (1-w) M (r/t)	7.0 (1-w)	Mod.	-	100	-	S, E	Laguna Niguel Bikeway (+ various return options)
12	Mission Viejo-San Juan Capistrano	E (1-w) E-M (r/t)	6.9 (1-w)	Flat	50	50	-	S, L, S/A	Doheny Bikeway
13	San Juan Capistrano-Dana Point	M	17.2	Mod.	60	40	10	S, N, L, S/A	Del Obispo Bikeway, San Juan Creek Loop

1,2 See footnotes on page 8

MASTER TRIP MATRIX

TRIP NO.	GENERAL LOCATION	LEVEL OF DIFFICULTY			ROUTE QUALITY			TRIP CHARACT.[2]	COMMENTS
		L.O.D.[1]	MILES	ELEV.	BIKE TRAIL (%)	BIKE LANE (%)	OTHER (%)		
14	Dana Point-San Clemente	M	17.1	Mod.	20	70	10	S, L, S/A	Doheny Beach-San Clemente Loop
15	Newport Beach-Corona Del Mar	M	10.1	Mod.	-	40	60	S, L, S/A	Newport Beach-Corona Del Mar Beach Loop
16	San Clemente-Oceanside-San Diego	S (1-w) VS(r/t)	67.2 (1-w)	Mod.-Steep	20	80	-	S, N, L, S/A, E, M	San Clemente-San Diego Bicentennial Bike Route
17	Santa Ana Canyon-Huntington Beach	M (1-w) S(r/t)	30.6 (1-w)	Flat	90	5	5	S, N, L, M	Santa Ana River Trail (Santa Ana Canyon-Ocean)
17A	Santa Ana Canyon-Yorba Linda	M (1-w) M(r/t)	7.4 (1-w)	Mod.	100	-	-	S, N	Green River Road to Yorba Regional Park
17B	Yorba Linda-Placentia-Orange	E(1-w) M(r/t)	10.0 (1-w)	Flat	100	-	-	S, L	Yorba Regional Park to El Camino Real Park
17C	Orange-Garden Grove-Huntington Beach	E(1-w) M(r/t)	13.4 (1-w)	Flat	100	-	-	S, N	El Camino Real Park to Huntington State Beach
18	Newport Beach-Irvine	E(1-w) M(r/t)	9.9 (1-w)	Flat	90	10	-	S, N	San Diego Creek
19	Seal Beach-Azusa	M-S S (r/t)	39.0 (1-w)	Flat	100	-	-	S, N, L, S/A, M	San Gabriel River (shore to mountains)
19A	Seal Beach-Long Beach	E (1-w) E (r/t)	5.6 (1-w)	Flat	100	-	-	S, N, S/A, M	Ocean to El Dorado Park
19B	Long Beach-Downey	E (1-w) M (r/t)	9.7 (1-w)	Flat	100	-	-	S, N, S/A, M	El Dorado Park to Wilderness Park
19C	Downey-Pico Rivera	E (1-w) M (r/t)	7.7 (1-w)	Flat	100	-	-	S, N, L, M	Wilderness Park to Whittier Narrows/Legg Lake
19D	Pico Rivera-Irwindale	E (1-w) M (r/t)	11.4 (1-w)	Flat	100	-	-	S, N, L, M	Whittier Narrows/Legg Lake to Santa Fe Dam

1,2 See footnotes on page 8

TRIP NO.	GENERAL LOCATION	LEVEL OF DIFFICULTY			ROUTE QUALITY			TRIP CHARACT.[2]	COMMENTS
		L.O.D.[1]	MILES	ELEV.	BIKE TRAIL (%)	BIKE LANE (%)	OTHER (%)		
19E	Irwindale-Azusa	E (1-w) M (r/t)	7.5 (1-w)	Flat	100	-	-	S, N, L, M	Santa Fe Dam to San Gabriel Canyon
20	Long Beach-Cerritos	E (1-w) M (r/t)	14.0 (1-w)	Flat	100	-	-	S, L, M	San Gabriel River-Coyote Creek
21	Cypress, La Palma, Buena Park	E-M	14.9	Flat	15	80	5	S, L	Cypress City Tour (loop)
22	Yorba Linda	E (1-w) M (r/t)	8.2 (1-w)	Mod.	80	-	20	S, N	El Cajon Trail
23	Brea, Chino Hills, Brea, Diamond Bar	S	23.3	Steep	-	20	80	S, N, E, M	Chino Hills Loop
24	Fullerton	M-S	15.4	Mod.-Steep	-	80	20	S, N	Fullerton Tour (loop), Craig Park, Tri-Cities Park
25	Anaheim Hills	E (1-w) M (r/t)	7.6 (1-w)	Mod.	-	100	-	S, M	Santa Ana Canyon Road
26	Orange	M (E)	10.2 (3.9)	Mod. (Flat)	10 (100)	80	10	S, N, L (S, N, L, S/A)	Orange/Irvine Park Loop (Irvine Park)
27	Santiago Canyon	S (1-w) S (r/t)	12.6 (1-w)	Mod.-Steep	-	-	100	S, N, E,	Santiago Canyon Road
28	Rancho Santa Margarita	E	7.4 (r/t)	Flat-Mod.	100	-	-	S, N	O'Neill Regional Park Tour
29	El Toro-Laguna Niguel	E (1-w) M (r/t)	15.9 (1-w)	Mod.	100	-	-	S, N, L	Aliso Creek Bike Trail
29A	El Toro-Lake Forest	E (1-w) E-M (r/t)	7.7 (1-w)	Mod.	100	-	-	S, N, L	Aliso Creek Bike Trail, Northern Segment
29B	Lake Forest-Laguna Niguel	E (r/t)	8.2 (1-w)	Mod.	100	-	-	S, N	Aliso Creek Bike Trail, Southern Segment

1,2 See footnotes on page 9

MASTER TRIP MATRIX

TRIP NO.	GENERAL LOCATION	LEVEL OF DIFFICULTY			ROUTE QUALITY			TRIP CHARACT.[2]	COMMENTS
		L.O.D.[1]	MILES	ELEV.	BIKE TRAIL (%)	BIKE LANE (%)	OTHER (%)		
30	Mission Viejo, El Toro, Laguna Hills	M-S	15.6	Mod.	30	70	-	S, N, L	Mission Viejo Bikeway (loop)
31	Laguna Hills, Irvine, Laguna Beach	M-S	14.3	Mod.-Steep	-	30	70	S, L, S/A	Laguna Hills Loop
32	Lake Forest	E	5.3	Flat-Mod.	20	80	-	S, N	Lake Forest Loop
33	San Gabriel Rvr.-Coyote Creek-Santa Ana River	S	63.5	Mod.	70	20	10	S, N, L, M	Western Orange County Loop
34	Santiago Cyn.-Aliso Crk.-PCH-Santa Ana Rvr.	VS	76.9	Mod.-Steep	30	60	10	S, N, L, S/A, E, M	Eastern Orange County Loop
35	Santiago Cyn.-Aliso Crk.-PCH-San Gabriel Rvr.-Coyote Crk.-El Cajon Trail-Villa Park	M	105	Mod.-Steep	40	30	30	S, N, L, S/A, E, M	Orange County "Century"
36	Irvine	M	4.3	Mod.	-	100	-	S, N	Turtle Rock Road (loop) + Class I spur trip
37	Irvine	E (E)	1.9 (2.4)	Flat (Flat)	100 (100)	-	-	S, N (S,N)	Mason Regional Park (west) (east grounds)
38	Orange County/ Newport Coast	S	8.1	Mod.-Sheer	-	45	55	S, E	Pelican Hill & Signal Peak (loop)
39	Laguna Niguel	S	8.4	Mod.-Steep	-	100	-	S, N, E	Laguna Niguel Tour (loop)
40	Capistrano Beach, San Clemente	M / M-S	9.7 / 15.1	Mod. / Mod.-Steep	30 / -	60 / 50	10 / 50	S, L / S, N, L	Hillside San Clemente (two loops)
41	Tustin	M	8.0	Mod.	-	100	-	S, S/A	Tustin Ranch Loop + Peters Canyon Bikeway

1,2 See footnotes on page 9

MASTER TRIP MATRIX

TRIP NO.	GENERAL LOCATION	LEVEL OF DIFFICULTY			ROUTE QUALITY			TRIP CHARACT.²	COMMENTS
		L.O.D.¹	MILES	ELEV.	BIKE TRAIL (%)	BIKE LANE (%)	OTHER (%)		
42	Mission Viejo	M	4.4	Mod.	100	-	-	S, N, L	Pavion, Jeronimo Gnbt, Oso Viejo & World Cup Parks
43	Yorba Linda	VS	23.6	Steep-Sheer	25	5	70	S, N, E	Yorba Linda Tour (three hill climbs)
44	Anaheim Hills, Orange	S	14.2	Steep-Sheer	-	10	90	S, E	Anaheim Hills Loop(s)
45	Lemon Heights	M-S	6.1	Steep	-	15	85	S, L, E	Lemon Heights Loop
46	Aliso Viejo	M	8.2	Mod.	-	100	-	S	Aliso Viejo Double Loop
47	Mission Viejo, Trabuco & Live Oak Canyons	S	13.2	Mod.-Steep	-	50	50	S, N, E	Cities and Canyons Loop
48	Silverado Canyon (Cleveland Nat. Forest)	M-S	11.3	Mod.	-	-	100	S, N	Silverado Canyon (up and back)
49	Modjeska Canyon (Cleveland Nat. Forest)	M-S	6.2	Steep-Sheer	-	-	100	S, N, S/A	Modjeska Canyon (loop)
50	Mission Viejo. Rancho Santa Margarita, SJC	S	27.1	Mod.-Steep	10	65	25	S, N, L, E, M	Arroyo Trabuco Loop
51	Coto De Caza	M	11.2	Mod.	-	-	100	S, L	Coto De Caza Loop (private: residents & guests only)

1 **L.O.D.** – Overall trip level of difficulty: **VS**-very strenuous; **S**-strenuous; **M**-Moderate; **E**-easy;
1-**w**-one way; **r/t**-round trip or up and back

2 **TRIP CHARACTERISTICS** - General trip features and highlights: **S**-scenic; **N**-nature trail; **L**-landmark(s);
S/A-sight-seeing attractions; **E**-elevation workout; **M**-mileage workout

TRIP DESCRIPTION/TERMINOLOGY

The trip descriptors in the "Master Trip Matrices" are described below in further detail. Several of these same descriptors are also used in the individual trip writeups.

GENERAL LOCATION: The general location of the bike trail is provided in terms of a city, landmark or general area description, as applicable. The "Master Trip Map" may be useful in conjunction with this general locator.

LEVEL OF DIFFICULTY: The rides are rated on an overall basis with consideration for elevation gain, trip distance and condition of the bike route.

A *very strenuous* trip can be of any length, has very steep grades and is generally designed for bikers in excellent physical condition. Trips are well enough described such that the biker might plan to ride the easier part of a stressing trip and link up with other easier trips.

A *strenuous* trip has some steep grades and/or relatively long mileage (on the order of 50 miles total). The trip is of sufficiently long duration to require trip planning and strong consideration of weather, water, food and bike spare parts. Some portions of the trip may be on surfaces in poor condition or on shared roadway.

A *moderate* trip may have mild grades and moderate mileage, on the order of 15-30 miles. The trip is typically of several hours duration and is generally on well-maintained bike route.

An *easy* trip is on the order of 10 miles or less, is relatively flat and is generally on well maintained bike trails or bike paths.

TRIP MILEAGE: Trip mileage is generally computed for the one-way trip length for *up and back* trips and full-trip length for *loop* trips. *Up and back* is specifically used for trips that share a common route in both outgoing and return directions. *Loop* specifically means that the outgoing and return trip segments are on predominantly different routes. *Round trip* is used without distinction as to whether the trip is an *up and back* or *loop* trip. In the trip writeups, the mileage from the starting point or "trailhead" is noted in parentheses to the nearest tenth mile, for example, (6.3).

Obviously, the one-way trips listed can be exercised with a planned car shuttle, ridden as an *up and back* trip, or biked in connection with another bicycle trip listed in this book. Connections with other trips are noted in the trip text or in a separate subsection for that trip titled, "Connecting Trips."

TRIP ELEVATION GAIN: The overall trip elevation gain is described in a qualitative fashion. *Flat* indicates that there are no grades of any consequence. Steepness of upgrades is loosely defined as follows: 1) *light* indicates limited slope and very little elevation gain; 2) *moderate* means more significant slope requiring use of low gears and may be tens of feet of upgrade; 3) *steep* indicates workout-type grades that require low gears and high physical exertion; 4) *sheer* indicates gut-buster grades that require extreme physical exertion (and a strong will to live!).

The frequency of upgrades is divided into the following categories: 1) *single* for flat rides with a single significant upgrade; 2) *periodic* for flat rides where uphill segments are widely spaced; 3) *frequent* where narrowly spaced upgrades are encountered (e.g., rolling hills).

Elevation contour maps are provided for trips with significant elevation change. A reference 5% (*steep*) grade is shown on all such maps.

BIKE ROUTE QUALITY: The trip is summarized with respect to route quality in the "Master Trip Matrices" and a more detailed description is given in the individual trip writeups. The following route terminology (which is similar to that used by CALTRANS) is used:

- *Class I* - off-roadway bike paths or bike trails
- *Class II* - on-roadway, separated (striped) bike lanes
- *Class III* - on-roadway, signed (but not separated) bike lanes

If the route is on-roadway and not signed (i.e., not marked as a bike route), it is arbitrarily referred to as *Class X*. All routes are paved unless otherwise noted.

TRIP CHARACTERISTICS: The overall highlights of the bike trip are provided in the "Master Trip Matrices" to assist in general trip selection. The trip may be scenic (*S*), with sweeping vistas, exciting overlooks or generally provide views of natural or man-made attractions such as cities. Alternatively, the trip may be a nature trail (*N*) or a path through areas which have an abundance of trees, flowers and other flora. The nature trips or portions thereof are generally on Class I bike routes. The trip may highlight historical or well-known landmarks (*L*) or may have one or more sightseeing attractions (*S/A*). An example of the former is the Prado Dam on the Santa Ana River (Trip #22C) while the latter might be the Laguna Museum of Art (Trips #9 and #10). Finally, some trips are potentially good workout trips in that there is significant elevation change (*E*) or lengthy mileage (*M*) if the entire trip is taken. Some trips may provide a mix of these characteristics and are so noted.

Several descriptors are unique to the individual trip writeups. Those descriptors are defined below.

TRAILHEAD: The general location of the start of the bike path is provided for a single starting point. Driving directions to that trailhead and/or directions for parking are included where there is a possibility of confusion. Always check to ensure that parking is consistent with current laws.

Note that for most trails, there are multiple points of entry beyond the primary point listed. For some of the trips in this book (particularly the river routes), alternate bicycle entry points are noted on maps by arrows ( ) along the bike route. Alternate trailheads may be found using information obtained from other bikers, or from state or local publications for more popular routes.

WATER: In the "Trailhead" description, general statements are provided about water needs. In the "Trip Description," available water along the route is noted where water is scarce. Particular emphasis is placed on public facilities for water and use of restrooms. Stores, shopping centers and gas stations are sometimes noted, although the availability of water or other facilities in these instances is subject to the policies of those establishments.

CONNECTING TRIPS: Where bike trips can be linked, they are so noted. *Continuation* trips are those where there is direct linkage at the beginning or end of the trip being described. *Connection* trips are either not directly linked (i.e., a Class X connector is required) or the linkage occurs at the interior of the trip being described. A brief "connector" route description is provided.

BIKE TRIP MAPS: Each ride in the book has an accompanying detailed bike map. A summary of symbols and features used in those maps is provided below.

— — — —	Bike trail in trip description (unless otherwise noted).			
. . . . . .	Alternate bike route (unless otherwise noted).			
SANTA ANA RIVER	River or creek when it is a major trip focus.	MAIN ST		Roadway
IRVINE	Nearby City		Park	Landmark #5 (5, 5)
W	Public Water Source	P	Parking	Entry Point to Trail
●—●	Locked Gate/ Limited Entry	++++++	Railroad Crossing or Overcrossing	School (as a trip point of interest)
Mission	Mission		Gravel Pit	Reference 5% grade

MAP SYMBOLS AND FEATURES

GENERAL BIKING CONSIDERATIONS

These are a collection of the thoughts that we've had in the thousands of miles of biking that we have done:

SAFETY: Use common sense when you are biking. Common sense when combined with courtesy should cover most of the safety-related issues. The four safety "biggies" are: 1) understand bike riding laws; 2) keep your bicycle in safe operating order; 3) wear personal safety equipment as required (a helmet is a must, bright or reflective clothes, and sunglasses); 4) ride defensively and always assume that moving and parked car inhabitants are not aware that you are there.

Common courtesy is to offer assistance to bikers stopped because of breakdowns. Point out ruts, obstructions, and glass to bikers behind you.

TRIP PLANNING/PREPARATION: We are absolute believers in advance planning. You minimize nasty surprises and have the joy of two trips for one (the anticipated trip and the physical trip itself). Familiarize yourself with the trip ahead of time; start by reading recent tour guides and talking to people who have been there before. For long-distance and/or more remote adventures, we do not recommend going alone.

Plan bicycle trips that are within your (or your group's) physical and technical abilities. Start with less-demanding trips and work your way up the difficulty ladder. Work on physical fitness and technical skills between trips to maintain or improve your abilities. Take rides with professional leaders and/or learn the necessary skills with an accomplished veteran in that activity area. As part of the training, learn first-aid techniques and use of the kit as appropriate for your activity.

The discussion which follows is applicable to both high-difficulty and/or extended-mileage day trips and multi-day tours. Look over the topographic maps and get a feel for the key areas of elevation change, and locate the key road junctions. Where relevant, check that the roads/river trails are open and available for public travel by making advance inquiries. Identify contingency routes if there is any doubt as to your ability to follow the nominal plan or if adverse weather or road conditions could require trip alteration.

Once you have identified your outdoor adventure, assess your gear needs for the trip. Work with your group to define individual responsibilities for group gear items. Ensure that you know how to use each piece of activity gear before departure. Maintain your gear, particularly that most critical to safety, and perform a pre-trip check that gear is in design-operable condition.

EQUIPMENT: This subject is covered in great depth in B-D Enterprises' publication, *Outdoor Recreation Checklists*. That reference covers gear needs for about every major outdoor activity, including on-road and mountain biking for both daytime and multi-day trips.

The discussion which follows focuses on day trips. The minimum biking equipment includes a water bottle or two, a tire pump, and a tool kit that typically includes tire irons, wrench(es), screwdriver(s), a patch kit, and (sorry to say) a bike lock. For longer day trips add a spare tube and a bike repair manual. We recommend a bike light even if there are no plans for night biking.

Necessary cyclist apparel includes a helmet, sunglasses, and clothes which will fit pessimistic weather conditions (particularly for longer trips). On all-day, cool or wet winter outings, we carry a layered set of clothes (this includes long pants, an undershirt, a long-sleeve shirt, a sweater, and a two-piece rain suit). Padded cycling pants and biking gloves are a must for long trips. Modern day, warm-when-wet clothes are light and extremely functional. For cool and dry days, we may drop the rain suit for a windbreaker (look for a windbreaker that folds up into a fanny pack). For other conditions, our outfits are normally shorts, an undershirt, a long-sleeve shirt, and a windbreaker. Laugh if you must, but wait until you find yourself biking home at night, in mid-winter, along a beach with a healthy sea breeze after you spent the day biking in the warm sun (an example of poor trip planning, we admit).

Bring a first-aid kit. For urban tours, our packaged, baggie-sealed kit has the following: sunscreen (15 SPF or greater), lip salve, aspirin, and band aids. For trips where help may not be so readily available, we add gauze (roll), ace bandage (roll) and butterfly clips, a small pair of scissors, moleskin, a needle, and an antiseptic such as hydrogen peroxide or iodine. Think about insect repellent if you think conditions may warrant.

If you are going to get your money out of this book, **get an automobile bike rack**! The cost of bike racks is cheap compared to most bikes. Besides, it just doesn't make sense to bike fifty miles to take the planned twenty-mile bike trip.

THE COAST

From Dana Drive in Dana Point Harbor

TRIP #1 - SEAL BEACH/SUNSET BEACH TOUR

GENERAL LOCATION: Seal Beach, Sunset Beach

LEVEL OF DIFFICULTY: Up and back - easy
Distance - 4.3 miles (one way)
Elevation gain - essentially flat

HIGHLIGHTS: A pleasant tour which concentrates on the beach community setting, this trip starts at the end of the Long Beach Marina, passes along the Seal Beach beachfront, transits a section of highway along the Anaheim Bay National Wildlife Refuge, and ends with a short cruise through the small beach community of Sunset Beach. The trip terminates at Bolsa Chica State Beach (see Trip #4 for the continuation route). This route is Class X through lightly traveled Seal Beach and Class II for about a 1.5-mile stretch of Pacific Coast Highway (PCH), as well as within Sunset Beach.

TRAILHEAD: Free public automobile parking is available at the Long Beach Marina along Marina Drive in Long Beach or along First Street in Seal Beach. From PCH in Seal Beach, turn west on Marina Drive (just west of Main Street) and continue roughly half a mile to First Street. In another quarter mile, cross the San Gabriel River and drive a short distance to the marina parking area near Seaport Village.

Public sources are scarce, however only a light water supply is needed for this short trip.

TRIP DESCRIPTION: **Seal Beach.** Leave the marina area and Seaport Village, cross the Marina Avenue bridge over the San Gabriel River (0.1) and turn right at First Street. Bike parallel to the San Gabriel River and take in the beautiful view of the marina breakwater and the fleet of pleasure craft. At the end of First Street (0.3), turn left on Ocean Avenue and cruise along the beachfront residences to the Seal Beach Pier and Eisenhower Park (0.8). Join the fishermen on the pier or take in the ocean view from the strand.

Pedal on Ocean Avenue until it begins curving to the left (northeast) and becomes Seal Beach Boulevard. Take a right at PCH (1.7) and start a small upgrade on a bridge with Anaheim Bay on the right and the U.S. Naval Weapons Station on the left. With some fortune, a large naval ship might be docked in Anaheim Bay. Cycle a second upgrade to another bridge and at (2.5) admire the vista from the highest point. Another excellent view of Anaheim Bay is to the right and Anaheim Bay National Wildlife Refuge to the left.

Surfside - Sunset Beach. Follow PCH past the private community of Surfside and the cluster of small eateries, making a right turn at Anderson Street in Sunset Beach (3.0). In a few hundred feet turn left at S. Pacific Avenue and bike along the long, snug

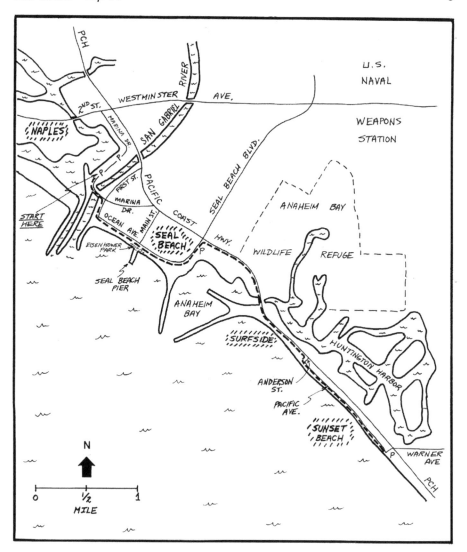

TRIP #1 - SEAL BEACH/SUNSET BEACH TOUR

row of beach residences. Coast on this Class II bike lane for about 1.3 miles to its terminus at Warner Avenue.

CONNECTING TRIPS: 1) Continuation with the Sunset Beach to Newport Beach Strand ride (Trip #4) - continue this trip south into Bolsa Chica State Beach; 2) connection with the bike route to the Anaheim Bay National Wildlife Refuge (Trip #2) - pedal east (away from the beach) on Warner Avenue; 3) connection with the PCH portion of Trip #4 to the Bolsa Chica Ecological Preserve - continue southward on PCH beyond Warner Avenue; 4) connection with the Belmont Shore/Naples area - from the parking area, take Marina Drive northwest and turn left (west) at 2nd Street.

TRIP #2 - SUNSET AQUATIC PARK/HUNTINGTON HARBOR TOUR

GENERAL LOCATION: Huntington Harbor (Huntington Harbour)

LEVEL OF DIFFICULTY: One way - easy; loop - moderate
Distance - 12.0 miles (loop)
Elevation gain - essentially flat

HIGHLIGHTS: The trip starts with a visit to the natural setting of Sunset Aquatic Park. From here, this free-form bike ride has only a suggested route which explores the "nooks and crannies" of the northern Huntington Harbor area. Cyclists can meander through housing areas set along lovely canals, enjoying many great views of the main channel and boat marinas, and visiting such enjoyable places as little Trinidad Island. There are opportunities to stop and rest at any one of several small parks along the way. The trip through Huntington Harbor is mostly Class X, but the roadway is generally lightly traveled. There is an option to return to Sunset Aquatic Park via a route along Saybrook Lane and Edinger Avenue, which is primarily Class II.

TRAILHEAD: From Pacific Coast Highway (PCH) turn east on Warner Avenue, drive about 1.5 miles, then turn left (north) on Bolsa Chica Street. Continue about 1.25 miles to Edinger Avenue, turn left (west), then proceed 1.75 miles and cross a small bridge (1.8). Stay on the road now named Sunset Way East for about 0.2 mile to the marina

Huntington Harbor (northwest)

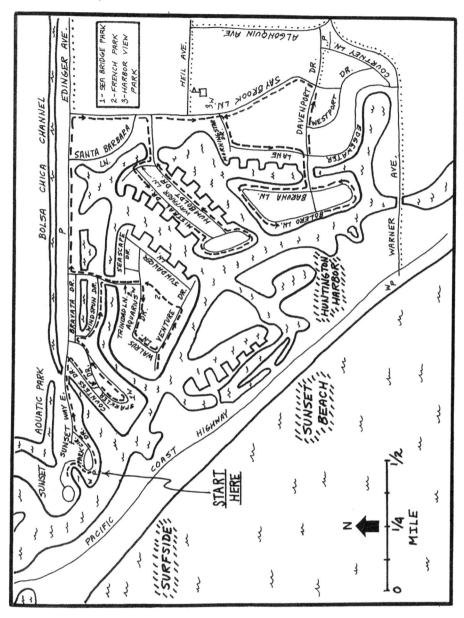

TRIP #2 - SUNSET AQUATIC PARK/HUNTINGTON HARBOR TOUR

<u>public</u> parking area at Sunset Aquatic Park. Do not use the permit parking spaces on Park Circle. (If the public lot is full, park along Edinger Avenue. Another option is to start from near the Huntington Harbor Mall. Park in the shade on the frontage road along Davenport Drive near Courtney Lane.)

From the San Diego Freeway, exit west at Westminster Avenue and go about 1.5 miles to Bolsa Chica Road. Turn left (south) and drive two miles to Edinger Avenue.

Turn right and continue as described above. From the Garden Grove Freeway, exit south at Valley View Street/Bolsa Chica Road and motor about three miles to Edinger Avenue. Continue as described above.

Public restrooms are located near the Harbor Patrol building in the park. Beyond this point, there is water at the three well-spaced Huntington Harbor parks noted on the trip map.

TRIP DESCRIPTION: **Sunset Aquatic Park.** From the parking/picnic area (a couple of open sites with benches and barbecues), bicycle through the boat launch entry (auto pay gate) on Park Circle that you passed when driving in. Cycle to the Harbor Patrol building and the boat launching area. Stop and watch the small cars pulling out big boats and burning up their tires! Ride just beyond the launch area, lock your bike to the nearby fence and take a walking tour of the natural (unimproved) Sunset Aquatic Park. There are numerous tidepools, interesting vegetation, and birds of many types. Return to the parking area and pedal across the bridge over the Bolsa Chica Channel (0.9) to Edinger Avenue.

Huntington Harbor (northwest). For this reference ride, turn right on Countess Drive (1.0) and make the first left turn, passing through the pedestrian fence onto Sparkler Drive. Pass Sea Bridge Park (water, restrooms, shade) and follow a loop which goes between a cozy network of quaint two-story homes. Just before returning to Edinger Avenue, turn right on Bravata Drive (1.8), then immediately right again on Windspun Drive. Cycle on that street to Trinidad Lane and turn right (2.4). In about 0.1 mile, take in the striking view of the long, home-surrounded canal.

Trinidad Island. Cross a small bridge, pass a shaded swimming/play area (with restrooms) to the right, and look head-on into the southern extremity of small, meandering French Park. This is Trinidad Island. Turn right on Aquarius Drive and cycle to the tiny grassy area at the western point of the island (2.9). A small path along the periphery of the island heads in either direction at this point. Turning left, the path proceeds along the main channel. Bike about 0.5 mile to French Park and wind through this grassy, compact park back to Trinidad Lane. Return to Edinger Avenue (4.5).

Huntington Harbor (east). Turn right on Edinger Avenue and right again on Saybrook Lane (5.7). Cruise about 0.3 mile on this pleasant but busy roadway to Humboldt Drive. Turn right (west) and cross a small bridge; there is a fine view from atop the bridge of the harbor, the nestled harbor "castles," and a cozy little beach (6.1). Tour the quiet island loop following Wayfarer Lane (to the right), Mistral Drive, the westernmost inner loop and return to the bridge via Humboldt Drive (7.7). There are only limited views of the harbor on this loop, as the large and sometimes beautiful residences are packed in side-by-side along the bay shore.

Return across the bridge to Saybrook Lane and turn right (south). Follow Class II Saybrook Lane 0.2 mile to Harbor View Park where there is water and shade (recreation/play areas and tennis courts). Just beyond the park and on the opposite side of the street, turn right (west) on Morningstar Drive (8.1).

The route returns to quiet residential streets and heads to Edgewater Lane (8.2). Turn left and continue to Davenport Drive (8.5). Turn right (west) and ride over a small bridge; the view from the bridge is almost a copy of that seen from Humboldt Drive. The island loop tour is a cruise through a quiet residential neighborhood on Baruna

Lane, around to Bolero Lane and back to the starting point at the bridge (9.5). Again, there are only scattered harbor views from the island due to blockage by the tightly packed residences. From Edgewater Lane, one option is for cyclists to repeat the incoming route.

Direct Return Route. A more direct return option is to follow Davenport Drive east to Saybrook Lane (9.8). Turn left (north), pass along the western edge of the Huntington Harbor Mall and follow Saybrook Lane 0.9 mile to Edinger Avenue. Turn left again and make a beeline of 1.3 miles on Class II bikeway to your parked car. The total trip mileage is 12.0 miles.

CONNECTING TRIPS: Connection with the beach bikepath to Sunset Beach/Seal Beach (Trip #1) or to the Sunset to Newport Beach Strand (Trip #4) - near the one-way trip terminus (Edgewater Lane and Davenport Drive), turn right (south) on Edgewater Lane and bicycle to Warner Avenue. Turn right (west) on Warner Avenue, cross PCH and turn north (Trip #1) or south (Trip #4).

TRIP #3 - HUNTINGTON CENTRAL PARK

GENERAL LOCATION: Huntington Beach

LEVEL OF DIFFICULTY: Loop - easy
Distance - 4.7 miles
Elevation gain - periodic light grades

HIGHLIGHTS: This short and pleasant trip takes in both east and west sections of Huntington Central Park, which has over four miles of fine Class I touring without even biking the innermost trails. The park offers a lovely treed area on the east side with Lake Talbert, the Huntington Central Library, and a duckpond. The west side has less tree cover, but is an equally nice area which sports Lake Huntington, a "Frisbee-golf" course, and the Donald D. Shipley Nature Center. There is a nice eatery on each side of the park, with Breakfast-in-the-Park on the west side providing lakeside dining under sun umbrellas. (We're suckers for this type of environment.) Also provided is a pleasant diversion trip around Lake Huntington.

TRAILHEAD: From the San Diego Freeway, exit south at Goldenwest Street and drive 3.5 miles to Slater Avenue. Continue another quarter mile and turn left into the east section of Huntington Central Park. From Pacific Coast Highway (PCH) southbound, drive four miles past Warner Avenue (Huntington Harbor) and turn left at Goldenwest Street. Go 2.5 miles north, passing Talbert Avenue. In another quarter mile, turn right into the park. From PCH northbound, drive two miles past Beach Boulevard (Huntington Beach) and turn right at Goldenwest Street. Proceed as described above.

Bring a light water supply since water is plentiful.

TRIP DESCRIPTION: **East Section.** Enter the bikepath and examine the spur trails off to the right which lead to the "Adventure Playground" and a picnic area above

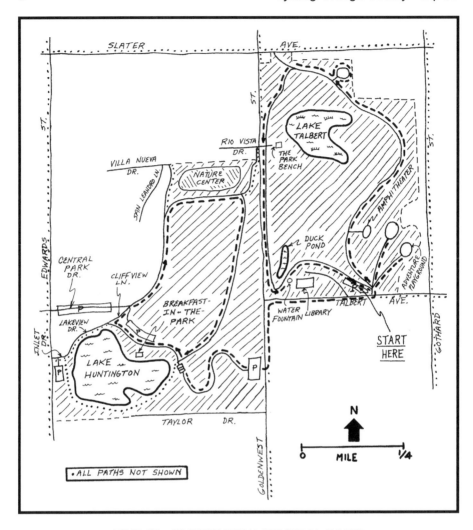

TRIP #3 - HUNTINGTON CENTRAL PARK

the small amphitheater. Return to the main path and bike into a relatively open area between the library and the amphitheater (0.4). Turn to the right and follow the park's outermost trail under the tall shade trees. Cruise around Lake Talbert (dry when we visited) and follow a short upgrade to the small loop and parking lot on Slater Avenue (1.6).

Return to the flat and bicycle past a small play area complete with "merry-go-round" horses anchored in the sand. Just beyond, the path reaches Goldenwest Street, parallels that road and reaches The Park Bench, a nice little rest stop for munchies. Note that there is a testy street crossing here (Rio Vista Drive) to reach the park's west section; it is not recommended for small children or inexperienced adults. However, our reference route continues south and reaches the southwest park edge, follows a 180-degree turn around a duckpond and passes alongside and below the Huntington Central Library and its beautiful water fountain. Return to the trip origin and turn right on Talbert Avenue, biking to Goldenwest Street (2.7).

Lake Huntington and Breakfast in the Park

West Section. For bikers who aren't wild about walking/carrying their bikes for short distances, turn right and cycle 0.3 mile to the crossing at Rio Vista Drive and enter the park from the Class I path. Otherwise, cross Goldenwest Street, turn left and pedal 0.15 mile to the parking entry to the more sparsely treed western park section. Proceed through the parking lot onto the Class I path into an area with strange little metal stanchions with chains on them; these are the "holes" that the Frisbee-golfers "sink" their Frisbees into. This is "disk golf" or "Frisbee-golf" country. Stop and watch a group of golfers drive through a hole or two.

Pedal to the stairway which leads to the lower level of the park (3.2). The options are to carry your bike down the steps or to walk it down a steep incline. Follow the Class I path at the base of the steps to the main western segment loop and veer left. (The option to turn hard left and do a ride around Lake Huntington is described below.) Cycle 0.15 mile to the lakeside and Breakfast-in-the-Park. Continue on the main path another 0.15 mile to Cliffview Lane, turn right and bike to its terminus at Central Park Drive, one of two westside park entries.

Turn right into a lengthy parking area, bike to the nearest northbound walkway/ bikeway, then turn left again at the intersection. Just short of the Donald D. Shipley Nature Center, stay right at a shaded junction (left leads to a park exit at Villa Nueva Drive) and cruise the periphery of the center, a neat place to learn about the local wildlife (3.8). Bike another 0.3 mile to the junction with the spur trail which heads north to Rio Vista Drive. Stay on the shaded main trail another 0.2 mile, pass a large children's play area and return to the Lake Huntington area just beyond.

Return Segment. Return via the reference route which means a bike carry up the steps and crossing at Talbert Avenue. The total trip distance is 4.7 miles. The alternative is to take the spur trail mentioned above and return via the Rio Vista Drive crossing and repeat the eastern park ride segment. This adds about a quarter mile to the trip length.

Excursion: Lake Huntington Spur. There are patches of packed dirt and sometimes short, soggy stretches on this 0.4-mile spur. At the base of the steps described
above, turn left and pedal around the eastern side of the lake. Follow the treed lakeshore
below Taylor Drive on the south side, swing north and reach the trail's end at Inlet
Drive. Bike on the sidewalk alongside the lake as the road curves left and becomes
Lakeview Drive. The roadway veers further left, then changes name to Cliffview Lane,
meeting the trail from Breakfast-in-the-Park.

CONNECTING TRIPS: Connection with the Sunset Beach to Newport Beach Strand
(Trip #4) - pedal 2.5 miles on Goldenwest Street to PCH. Bike on the highway or the
beachside Class I path just beyond in either direction.

TRIP #4 - SUNSET BEACH TO
NEWPORT BEACH STRAND

GENERAL LOCATION: Sunset Beach, Huntington Beach, Newport Beach

LEVEL OF DIFFICULTY: One way - easy; up and back - moderate
Distance - 13.8 miles (one way)
Elevation gain - essentially flat

HIGHLIGHTS: Orange County's answer to Los Angeles County's South Bay Bike
Trail, this trip is entirely along the beach and almost entirely a Class I route. This is a
very pleasant tour which mixes open areas with great ocean views along the well-
populated strand. The trip passes three piers, scattered surfing areas, and several state
or local parks and beaches, and has numerous locations for food/water/rest stops. Parts
of the trip are well populated, particularly near the piers and especially in summertime.
The Bolsa Chica State Beach portion of the route is lighted for those folks who like
"moonlight" bike rides. An optional partial loop trip is possible by riding portions of
Pacific Coast Highway (PCH) on the return leg. This optional leg passes near the Bolsa
Chica Ecological Reserve.

TRAILHEAD: Limited free public parking is available along Pacific Avenue in Sunset Beach, or if one is willing to pay, at Bolsa Chica State Beach. To park at Sunset
Beach, turn off of PCH toward the ocean on Warner Avenue and turn right a short distance later at N. Pacific Avenue. The state beach entrance is almost 1.5 miles further
south from Warner Avenue on PCH, across from the Bolsa Chica Ecological Preserve.

TRIP DESCRIPTION: **Bolsa Chica State Beach to Huntington Beach Pier**
(5.2 miles). The Class I Bolsa Chica State Beach portion of the bike trip begins at
Warner Avenue within the state park. Immediately, one has open beach area and a view
across San Pedro Channel to Long Beach, Los Angeles Harbor, and on a clear day, Santa

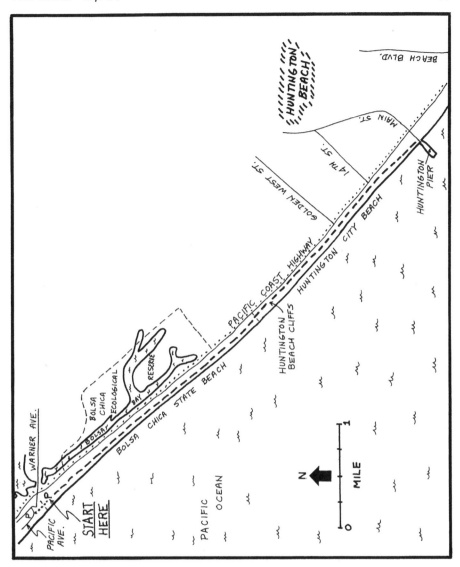

TRIP #4A - SUNSET BEACH TO NEWPORT BEACH STRAND (NORTHERN SEGMENT)

Catalina Island. The roomy bikepath passes the state beach entrance at (1.6) and continues to an area where beach sand has been piled high on either side of the path (2.2). This should give some hint as to what high tide means in this area during heavy storms!

Next, the route climbs gradually for a short distance to the Huntington Beach Cliffs above Huntington City Beach (2.3). Take a break and hike to the cliff edge for a guaranteed view of surfer heaven, morning to evening. The bikepath stays on the bluffs and includes a palm-tree-lined portion of path, as well as a small park/rest stop.

At (4.7) the path heads downhill and returns to the beach. For the next mile, this area is occupied year round by bathers, swimmers, bikers, walkers, and other folks

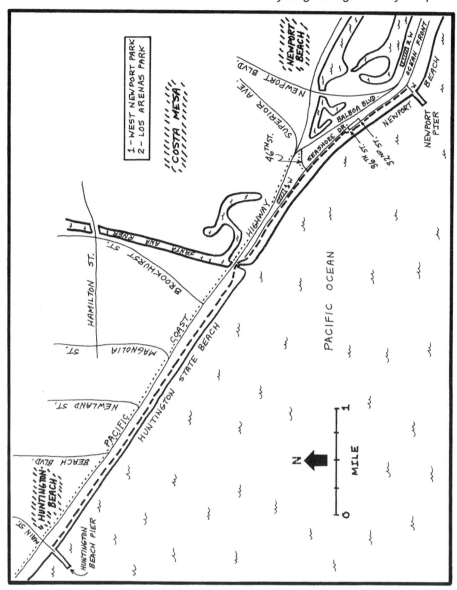

**TRIP #4B - SUNSET BEACH TO NEWPORT BEACH STRAND
(MIDDLE SEGMENT)**

who are interested in being near the Huntington Beach Pier. At (5.2) the trail reaches the pier. A short walk to its end leads to some excellent views of the surrounding beach areas, plus the camaraderie of ever-present fishermen. On the other side of the pier, stop and check out the surfers riding the waves to the beach, and sometimes under the pier.

Huntington Beach Pier to Newport Pier (5.4 miles). Cycle south through Sunset Vista Beach to the Huntington State Beach entrance at Beach Boulevard (Highway 39) (6.1). In about two miles, the state beach ends and the route reaches the Santa

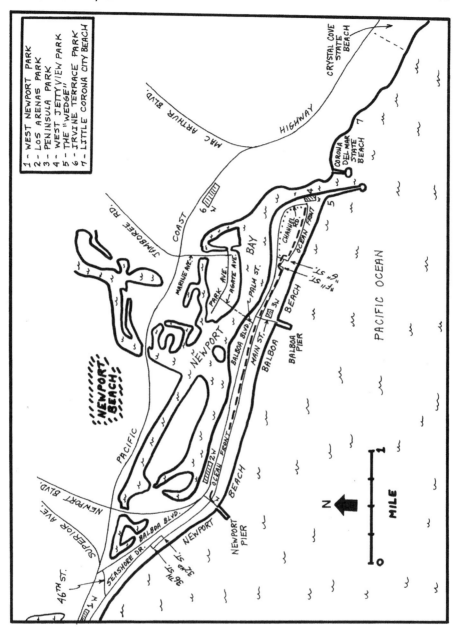

TRIP #4C - SUNSET BEACH TO NEWPORT BEACH STRAND
(SOUTHERN SEGMENT)

Ana River. This is the junction with the Santa Ana River bike route (see Trip #17). Cross the wooden foot bridge and take the right branch of the bikepath a short distance to Seashore Drive, then travel a Class II path along the beachside community homes.

At (9.0) pass the eastern edge of West Newport Park (water, restrooms, children's playground, and athletic courts) at 56th Street, and at (9.9) reach 36th Street. Take a right turn (toward the beach) and ride a short distance to a Class I bikepath along the strand. On this part of the trip to the end of the bikeway, bikers effectively share the living rooms of all those beach folks living along the strand. The strand path reaches the Newport Pier at (10.6). Try the shops at the pier for some excellent munchies. (We are fans of Charlie's Chili.) Take a tour down the pier or watch the surfers just north of the pier.

Newport Pier to Balboa Peninsula Point (3.2 Miles). Bicyclists who by-pass Newport Pier have another chance for a break at Balboa Pier (12.4). In addition to good munchies and a tour of the pier, there are the additional options of shopping at the nearby mall or lying in the grass at Peninsula Park (restrooms, picnic benches, and children's playground). Another 0.4 mile further down the path, the route ends abruptly at the wall of a beach house. Return a short distance to "F" Street and turn away from the beach. Pedal a short distance to Balboa Boulevard, turn right soon after at "G" Street, then continue as "G" Street fuses into Ocean Front.

Cruise on this pleasant little street on Class X roadway until it ends at West Jetty View Park near Balboa Peninsula Point (benches, grass, and water fountain) (13.8). This is the scenic highlight of the trip! Take in the views across the channel to Corona Del Mar State Beach and Little Corona City Beach, or across Newport Bay. A short walk out toward the ocean to the West Jetty provides a great view down the coast. Just north of the jetty is "The Wedge," an area with unusual and dangerous currents and tides, one of the prize areas for surfers who want to challenge "Mother Nature."

Alternate Return Route. From West Jetty View Park, take Channel Road to-ward Newport Bay to its end at Balboa Boulevard. Bike on Balboa Boulevard until it meets "F" Street, roughly 0.75 mile from the park. There are frequent "peeks" between the residences into Newport Bay and of Balboa Island. Reverse the incoming bike trip along the strand. Turn northwest (inland) on 46th Street and bicycle several blocks to Balboa Boulevard. Turn left and in a few hundred feet make a left turn onto PCH.

West Jetty View Park

The remaining return trip can be made on PCH, which is a mix of Class II and Class X routes. This is the choice for more experienced cyclists who are looking to "air it out." However, the Class X portion of PCH, for a several-mile stretch surrounding the city of Huntington Beach, is a narrow roadway with high-speed traffic. To bypass this segment, use the strand bikepath described on the "up" leg between Huntington State Beach (at the Beach Boulevard entrance) and the Huntington Beach Cliffs.

On the PCH return leg, stop at the Bolsa Chica Ecological Reserve, which is just 0.4 mile from the trip origin at Warner Avenue. The Reserve is entered via a walking bridge (no bikes) across Bolsa Bay and contains an abundance of bird wildlife over miles of walkways.

CONNECTING TRIPS: 1) Continuation with the Seal Beach/Sunset Beach Tour (Trip #1) - go north from the trailhead; 2) connection with Sunset Aquatic Park/Huntington Harbor Tour (Trip #2) - cycle east on Warner Avenue from the trailhead; 3) connection with the Newport Beach/Corona Del Mar Tour (Trip #15) and Upper Newport Bay route (Trip #6) - from the junction of PCH and Balboa Boulevard, proceed southeast on PCH to Tustin Avenue and Jamboree Road, respectively; 4) connection with the Santa Ana River Trail (Trip #17) - from Huntington State Beach, take the bike trail from the north side of the Santa Ana River which passes under PCH.

TRIP #5 - MILE SQUARE PARK

GENERAL LOCATION: Fountain Valley

LEVEL OF DIFFICULTY: Loop - easy
Distance - 8.7 miles (outer plus inner loops)
Elevation gain - essentially flat

HIGHLIGHTS: This trip is a family delight! Los Angeles County has El Dorado Park, but Orange County has Mile Square Park, and there's no major roadway to divide it. As advertised, it is about a mile on each of its four sides. Along with great Class I bike trails are picnic grounds with covered picnic sites, small lakes, playgrounds, sports courts, baseball diamonds, soccer fields, and separated archery and nature areas. The park also sports two adjoining golf courses, one of which has a coffee shop.

The mileage shown is for a fixed route consisting of a tour around the exterior boundary of the park, followed by two "inner loops." The route is actually free-form and at the discretion of individual bikers. The bikeways throughout are lightly used and generally in excellent condition.

TRAILHEAD: From the San Diego Freeway, exit at Warner Avenue and head north about half a mile. For the trip as described here, turn left at Brookhurst Street and drive about half a mile to Heil Avenue. There is free parking within the park in this area.

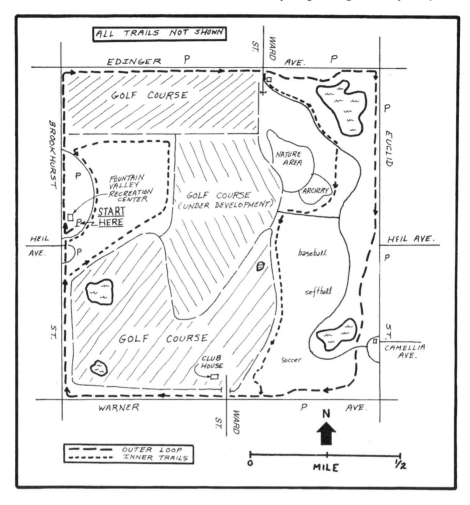

TRIP #5 - MILE SQUARE PARK

There are also numerous places to park free on the periphery (see the map). Finally, there is pay parking within the eastern section, accessed through the entries across from Ward Street and Camellia Avenue.

Bring a light water supply. There are water and restroom facilities throughout the park.

TRIP DESCRIPTION: **Outer Loop.** Return to Brookhurst Street and turn right (north) on the bikepath. Pass the handball courts, tennis courts, and the western edge of the Baker Golf Center. There is a fine view of both Mount San Antonio and Mount Saddleback from this area on a clear day. Turn right at Edinger Avenue (0.5) and cruise along the golf center. Cross an auto entry at Ward Street (1.2) and follow the bikeway/ walkway past the auto entry. For the outer loop, stay to the left at each trail junction on the park's eastern side.

Enjoy this grassy, tree-studded section while passing a long string of picnic kiosks and scattered park benches. Cycle to the western edge of a small lake with several bridges over to a small island playground. Then pedal along the outside park path to Euclid Street and turn right (1.6). In the next 0.9 mile along Euclid Street are many picnic areas, grassy knolls with plentiful tree cover, a second lake near the park's southeastern edge, and the Euclid Street auto entry.

There is a gradual turn around the southernmost lake, and the bike trail begins to parallel Warner Avenue (2.6). Bicycle past a collection of soccer fields, pass through a small parking area, go by the maintenance yard and then hug Warner Avenue. In about 0.6 mile, the path crosses the Ward Street entry to the Mile Square Golf Course and a coffee shop. The bikeway continues along the golf course all the way to Brookhurst Street (3.5). Turn right, bike along the course's western edge (noting the "reference junction" to the right) and return to the parking area entrance at Heil Avenue (4.0).

Westside Inner Loop. Reverse direction and head back to the "reference junction." Make a sharp left onto that path and pedal alongside the fenced-in golf course. Follow a wide semicircle which encloses numerous baseball fields and cruise alongside the fence which encloses a future addition to the golfing areas. (This region used to contain an old airstrip which was used for radio-controlled model cars and high-speed aerodynamic bicycles, and the middle area between strips was used for model airplanes. Though a national focal point for these activities, it lost out to "progress.")

Near the northernmost point, work back toward Brookhurst Street, using both trails and roadway. (Our preference was to take an existing path eastward to Ward Street and the east side of the park, but it was gated when we passed through.) Return to the Heil Avenue trip start point at (5.2).

Eastside Inner Loop. Repeat the outer loop, turning right again at the Edinger Avenue auto entry. Follow the entry road alongside the fenced Nature Area, pass through a parking lot and find the bikeway/walkway at the lot's southeastern edge. (From this point, keep the main auto roadway to your left.) Bike alongside the archery range, then steer toward the separator fence, passing to the west of a succession of baseball, softball, and soccer fields, in that order. Pass through the parking lot to Warner Avenue again, then repeat the exterior park circuit along Warner Avenue and Brookhurst Street (8.7).

CONNECTING TRIPS: 1) Connection with the Santa Ana River Trail (Trip #17C) - take Warner Avenue, Heil Avenue, or Edinger Avenue east (1 to 1.5 miles); 2) Spur trips - there are numerous Class II bike routes in the Fountain Valley/Huntington Beach area which pass through predominantly residential areas. For example, take Heil Avenue about half a mile west to Bushard Street and head either north or south at that junction. Ward Street is Class II from below the park to Yorktown Avenue in Huntington Beach.

TRIP #6 - UPPER NEWPORT BAY

GENERAL LOCATION: Newport Beach

LEVEL OF DIFFICULTY: Loop - moderate
                         Distance - 6.2 miles
                         Elevation gain - periodic moderate grades

HIGHLIGHTS: This is a pleasant loop trip with a highlight of natural scenery together with a tour through some varied residential areas. It visits the Upper Newport Bay Wildlife Preserve, offering a chance to see a large variety of bay scenery and wildlife. The bay area roadway is flat, while the residential portion of the trip offers a couple of challenging uphills. There is an excellent lookout vista at the northern end of Upper Newport Bay. The trip is almost completely Classes I and II if taken in the counter-clockwise direction as written. There are also two excellent spur trips off of this "looper" with an abundance of parks off those excursions.

   Note that the Newport Dunes Waterfront Resort itself might serve as a fine base of operations for a family ride. The area is scenic; it has a nice Class I path at its periphery and a much larger Class I area with light, slow-moving traffic.

TRAILHEAD: Jamboree Road begins at Pacific Coast Highway (PCH) in Newport Beach. It is roughly 2.5 miles east of Newport Boulevard (the outlet of the Costa Mesa Freeway) and 1.25 miles west of MacArthur Veteran's Memorial Boulevard. Take Jamboree Road 0.25 mile northeast to Backbay Drive and turn left. Drive about 100-200 yards past the Newporter Inn grounds and turn left into the pay parking area at Newport Dunes Waterfront Resort. There are picnic, recreation, and restroom facilities within the park, as well as a market. Nearby is a boat marina and a pedestrian bridge which crosses a lagoon. Finally, there is a Class I path on periphery of the eastern and northern sections which goes from Jamboree Road to Bayside Drive. Other options are to use the very limited free parking in surrounding residential areas or at Fashion Island, or to start the trip from the Eastbluff Drive area. (Read the roadsigns carefully before parking.)

   Load up with water at the trailhead, as there are no public facilities directly on this route. Take a diversion to Eastbluff Park or Eastbluff Village Shopping Center if water is needed.

TRIP DESCRIPTION: **Jamboree Road.** Leave the parking area and follow Backbay Drive to Jamboree Road. Turn left (north) onto the Class I path and head up a grade, passing Santa Barbara Drive (0.4). This is an entrance to Fashion Island Shopping Center. Continue uphill to a plateau at San Joaquin Hills Road (0.9), then navigate a steep downhill, followed by another moderate-to-steep uphill. Near the top of the grade, turn left at Eastbluff Drive (1.4) and pedal through a pleasant residential neighborhood. Pass a large recreation field at Corona Del Mar High School, then Vista Del Sol (an entry to Eastbluff Park which has restrooms, athletic fields, children's play areas), and then cruise by Eastbluff Shopping Center (2.1). The route passes along a pleasant palm-tree-lined bluff, then heads downhill. Partway down this grade is Backbay Drive (2.9).

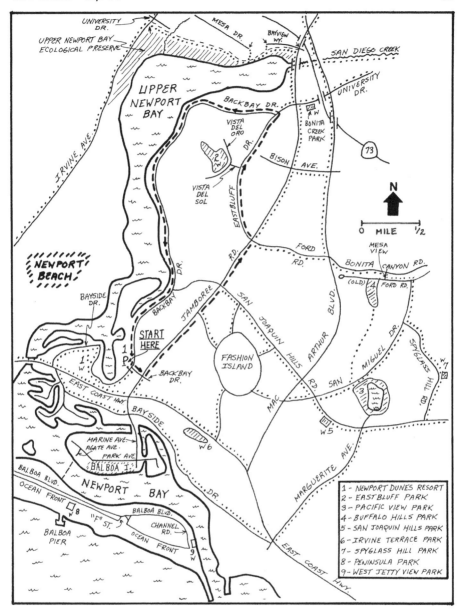

TRIP #6 - UPPER NEWPORT BAY

Backbay Drive. At this junction stop and enjoy one of the premier views of the north end of Upper Newport Bay. Bike down a moderate to steep grade on Backbay Drive and travel along the bay itself. There is a one-way bike lane on the west side of the road only (thus, our counterclockwise route), which continues to the starting point. The route passes a large, open, marshy flat with thousands of birds (3.2) and continues to twist and wind along the bay. There are continuous, excellent views into the mud flats, marshes, open bay, and the bluffs on both sides of the bay.

In three quarters of a mile, the view opens into an expansive sweep, including the high bluffs across the bay. There are numerous turnouts along the way, some of which are occupied by bird-watchers and a few tame ducks. There is a series of light "ups and downs" in this area with signs to indicate that the road may be flooded during storms (4.7). The route snakes past a relatively low but scenic turnout/overlook (5.6) and returns to the aquatic park entry (6.2).

Excursions: **Upper Bay Excursion.** At Eastbluff Drive and Backbay Drive go east on the former street to Jamboree Road. Turn left (north) onto the Class I connector on the road's west side, follow that path on the bridge across San Diego Creek and cycle alongside the eastern edge of the Upper Newport Bay Ecological Preserve. The trail swings west alongside Bayview Way then passes a junction which goes north to the end of that street in 0.2 mile from Jamboree Road. Note that the path is shared by walkers, bikers, and equestrians, with the horse people using the paralleling dirt path. There are numerous foot trails below and nearer the water's edge, as well as walking and horse trails coming from the rustic hillside residences above.

Pass the junction, continuing west, and enjoy the views to the left of the upper bay and the distant bluffside residences. Pedal by an entry from Mesa Drive (0.4), cruise another 0.6 mile, then use the extensive wooden footbridge to cross this sometimes marshy area of the bay. Go over the Delhi Channel on a less-spectacular bridge and bike parallel to the western segment of University Avenue. The path reaches Irvine Avenue in another 0.4 mile (about two miles total from the Eastbluff Drive/Backbay Drive junction.)

Special Scenic Connection. To connect with the Sunset Beach to Newport Beach Strand tour (Trip #4), bike south on Jamboree Road, cross PCH and follow the roadway onto Balboa Island. Take the ferry from the south end of Agate Avenue across the bay to the Balboa Peninsula.

Backbay Drive in Upper Newport Bay

CONNECTING TRIPS: 1) Continuation with the Newport Beach/Irvine Tour (Trip #7) - the tours share a common segment from the trip origin; 2) connection with the Newport Beach/Irvine Tour (Trip #7) - take the **Upper Bay Excursion** described above to Irvine Avenue and continue south; 3) connection with the San Diego Creek Trail (Trip #18) - at the scenic overlook at Backbay Drive and Eastbluff Drive, continue downhill on Eastbluff Drive (use the sidewalk on the north side) to Jamboree Road. Turn left at the trail sign at that intersection and bike to the creek entry near the bridge; 4) connection with William R. Mason Regional Park (Trip #37) - at Eastbluff Drive and Backbay Drive, follow the former street across Jamboree Road where it becomes University Drive and bike 1.5 miles to the park main entrance.

TRIP #7 - NEWPORT BEACH/IRVINE LOOP

GENERAL LOCATION: Newport Beach, Irvine

LEVEL OF DIFFICULTY: Loop - moderate
Distance - 24.4 miles
Elevation gain - periodic moderate-to-steep grades

HIGHLIGHTS: This jim-dandy biking experience on mixed Class I/II/III bikeway takes a "slice" out of several different Newport Beach and Irvine areas. The tour leaves from inviting Newport Dunes Waterfront Resort, visits the Fashion Island area, tours posh and scenic Spyglass Hill, and passes over San Diego Creek. Next is an eight-mile circuit through a modern light commercial area (into Irvine), a cruise alongside John Wayne Airport, a westside tour of Upper Newport Bay, visits to sightseers' Galaxy Park and sportsmen's Mariner's Park, and a scenic return on Dover Drive and Pacific Coast Highway (PCH). The Spyglass Hill area climb and the collection of moderate upgrades throughout the route place this trip at the upper end of a moderate rating.

TRAILHEAD: Jamboree Road begins at PCH in Newport Beach. It is roughly 2.5 miles east of Newport Boulevard (the outlet of the Costa Mesa Freeway) and 1.25 miles west of MacArthur Boulevard. Take Jamboree Road a quarter mile northeast to Backbay Drive and turn left. Continue alongside the Newporter Inn grounds and turn left into the pay parking area at Newport Dunes Waterfront Resort. There are picnic, recreation, and restroom facilities within the park, as well as a market. Nearby is a boat marina and a pedestrian bridge which crosses a local lagoon. Other (free) options are to use Fashion Island, the very limited free parking in the surrounding residential areas, or the Eastbluff Drive area. (Pay close attention to local parking laws.)

Bring a full water bottle. There are scattered water sources throughout the route, although no public water sources were found in the 8.3-mile northern industrial segment.

TRIP DESCRIPTION: **San Joaquin Hills Road.** Leave the park, return to Jamboree Road and turn left (north). Bike on the sidewalk (marked Class I) through a series of workout roller-coaster grades and turn right at San Joaquin Hills Road near the top of the grade (1.1). Pass the gas station and bike on this wide road with plenty of shoulder or use the sidewalk where marked. (There are numerous areas in Newport Beach where signs designate bikeable sidewalks.) The uphill route passes Santa Cruz Drive (an entry to the Newport Harbor Art Museum), then several impressive buildings in the Fashion Island complex, and reaches a crest soon after (1.5). There is an excellent view into the canyons to the northeast, as well as a long-distance view to Mount Saddleback.

Cruise through a residential area and pass Santa Rosa Drive, MacArthur Boulevard, and San Miguel Drive. Next is an uphill pedal which takes riders to Crown Drive and a lawn bowlers' paradise at San Joaquin Hills Park. Shortly, the road passes Marguerite Avenue and begins a steep upgrade. During this workout, bikers are treated to the well-manicured and flowered Pacific View Memorial Park Cemetery (3.1) to the left. The path flattens in a short distance.

Spyglass Hill Road. Turn left onto Spyglass Hill Road and enjoy the prestigious and well-maintained neighborhood while heading uphill. Use the Class I sidewalk or the wide road. Near the crest at El Capitan Drive is cozy Spyglass Hill Park (actually a children's play area with grass, light shade, and a water fountain). Just beyond is a downgrade that leads to an area with an expansive view to the west near Ridgeline Drive. Spread out before you are Fashion Island, Newport Bay, the surrounding Orange County flatlands, and a long-distance view to Catalina Island. Follow a steep downhill that flattens near San Miguel Drive and turn right (north) (4.5).

Upper Newport Bay-East. Follow Class II San Miguel Drive one-half mile to its terminus; turn left on mixed Class I (Old) Ford Drive. Turn right at Mesa View, left at Bonita Canyon Drive and follow what is a general downgrade through a mixed

Spyglass Hill Road

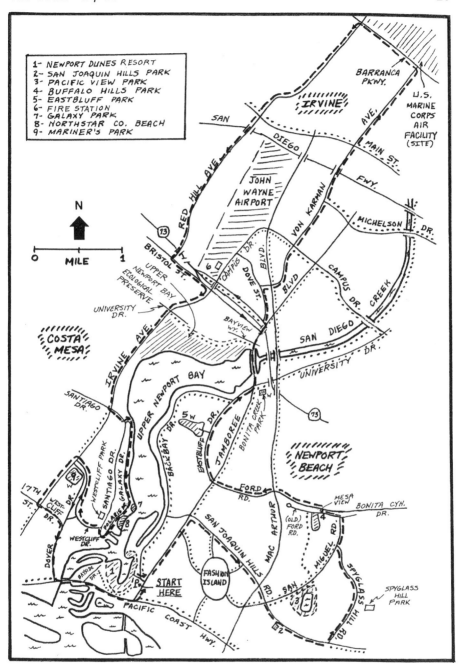

TRIP #7 - NEWPORT BEACH/IRVINE LOOP

residential/light commercial area to Jamboree Road (6.5). Cross Jamboree Road on the Class II street now named Eastbluff Drive and bike 1.3 miles through a well-groomed residential neighborhood, passing Vista Del Sol (entry to Eastbluff Park which has restrooms, athletic fields, and children's play areas) and the Eastbluff Shopping Center. The bikeway transits a pleasant tree-lined bluff, then heads downhill and returns to Jamboree Road.

Across Jamboree Road, Eastbluff Drive becomes University Drive, which leads shortly to super Bonita Creek Park (restrooms, snack shop, recreation fields/courts, and limited tree cover). However, the reference game plan is to bike across the bridge over San Diego Creek on the west side of Jamboree Road and to note the Class I bike trail just north of the bridge at Bayview Way. Turn left and follow that path along the northern periphery of the bay if you desire to take the shorter 14.8-mile Newport Bay Loop. (See the **Upper Bay Excursion** in Trip #6.) However, our reference route continues north on Jamboree Road and turns left at Bristol Street (north direction of that divided road) (8.1).

Irvine. At the first intersection, turn right at Dove Street and begin an 8.3-mile arc that passes through light industrial/high-tech territory with plenty of biking room. This portion of the tour is more scenic than expected, particularly for "building watchers" and "sidewalk superintendents." Note that Class I sidewalk biking is allowed where posted. Pedal 0.4 mile to Newport Place Drive and cross MacArthur Boulevard onto what is now Von Karmen Avenue.

Bike northwest on the Class I sidewalk past a variety of interesting building architectures and clever landscaping. In succession cross the main intersections at Campus Drive (transition to Class II), Michelson Drive, pass over the freeway, and cruise to Main Street. The number of stoplights on this industrial area tour are limited to the major intersections. The density of industrial complexes tails off north of the freeway, and this beeline route stays on lightly used roadway to Barranca Parkway (12.1). The gigantic blimp hangers of the now-closed Marine Corps Air Facility are clearly visible from here.

Turn left and bike on the Class II road 0.7 mile to Red Hill Avenue and turn left again. Pedal past a gas station at MacArthur Boulevard. Cycle 2.7 miles on the Class II route through an array of modern, light commercial complexes, passing over both the San Diego Freeway and the San Joaquin Transportation Corridor (State Highway 73). Along this segment are stowed aircraft and support facilities, as well as the arriving and departing flights of the John Wayne Airport.

Upper Newport Bay-West. Turn left at S. Bristol Street (16.8) and bike 0.4 mile to Irvine Avenue, then turn right and pedal downhill past the Newport Beach Golf Course. Near University Drive on the Class II road is the first peek into Newport Bay. (Note that there is a Class I path on the east side of the road below University Drive. This is the outlet of the **Upper Bay Excursion** in Trip #6.) Irvine Avenue winds through some small rolling hills and in 1.3 miles from Bristol Street reaches an open area with a view across the bay with Mount Saddleback in the background that will "knock your socks off."

Pedal a short distance to Santiago Drive through more small rolling hills. One option is to continue 0.7 mile south to Mariner's Park on Irvine Avenue. However, the reference route turns left at Santiago Drive, left again at Galaxy Drive and proceeds on the latter road through a quiet residential neighborhood. In just short of a mile is little Galaxy Park with a fountain, benches, and a dynamite view of Upper Newport Bay.

Continue on winding Galaxy Drive, turn left on Polaris Drive and bike past Northstar Lane (this road leads to a small marina and little Northstar County Beach) (20.2) and Westcliff Park (grassy scenic site at the end of Westwind Way). The road turns sharply right and follows a short and steep uphill to Westcliff Drive. Follow this road 0.4 mile and veer left onto a short spur that leads to Dover Drive. Follow this street as it bends to the left and returns to Irvine Avenue at Mariner's Park (recreation fields, playgrounds, shade, and water).

Return Segment. Turn left (south) and bike 0.7 mile to 17th Street/Westcliff Drive. Turn left, pass Westcliff Plaza (shopping center) and turn right at a "T"-intersection back onto Dover Drive. Freewheel another 0.4 mile of mostly downhill to PCH (23.2). Follow the Class I path on the east side of Dover Drive under the west end of the bridge to reach PCH eastbound (got that ?!). The territory on the return segment changes from residential to a mix of open and commercially developed land and higher density traffic on PCH.

Cross the bridge eastbound on the sidewalk or the Class II path on PCH. There is a fine view from the bridge of both the bay and the boaters below. Docked at the east end of the bridge is the Pride of Newport sternwheeler, a floating restaurant/nautical museum. The path crosses Bayside Drive, then follows a 0.4 mile upgrade that provides a grand view of Upper Newport Bay and Newport Dunes Waterfront Resort from the crest. In 0.6 mile, turn left on Jamboree Road, left again at Backbay Drive and return to the parking area (24.4). (A turn north at Bayside Drive at the signal and short ride almost to the resort entry booth will provide a "backdoor" Class I alternate entry to Newport Dunes Waterfront Resort and the trip origin. The Trip #6 map has the detail.)

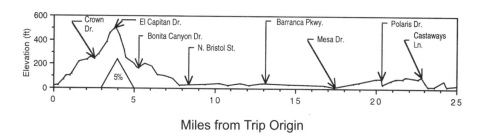

Miles from Trip Origin

CONNECTING TRIPS: 1) Continuation with the Upper Newport Bay tour (Trip #6) - the two trips share a common route from the start point; 2) connection with the Newport Beach/Corona Del Mar Tour (Trip #15) - at PCH and Jamboree Road, bike east on PCH; 3) connection with the Sunset Beach to Newport Beach Strand route (Trip #4) - at Dover Drive and PCH, bike west on PCH, turn toward the ocean at Balboa Boulevard and turn right at 46th Street; 4) connection with the San Diego Creek tour (Trip #18) - at the south side of the bridge over San Diego Creek, follow the Class I trail on the west side of Jamboree Road down below the bridge; 5) connection with William R. Mason Regional Park (Trip #37) - at Eastbluff Drive and Jamboree Road, follow the former street east where it becomes University Drive and bike 1.5 miles to the park main entrance.

TRIP #8 - IRVINE BIKEWAY

<u>GENERAL LOCATION</u>: Irvine

<u>LEVEL OF DIFFICULTY</u>: Loop - easy to moderate
                            Distance - 15.6 miles
                            Elevation gain - essentially flat

<u>HIGHLIGHTS</u>: This 100 percent Class II, all-residential multi-looper explores a community that has to be the biker's and walker's dream. Wide sidewalks, Class II paths, and public parks are seemingly everywhere. Add three Class I paths that cross the locale and two pristine lakes, and you've got to feel like somebody actually planned this area to be lived in! This is a pleasant, flat, moderate-mileage trip which takes in the Northwood-Westwood-Southwood-Eastwood Loop north of the Santa Ana Freeway and the West Yale-East Yale Loop to the south. A multitude of spurs can be taken off the main route, particularly off Yale Avenue. Several excellent spurs off the main route are provided as excursion rides. Finally, there are many excellent marked bikeways in the adjacent city of Tustin.

<u>TRAILHEAD</u>: From the Santa Ana Freeway, exit at Culver Drive and head northeast about 1.75 miles to Portola Parkway. Turn right and drive 0.6 mile to Yale Court. Turn right (south) and drive to street's end at Meadowood Park. The park is equipped with a small community center, restrooms, trees, and a children's playground, as well as picnic and barbecue facilities.

From the San Diego Freeway, exit northeast at Culver Avenue and motor 5.25 miles to Portola Parkway. Continue as described above. From the Eastern Transportation Corridor (State Highway 261), go southeast at the Portola Parkway off-ramp and motor 1.5 miles to Yale Court. Turn right as described above.

Only a light ration of water is needed since there are many parks, gas stations, and shopping centers along the way.

<u>TRIP DESCRIPTION</u>: **The Northern Half-Section.** Proceed down Class II Yale Avenue and cross over Hicks Canyon Wash and the Class I Hick's Canyon Bikeway, turning right at Hick's Canyon Road (0.3). Follow the arc through a nicely landscaped residential area to its halfway point where the street name becomes Park Place. Return to Yale Avenue (1.3) and turn right, cross Irvine Boulevard, then pass a shopping center. At (1.7), turn right on Northwood and follow this semicircle 0.3 mile to Silkwood Park. The park has a water fountain, trees, grass, a children's playground, a picnic area with barbecue facilities, and a section of the Class I Ventu Spur Trail.

As the road swings southwest its name changes to Westwood and it passes Brywood Park at (2.5). There is water near the baseball field and a restroom on the side of the elementary school facing the park, as well as limited picnic and barbecue facilities, tree cover, a children's play area, and other sports fields. In about 0.4 mile, the roadway is now Southwood and it returns to Yale Avenue at (3.1). Turn right, bike 0.3 mile and

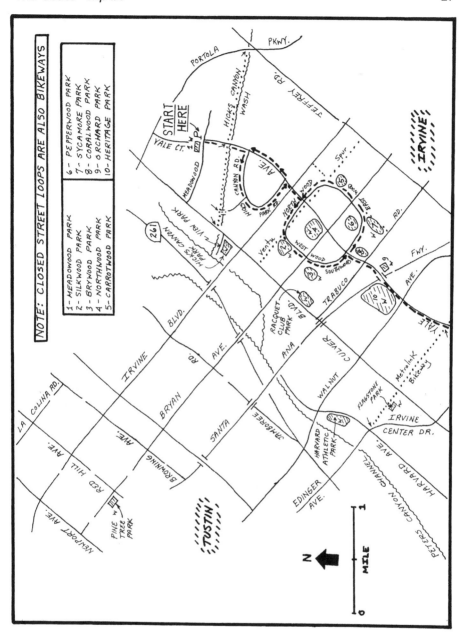

TRIP #8A - IRVINE BIKEWAY

pass Orchard Park (just off of Roosevelt), then cross over the Santa Ana Freeway soon after. The park has limited tree shade, restrooms, grass, and a children's playground.

The Southern Half-Section. Just after the freeway crossing is the area's granddaddy, Heritage Park. Besides all the amenities of the prior parks, it also has an aquatic park, library, fine arts center, and community center. Pedal past Walnut Avenue

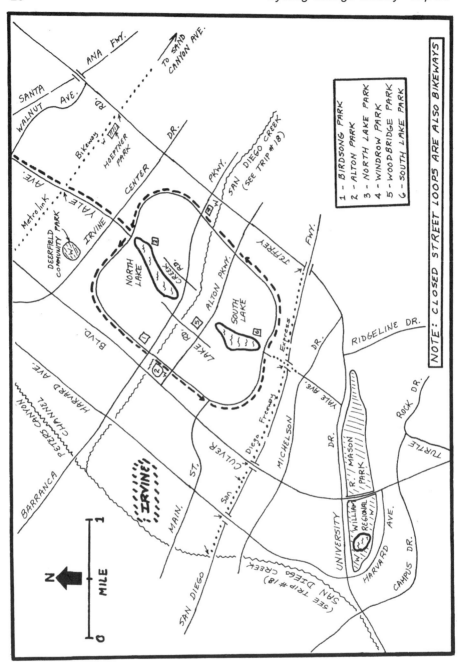

TRIP #8B - IRVINE BIKEWAY

(3.8) and reach Presley Park, with facilities like those at Silkwood Park, then follow a bridge over the Orange County Transportation Authority (OCTA) Metrolink railroad tracks with their paralleling Class I bikeway.

At (4.8), Yale Avenue ends at the northern tip of North Lake and cyclists head right onto West Yale Loop. Almost the entire loop is through residential environs with scattered parks and open grassy areas with single-family residences and some townhouse complexes. A mile-plus of pedaling leads across Warner Avenue, a pass-by of Birdsong Park (numerous facilities but no water) (6.4), followed by Barranca Parkway and a shopping center. At (6.7), pass over San Diego Creek (see Trip #18) and the northern edge of Alton Athletic Park (trees, water, restrooms, and numerous athletic fields).

Soon cross Alton Parkway followed by Main Street (7.3). *Note:* Below Alton Parkway, all parks we investigated are off the main loop and private. Bicycle around to the southern edge of the loop to the tip of South Lake and pass a small segment of Yale Avenue to the south. Nearby is Springbrook on the north side, which is an entry to South Lake (8.4).

Closing the Loops. Not far beyond, cyclists find themselves on East Yale Loop, heading northeast past Alton Parkway and a couple of shopping complexes (9.8). In 0.2 mile recross San Diego Creek and look for the signed entry to Windrow Park. (See Trip #18 for the park description.) Cross Barranca Parkway and follow the loop as it arcs 0.8 mile before returning to Yale Avenue (11.0). Nearby is a shopping complex and Ruby's, an upscale burger, fries, and milkshake diner with a North Lake vista.

Retrace the incoming route across Irvine Center Drive (11.2), Walnut Avenue (12.3), and the Santa Ana Freeway (12.6), then cruise 0.4 mile to Southwood. Turn right and

East Side of South Lake

follow the semicircle back around to Yale Avenue (14.4), then bike north 0.3 mile to Irvine Boulevard. (Near where Southwood becomes Eastwood on the semicircle, look to the right for Sycamore Park with a water fountain on the park's southern edge and tree cover, covered picnic areas, barbecues, park benches, and a children's playground.) All that remains is a 0.9-mile pedal on Yale Avenue back to Meadowood Park (15.6).

Excursions: Hicks Canyon Bikeway. The Class I path is enclosed within a pristine, shaded, nature-surrounded swath along the Hicks Canyon Wash. It starts at the intersection of View Park and Central Park at the western edge of Hick's Canyon Community Park and goes east to Portola Parkway, a distance of about two miles. Access from the southside residential area is at Culver Boulevard, Yale Avenue, and Portola Parkway, all of which also have street underpasses. There is one walkway/bikeway over the wash off of Hicks Canyon Road. In addition to the underpass accesses, there are numerous gated entries from the private community on the north side.

Cyclists planning an up-and-back ride should consider starting from the west in order to tackle the steady but mild uphill on the outbound leg. The natural start point is Hick's Canyon Community Park, which has a small community center, water, restrooms, Class I bikeway/walkways throughout the park, a children's play area, covered and uncovered picnic facilities, and sports fields.

Ventu Spur Trail. This Class I mini-trail is used by local walkers and bikers to access both sides of the northern loop area. It meanders between residences from just east of Culver Boulevard at Matera and continues southeast 1.5 miles to Jeffrey Road. It passes through the north end of both Silkwood Park and Pinewood Park near the western and eastern ends of the trail respectively. There are marked street crossings at Westwood, Yale Avenue, and Eastwood.

Metrolink Bikeway. The western and eastern entries to this three-mile Class I path alongside the OCTA Metrolink railway are off of Harvard Avenue, just north of Irvine Center Drive and Sand Canyon Avenue, just south of Burt Road respectively. There are also entries at Culver Road, Yale Avenue, and Jeffrey Road. Though removed from traffic elsewhere, there is a single road crossing at Jeffrey Road.

Yale Loop North-South Connector Trail. This 1.7-mile Class I path cuts through the heart of the Yale Loop heading roughly north-south. The northern and southern entries are near the northern and southern Yale Avenue/Yale Loop intersections, respectively. The trail skirts the western periphery of North Lake and the eastern side of South Lake. It bypasses Barranca Parkway on a walker/biker overpass, cruises through Woodbridge Village Center (eateries, shopping), crosses San Diego Creek on a walkway/bikeway bridge, cuts through Woodbridge Community Park and follows a second overpass on Alton Parkway.

San Diego Freeway Express. This Class I trail (name unknown) parallels the San Diego Freeway on its north side, going uninterrupted 1.1 miles from Jeffrey Road to Culver Boulevard. Reaching the straight-through 0.8-mile western segment requires crossing Culver Boulevard at a marked, signal-lighted intersection. The entire path follows beneath the power towers/transmission lines through brush-lined (east side) or grass-surrounded (west side) environs. The entries to the east side are at Jeffrey Road, Yale Avenue, and Culver Boulevard, and to the west side are Culver Boulevard, Reed Avenue, Harvard Avenue, and the path terminus at San Diego Creek.

CONNECTING TRIPS: 1) Connection with the San Diego Creek ride (Trip #18) - at the creek crossings, look for the entry on the north side of Alton Park or south side of Windrow Park; 2) connection with the Turtle Rock Drive (Trip #36) and William R. Mason Regional Park (Trip #37) tours - follow Yale Avenue south of Yale Loop and take the pedestrian/bike crossing over the San Diego Freeway. Continue on Yale Avenue to its end at University Drive, cross the street and take the Eastern Mason Park Bikeway westbound to "The Triangle Junction." Turn east or west for the Mason Park tour or south to reach Turtle Rock Drive; 3) connection with the Tustin Ranch Loop (Trip # 41) - from the Irvine Boulevard intersection, bike northwest 1.75 miles to Jamboree Road.

TRIP #9 - LAGUNA CANYON ROAD

GENERAL LOCATION: Irvine, Laguna Canyon, Laguna Beach

LEVEL OF DIFFICULTY: One way - moderate; up and back - moderate to strenuous
Distance - 10.6 miles
Elevation gain - frequent moderate grades

HIGHLIGHTS: This sun-exposed canyon route starts from Irvine in the Orange County interior and dumps out at breezy Laguna Beach. The first 1.9 miles is on Class II roadway which passes through light-industrial complexes, followed by a 1.2-mile ride through open agricultural area on Class X roadway. The remaining Class III portion within Laguna Canyon traverses a series of rolling hills through 3.1 workout miles before cruising downhill into the city of Laguna Beach. The highlights of the trip are the canyon vistas and the points of interest near Laguna Beach. The latter include Irvine Bowl and Irvine Bowl Park, as well as Laguna's Main Beach. Just to the north off of Pacific Coast Highway (PCH) are Heisler Park and the Laguna Art Museum.

TRAILHEAD: From the Santa Ana Freeway, exit southwest at Jeffrey Road and drive 1.5 miles to Barranca Parkway. Turn right and then left at Yale Loop East (the first street) and motor about 200 yards. Turn left at the signed entrance to Windrow Park and drive to the park's edge on Jeffrey Road. From the San Diego Freeway, exit northeast at Jeffrey Road/University Drive and go one mile to Barranca Parkway. Turn left and follow the directions above. The park has water and restrooms near the athletic fields (cross the wooden pedestrian bridge for access), shade trees, and a gymnasium.

Bring a filled water bottle, two if you are doing an up-and-back ride. There are public water sources at Windrow Park and in Laguna Beach, with nothing in between.

TRIP DESCRIPTION: **Windrow Park to Laguna Canyon Road.** From the park's eastern edge, follow the Class I San Diego Creek Bikeway under Jeffrey Boulevard. Continue along the creek for a 1.3-mile amble to Laguna Canyon Road or leave the creek and bike roughly the same distance along the light-industrial complexes on Class II Barranca Parkway. Turn right onto Class II Laguna Canyon Road, which becomes Class X at Pasteur. Bike over the San Diego Freeway and cycle through agricultural environs.

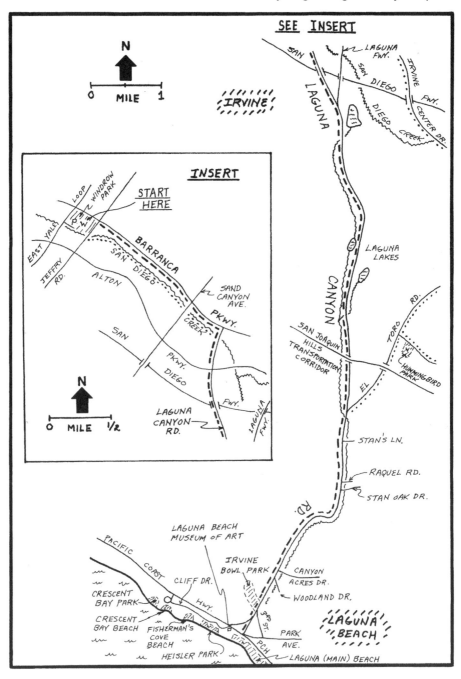

TRIP #9 - LAGUNA CANYON ROAD

Laguna Canyon Entry. Laguna Canyon Road fuses with the Laguna Freeway outlet traffic in an area surrounded by open fields (2.8). In 0.1 mile, the bikepath starts heading into the canyon opening; the Laguna Reservoir is high on the hillside to the left. There are rolling hills and a small creek along the roadway as the route proceeds into the canyon proper. The roadway becomes a signed Class III at (3.1).

The Canyon Tour. Follow a moderate upgrade (3.7) and reach the crest in an area with a few small shade trees (4.0). In another 0.4 mile, pass a small hamlet to the left (east); to the right are small tree stands and overgrowth. In about 1.3 miles of light rolling hills and nearly treeless roadway, pass over the outlet creek from North Laguna Lake (5.7). This creek parallels the road through much of the canyon.

Bike over the rolling hills within the canyon and head up a grade with a "Laguna Beach City Limit" sign near the summit (6.1). At the time of our initial trip, there were a large number of hawks circling the area. In 0.3 mile, pass under the San Joaquin Hills Transportation Corridor, then observe the interesting rock formations just beyond and to the right. Pass the El Toro Road terminus (7.2) and, soon after, a small community to the left (east).

In succession, the uphill-downhill route passes Stan's Lane (7.6), opens up to a view of a ridgetop community to the east, then passes through a small roadway community with an adjacent cattle grazing area near Raquel Road (8.1). The terrain flattens out and passes a parklike area to the east, meets another small community (8.4), then proceeds through a 1.2-mile narrow canyon segment with no other cross-streets. Just beyond Canyon Acres Drive, the canyon opens up to some strong indications that the "big city" is near.

Laguna Beach. The now flat route begins to exit the canyon and passes through heavier residential/commercial areas, the site of the seasonal Sawdust Festival, then meets the turnoff to the Irvine Bowl and Irvine Bowl Park (10.2). Just beyond is a view into the commercial heart of Laguna Canyon Road and a "peek" at the local beach. At (10.6) from the trip start, the bikepath ends at PCH and enticing Laguna Beach's Main Beach.

Return Route Options. The options at this point are to return directly back up the canyon, take a lengthy tour of the city of Laguna Beach or plop down at the beach. The Laguna Beach tour might include a trip to Heisler Park and the Laguna Art Museum; they are reached via Cliff Drive, just north on PCH. A shadier option is to return to Irvine Bowl Park.

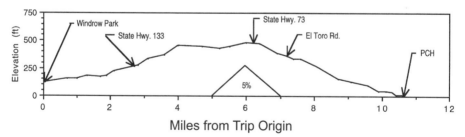

Miles from Trip Origin

CONNECTING TRIPS: 1) Continuation with the Laguna Beach Tour (Trip #10) - at the trip terminus take PCH to the right (northwest) towards Crystal Cove State Park or left towards Aliso Beach County Park; 2) continuation with the San Diego Creek route (Trip #18) - from the trip origin, bike east as described in the tour description or west toward the Yale Loop; 3) connection with the Irvine Bikeway (Trip #8) - from the trip origin, bike west to the Yale Loop on the San Diego Creek bikeway, Barranca Parkway, or Alton Parkway; 4) connection with the Laguna Hills Loop (Trip #31) - at the junction with El Toro Road, head northeast on that road.

TRIP #10 - LAGUNA BEACH TOUR

<u>GENERAL LOCATION</u>: Corona Del Mar - Laguna Beach

<u>LEVEL OF DIFFICULTY</u>: One way - moderate; up and back - moderate to strenuous
Distance - 9.1 miles (one way)
Elevation gain - frequent moderate-to-steep grades

<u>HIGHLIGHTS</u>: This is one of the finer beach tours, provided that a continuous diet of hills and limited stretches of "tight" biking quarters on Pacific Coast Highway (PCH) aren't a turnoff. There are excellent beach vistas spread throughout the route, including at the Crystal Cove State Beach area, Crescent Bay Point Park, and Heisler Park. The route passes through pleasant Laguna Beach and some of the local hillsides and ends at scenic Aliso Beach County Park. Most of the route is Class II or III, although there is a short section near the center of Laguna Beach that rides more like a Class X route.

<u>TRAILHEAD</u>: Proceed south from Newport Beach on PCH. Roughly 1.25 miles from MacArthur Boulevard, turn right (south) on Seaward Road and find parking in that residential neighborhood. From Laguna Beach continue three quarters of a mile north beyond the northern boundary of Crystal Cove State Beach to Seaward Road. (If you pass Poppy Avenue, you've gone too far.)

<u>TRIP DESCRIPTION</u>: **Crystal Cove State Park.** Return to PCH and turn right (south). This is the start of a Class II route through residential areas. Just beyond Cameo Shores Road/Cameo Highlands Drive (0.3), the development thins. There are hills to the left (northeast) and the bluffs of Crystal Cove State Park on the ocean side. (At the park's western edge is a Class I trail which, when connected with the park roads, covers almost three miles alongside PCH.) Pass the park entrance near Newport Coast Drive (1.0), Los Trancos Canyon (1.5), and then start a steep downhill. In another 0.1 mile is another entry to the park near the Crystal Cove area, followed by a short, steep upgrade. There is a nice peek at one of the many coves in the area near the crest (2.1).
  The Hills. In another 0.5 mile, cyclists pass near Reef Point. Head steeply downhill and enjoy a spectacular view into El Moro Cove. (Stop and admire the cove surroundings.) Near the bottom of the grade, there is a roadside snack stand, just at the point where another short, steep upgrade starts (3.3). (Those clever devils!) Work through steep rolling hills, pass Irvine Cove Way, then Bay Drive, and reach a crest at McKnight Drive (4.7). Just beyond is Crescent Bay Drive where cyclists can divert 0.1 mile to the right (toward the ocean) to take in Crescent Bay Point Park and one of the great vistas along the coast. There is also a water fountain here.
  Cliff Drive. In less than 0.2 mile, the bikepath leaves PCH and turns toward the beach on Class III Cliff Drive. The short tour along this lightly traveled, mild roller-coaster residential street is one of the premier parts of this trip. Bikers pass large groups of scuba divers preparing for the trip down to the coves, get periodic peeks down to those coves, then pass on the city side of Heisler Park (5.7).

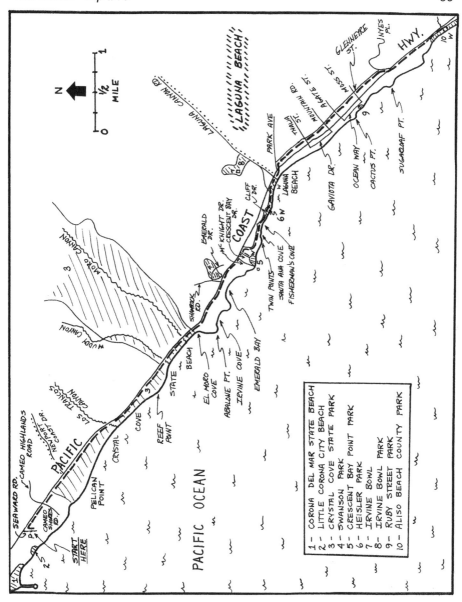

TRIP #10 - LAGUNA BEACH TOUR

This pleasant, long and thin park has a number of fine vista points supplied with benches. Walkways are distributed across the grounds. Stop and watch the scuba divers and scuba school in Diver's Cove. There are nice picnic spots with barbecues and water, too. Beyond is the Laguna Lawn Bowling Green, more park benches with a beach overlook, beach access at the south end of Heisler Park (a great view to the south beaches), and the Laguna Beach Museum of Art (5.8).

View from Heisler Park

Central Laguna Beach. The route returns to PCH in 0.1 mile and heads down-hill to the busiest part of town (and some of the tightest Class III bikeway we've seen). Pass Laguna Beach at the foot of Broadway, which is the local sunbathers' Mecca. There is water here and also pleasant outdoor dining at Greeter's Corner Restaurant next to the beach.

Paralleling PCH. Shortly, the path again leaves PCH and follows Park Avenue two blocks to Glenneyre Street (another block east on Catalina Street is the marked Pacific Coast Bicentennial Bike Route). We do not recommend riding PCH in the next mile or two because of the heavy traffic and absence of a usable shoulder! Instead, turn right on Glenneyre Street (6.3) and return southbound through a commercial district with light traffic and plenty of bike room. Pass through rolling hills past Thalia Street (6.7) and Cress Street (7.0). The road tightens down into a small one-lane road through more rural area near Calliope Street (7.1).

Beyond Agate Street (7.4) is a steep upgrade; in another 0.3 mile, the path reaches Diamond Street and a decision junction. Continue on Glenneyre Street if you want some challenging uphill and exciting downhill, turning right at Alta Vista Way, left at Solana Way, left at Victoria Place, then right at Nyes Place, to return to PCH (8.2). The easier option is to turn right toward the ocean and return to PCH at Diamond Street.

Aliso Beach County Park. Beyond Nyes Place, head downhill past a mobile home park in the hillsides and Aliso Creek Plaza (8.3). Pass Wesley Drive (8.8), then coast a steep downhill to the Aliso Beach County Park entrance (9.1). The park sports a pavilion with seasonal snack stand and restrooms, a fine and lightly used beach, children's playground, scattered palm trees, fire pits, and a real, live creek that runs through the park to the beach.

Return Route Options. On the return trip, follow the bikeway/walkway along the north side of Aliso Creek under PCH. Return by the same route unless there is a desire for some fun diversions. They are as follows: 1) at Moss Street and PCH, turn west on Moss Street to Ocean Way; follow that pleasant street up on the ocean bluffs to Agate Street. Cross PCH there and return to Glenneyre Street, then proceed to Mountain Street; 2) turn west and recross PCH to Gaviota Drive (a little road behind a bunch of garages that has limited but classy ocean views). Continue on Gaviota Drive to Thalia Street and again cross PCH, returning to Glenneyre Street. The remainder of the trip is a backtrack to the starting point.

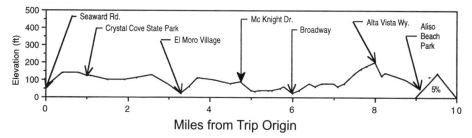

CONNECTING TRIPS: 1) Connection with the Laguna Canyon Road tour (Trip #9) - turn inland (north) in Laguna Beach proper at Broadway (State Highway 133) and continue north; 2) connection with the Newport Beach/Corona Del Mar Tour (Trip #15) - go two streets north on PCH beyond Seaward Road to Poppy Avenue. Turn toward the coast and bike 0.3 mile to Ocean Boulevard above Little Corona City beach; 3) connection with the Signal Peak and Pelican Hill ride (Trip #38) - turn north at Newport Coast Drive.

TRIP #11 - LAGUNA NIGUEL BIKEWAY

GENERAL LOCATION: Mission Viejo, Laguna Niguel

LEVEL OF DIFFICULTY: One way - moderate; up and back - moderate
Distance - 7.0 miles (one way)
Elevation gain - frequent moderate grades

HIGHLIGHTS: This tour explores territory ranging from the dryer interior hills to the breezy west-facing beaches. The route has an initial exposed section followed by a lengthy, lush tree-lined segment. There are scattered undeveloped sections, as well as large shopping centers at the trip origin, middle segment, and terminus. The one constant of this trip is mildly hilly terrain. There are several excellent vista points, particularly late in the trip.

There is an excellent spur trip off the main Class II Crown Valley Parkway route. It is a Class I hillside trail along the lower part of the Salt Creek Trail, reached via Camino Del Avion, that winds alongside the Monarch Beach Golf Links and lets out at Salt Creek Beach Park. There is additional (directly connected) fun biking near the

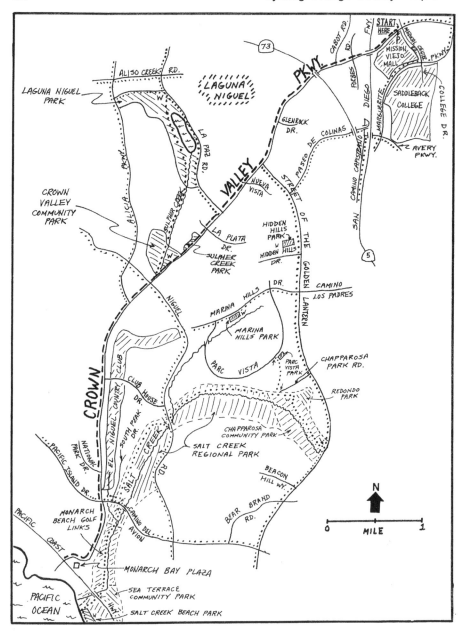

TRIP #11 - LAGUNA NIGUEL BIKEWAY

beach below the awesome Ritz Carton Hotel, within the upper park, and across PCH at Sea Terrace Community Park.

For round-trip riders, there are several classy return options which use some combination of Camino Del Avion, the Salt Creek Trail, Niguel Avenue and the Street of the Golden Lantern (SGL). All are more difficult than the basic up-and-back tour, but offer some interesting return trip variety. The **Salt Creek Trail to Street of the Golden Lantern** is a particularly appealing, sight-filled option.

TRAILHEAD: From the San Diego Freeway, exit east on Crown Valley Parkway and proceed about one-half mile to Medical Center Road (El Regateo to the north). Turn right (south) and find parking within the Mission Viejo Mall. From the San Joaquin Transportation Corridor (State Highway 73), exit at Greenfield Drive and turn south. In about one-third mile, take Crown Valley Parkway left (east) and cross over the San Diego Freeway. Continue as described above.

Bring a moderate water supply and plan to resupply at Crown Valley Community Park near the trip midpoint and/or Salt Creek Beach Park at the spur trip end point.

TRIP DESCRIPTION: **Mission Viejo.** Exit the Mission Viejo Mall and turn left (west) on Crown Valley Parkway. For the next one-fourth mile the Class II route remains alongside the mall, heading downhill, with residences in the hills to the right. Just beyond the passage over the San Diego Freeway (0.2), the road becomes Class III and the surrounding territory begins to transition to a drier, less-developed look. The route passes Forbes Road, crosses over Oso Creek (0.3), goes under State Highway 73 just beyond Cabot Road (0.7), then passes The Center at Rancho Niguel.

The Foothills. Cycle uphill, reaching the top of the upgrade in about another half mile. This is Class II roadway, as it will stay for the trip's remainder. There is a nice view out of the small canyon, back toward Mission Viejo proper, which includes the distant mountains and foothills.

Proceed through this partially developed, hill-enclosed section, pass Glenrock Drive (1.7) and head downhill to Moulton Parkway/SGL (2.1). Crown Valley Parkway has paralleled Sulphur Creek for the last half mile and will continue to do so for another 1.5 miles. There is a Class I bikeway along the creek for most of this stretch.

Laguna Niguel. In another 0.2 mile, bike past Nueva Vista where there are newer residential developments in the hills to the right (northwest) and a small shopping center to the left. Cross Adelanto Drive (2.6), continue uphill to La Paz Road, then follow a long

Lower Salt Creek Trail

downgrade past La Plata Drive to the Sulphur Creek Reservoir (3.1), where Sulphur Creek pulls away from the roadway. In another 0.3 mile is Crown Valley Community Park, a nice shade park with water and restrooms; it's a great place for a rest break. Pedal up to Niguel Road (3.7) to a flat, reaching Alicia Parkway. In this 0.3 mile there are many places to stop and snack, including "The Village" and the Crown Valley Mall.

The hilly route continues uphill just north of Alicia Parkway, and the surroundings change from one of the dryer interior to more coastal and treed. The road curves south in this area. Bike in a tree-lined section which crests at a point above the El Niguel Country Club and Golf Course (4.5). Follow a roller-coaster stretch by Club House Drive (4.9) and Laguna Woods Drive (5.2), then enjoy the views into the surrounding hills. Crown Valley Parkway meets Camino Del Avion (east)/Pacific Island Drive (west) at (6.1).

The Coast. There is an exceptional spur trip off of Camino Del Avion which is described below. However, our reference route continues on a workout upgrade to a crest near Sea Island Drive (6.5). As a diversion, cross the roadway for a vista that takes in a wide coastal area. Begin a long steep descent from this crest and enjoy the periodic "peeks" at the ocean. In 0.35 mile, the route passes the Monarch Bay Plaza entrance and, in another 0.15 mile, meets PCH (7.0) at the plaza's southern edge.

Return Route Options for Up-and-Back Riders. Retrace the incoming Crown Valley Parkway route to Class II Camino Del Avion (7.7). At this juncture, simply retrace the incoming ride or turn right (east) and take one of the alternates below:

Surface Street Return. (See the elevation contour below for the "Alternate Return Leg.") Cross the bridge over Salt Creek and make a short climb, then coast to Niguel Road (8.4). A short easy pedal is followed by a serious climb to Class II SGL. Turn left (north), coast another short stretch, then pump a steep grade for the next mile past a succession of gated communities. The initial crest is reached just after Old Ranch Road/Bear Brand Road, followed by Beacon Hill Way in 0.3 mile (9.9).

Pass a fire station and the Salt Creek Trail outlet just south of Sardina/ Saint Christopher (10.6). Reach another local crest near Dunes in 0.4 mile, cruise to Marina Hills Road, then tough out a final climb to the trip high point near Duchess Street (12.5). (On the way up at the northwest corner of Hidden Hills Road, is Hidden Hills Neighborhood Park, a cozy park with a water fountain, picnic benches, gazebos, limited shade, and a children's play area.) Pass the sign noting the pending 10 percent downgrade, then glide by Paseo De Colinas in 0.4 mile and reach Crown Valley Parkway at (13.4). Turn right and retrace the outgoing route back to Medical Center Road (15.5). Of the three return options, this is the hardest and the full loop is rated strenuous.

Salt Creek Trail to Niguel Avenue. Look for the trail at street level to the west side of the bridge on the north side of Camino Del Avion. (It is just east of private South Peak Drive.) This up-and-down trail stays partway up the western side of the canyon. The canyon bottom is in a relatively natural state and both east and west ridgelines are topped with upscale residences.

In one mile, coast downhill to Niguel Avenue and find the street's undercrossing. Parallel the street and take the Niguel Avenue return trail exit, heading northeast. Once on Niguel Avenue northbound, climb steeply to a false crest in 0.3 mile (just beyond Club House Drive), then resume a less testy 0.95 mile pull to a second summit just near La Hermosa Avenue. A 0.25-mile steep coast leads to Crown Valley Parkway. Turn right and just reverse the incoming route from Niguel Avenue to Medical Center Road. The total loop is 14.1 miles. The return via this route makes for a moderate-to-strenuous round trip.

Salt Creek Trail to Street of the Golden Lantern. Follow the Salt Creek Trail as described above, but rather than taking the fork northeast to Niguel Avenue, take the trail eastward into San Juan Canyon. A steady light upgrade on the canyon's northern face leads to a large sports complex at the western edge of Chapparosa Community Park in 1.1 miles, which has restrooms, several baseball diamonds, athletic courts and fields, picnic facilities, and a children's playground.

Skirting the park on its northern edge leads to a steep exit path north to scenic Parc Vista Park and Parc Vista (a roadway) near Minori. Continuing past this exit path leads to the auto outlet at Chapparosa Park Road on the park's eastern edge. Cross the road and look for an entry gate heading uphill to the right. A quarter-mile section of steep uphill leads to a milder, winding, canyon-hugging grade where the views back down the incoming Salt Creek Trail just get better with altitude. In 1.1 miles from Chapparosa Road is the trail's end at SGL just south of Sardina/Saint Christopher. (There is parking just across the small canyon at SGL for Dog Park users and bikers who want to explore upper Salt Creek Trail.) The SGL segment (left) to Crown Valley Parkway is described in the **Surface Street Return** above. The total loop is 16.0 miles and is rated strenuous.

Excursion: Salt Creek Beach via Salt Creek Trail. On the incoming route, turn east on Camino Del Avion and bike 0.1 mile, then look for a steep Class I trail on the west side of the bridge over Salt Creek. (There is also an entry on the north side of the street at the east end of the bridge.) Take the trail down to Salt Creek Regional Park and head south. There is a great view to the ocean and surrounding classy residential territory at this point. Bike the Class I path another 1.3 miles down a winding canyon path alongside the Monarch Beach Golf Links, pass under Pacific Coast Highway (PCH), and cruise to Salt Creek Beach.

Once at the coast, the trail proceeds southeast about 20 to 30 feet above the beach and reaches Bluff Park (picnic tables, barbecues, and supreme view). A short distance beyond is the steep (private) trail to the Ritz Carlton Hotel and a second steep (public) trail that heads north toward PCH. The latter trail passes under Ritz Carlton Drive and reaches a parking area with restrooms, tree shade, and an adjacent landscaped park area. Biking further north leads under PCH to Sea Terrace Community Park with its grassy knolls, picnic benches, and library. (Bikers who follow the full spur tour can return to Salt Creek most conveniently via PCH.)

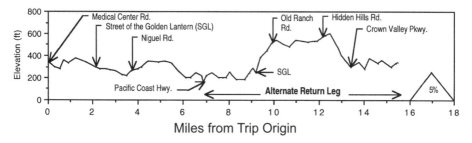

CONNECTING TRIPS: 1) Connection with the Aliso Creek Trail (Trip #29) - Option A: Exit Crown Valley Parkway at La Paz Road - Option B: Exit Crown Valley Parkway at Crown Valley Community Park and ride north on the bike trail; 2) Connection with the Mission Viejo Bikeway (Trip #30) - from the Mission Viejo Mall, turn right (east) on Crown Valley Parkway, continue about half a mile to Marguerite Parkway and turn left (north); 3) connection with the Westside Laguna Niguel tour (Trip #39) - the two trips share a common segment on Crown Valley Parkway; 4) connection with the Aliso Viejo Figure "8" (Trip #46) - at Crown Valley Parkway and La Paz Road, bike north on the latter street to Aliso Creek Road; 5) connection with the Arroyo Trabuco Loop (Trip #50) - at Crown Valley Parkway and Medical Center Road, bike southwest on the latter street to Marguerite Parkway.

TRIP #12 - DOHENY BIKEWAY

GENERAL LOCATION: Mission Viejo, San Juan Capistrano

LEVEL OF DIFFICULTY: One way - easy; up and back - easy to moderate
Distance - 6.9 miles (one way)
Elevation gain - essentially flat

HIGHLIGHTS: This is a pleasant trip on mostly Class I and Class II bikeways along Oso, Trabuco, and San Juan Creeks. Included is a segment which passes near historic San Juan Capistrano Mission and a ride terminus at scenic Doheny State Beach, which has plentiful facilities. The route starts at the southern edge of Mission Viejo and cruises the periphery of Laguna Niguel, then visits San Juan Capistrano, Dana Point, and Capistrano Beach. There are several pleasant parks for rest spots south of Junipero Serra Road.

TRAILHEAD: From the San Diego Freeway, exit at Avery Parkway. One option is to drive west a short distance to the end of Avery Parkway, turn left (south) and find parking on Camino Capistrano. A second option is to drive east on Avery Parkway, cross Marguerite Parkway and proceed steeply 0.2 mile up to Los Ondas Avenue. Turn left and drive 0.1 mile to Coronado Park. There are scattered trees, park benches, and barbecues, as well as a children's playground, but no water.

From the San Joaquin Hills Transportation Corridor (State Highway 73) south-bound, continue onto the San Diego Freeway transition and exit east at Junipero Serra Road. Turn north onto Rancho Viejo Road and drive two miles to Avery Parkway. Proceed as described above.

Bring a light water supply. There are commercial water stops near the Avery Parkway western terminus and public sources at several parks along the way.

TRIP DESCRIPTION: **Camino Capistrano.** From Coronado Park, return to Class II Avery Parkway and coast on a steep downhill past Plata Place (an entrance to Saddleback College) to Rancho Viejo Road (0.2). Cross that street and go under the

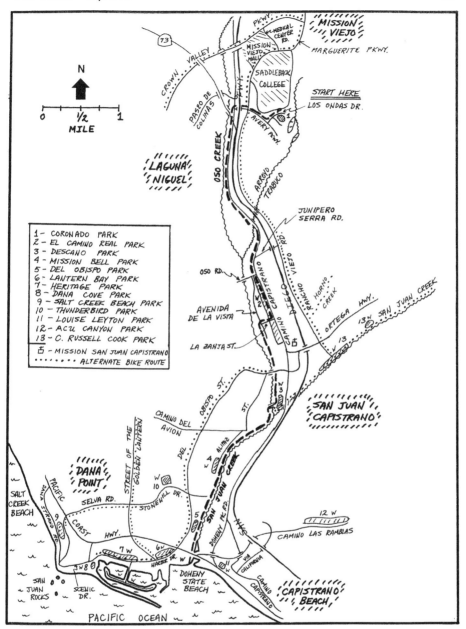

TRIP #12 - DOHENY BIKEWAY

San Diego Freeway on a short Class X stretch, turning left (south) at the Avery Parkway terminus. Proceed south on Class III Camino Capistrano under Highway 73, passing numerous roadside businesses and fast-food stops into a more open countryside
(0.5). Here the route transitions to Class II.

   For the next couple of miles, the surrounding backdrop is the hills to the right
(west) and the San Diego Freeway to the left. There is a short stretch of highway that

has been blocked to auto traffic for several years but is passable by bikers and pedestrians. Beyond the road closure, pass the Rancho Capistrano Cemetery (0.7) and orange groves, then cross over the Arroyo Trabuco (1.4). South of the confluence of Oso and Trabuco Creeks, the waterway takes the name of the latter. The route crosses Junipero Serra Road (2.3) and Oso Road, then reaches the northern end of El Camino Real Park (2.7).

El Camino Real Park and Trabuco Creek. The Class I bikepath travels along the edge of this well-shaded park. There are scattered park benches and tables, and a restroom is located near the park's midpoint across from Calle Bonita. About a quarter mile further down Camino Capistrano is Mission San Juan Capistrano. However, the marked bike route turns right (west) at La Zanja Street and proceeds shortly to a terminus at Avenida De La Vista (3.3). Turn left onto this Class III route and bike through a residential neighborhood to a cul-de-sac (3.5).

Pedal onto the small path that returns to the east side of Trabuco Creek. That Class I bikeway follows the cement-walled creek into a more open valleylike area, passes under Del Obispo Street (4.0) and then cruises along a light industrial area to the left (east). Soon, cyclists pass alongside conveniently located Descanso Park with its shade trees, grassy rest area, full picnic facilities, restrooms, and water (4.4).

San Juan Creek. Cross the creek on a little bikeway/walkway. The crossing is just upstream of the point where Oso Creek and San Juan Creek join, and the waterway takes the name of the latter. Soon there is a long-distance view down the creek with a good look at the foothills to both the east and west. There are several entry points at Via Mistral and beyond (5.0-5.2) and a passage alongside Mission Bell Park (5.5). (The long, thin park is broken into several sections, with the southernmost having water fountains and porta-potties.) Dip under Stonehill Drive, pass additional bike entries at (5.9-6.0) and note the increasing housing density along the path. The route passes a large group of condominiums and later the entry to Del Obispo Park (6.5). This park has light shade, baseball diamonds, tennis courts, and a seasonal concession stand.

San Juan Creek Outlet at the Ocean

Doheny State Beach. In another quarter mile, follow a passage under Pacific Coast Highway (PCH). If the path is not flooded, stay on the trail alongside the marsh-land (frequently there are ducks in this area). Stop near the beach and enjoy the sweeping view, particularly south (6.9). Finally, take a leisurely spin through expansive Doheny State Beach Park. There are picnic and barbecue areas, trees, water, a beach, concession stands, and plenty of people.

If the bikeway is flooded, cyclists must divert to the surface streets to reach the ocean. Backtrack to the nearest trail entry point to PCH. Travel west to Del Obispo Street and take that street across PCH to the main park entrance. (On the south side of PCH, the street's name is Dana Point Harbor Drive.)

Alternate Return Route. Round-trip bikers can repeat the incoming route or opt for a short 1.5-mile segment on Rancho Viejo Road on the east side of the San Diego Freeway. The freeway walker/biker underpass is located where Camino Capistrano crosses Trabuco Creek. Having transited the freeway, bike north on Class II Rancho Viejo Road to Avery Parkway, then return to the trip start point.

CONNECTING TRIPS: 1) Continuation with the Del Obispo Bikeway (Trip #13) - return to the main entrance of Doheny State Beach/Park and turn right (north) at Dana Point Harbor Drive, then continue north across PCH; 2) continuation with the Doheny/San Clemente Bike Route (Trip #14) - from Doheny State Beach/Park, follow the frontage road along PCH south towards Capistrano Beach; 3) connection with the Arroyo Trabuco Loop (Trip #50) - at Junipero Serra Road and Camino Capistrano, go east on the former street under the San Diego Freeway.

TRIP #13 - DEL OBISPO BIKEWAY

GENERAL LOCATION: San Juan Capistrano-Dana Point

LEVEL OF DIFFICULTY: Loop - moderate
Distance - 17.2 miles
Elevation gain - periodic light upgrades; single, short, and steep upgrade

HIGHLIGHTS: This is a "must do" adventure! The outbound leg is built around the Del Obispo Bikeway with an alternate return leg provided for variety. Most of the trip is on Class I or Class II bikeway. Far and away, the tour highlight is the Dana Point Harbor tour at the end of the outbound leg. The route also passes next to historic Mission San Juan Capistrano. In addition, there is a pleasant cruise on Del Obispo Street, several park visits, and a tour into the "far reaches" of San Juan Creek. Finally, there are fine scenic views from atop Lantern Bay Park and some super-duper vista points from a very strenuous spur trip off of Scenic Drive.

TRAILHEAD: From the San Diego Freeway, exit at Ortega Highway and head west about a quarter of a mile to Camino Capistrano. Turn right (north) and continue a

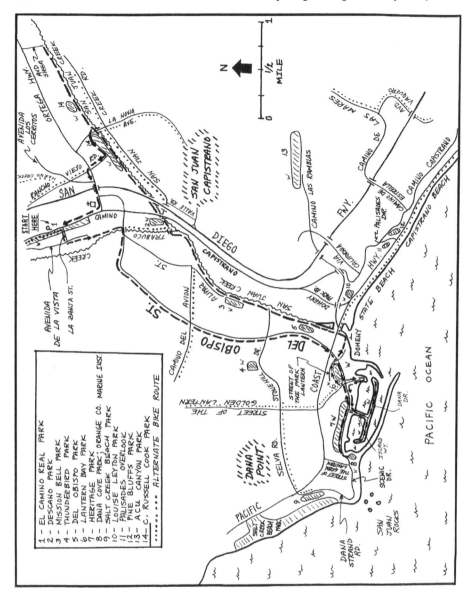

TRIP #13 - DEL OBISPO BIKEWAY

quarter of a mile to El Camino Real Park. Find a turnaround point north of La Zanja Street and pick a spot alongside the shaded park. (The park also has benches, grass, and a restroom near the park's midpoint across from Calle Bonita.) From Pacific Coast Highway (PCH), turn north at Del Obispo Street (Dana Point Harbor Drive to the south) and drive half a mile to the park.

Bring a moderate water supply. There are shopping centers and parks with water scattered about this bike route. For additional details on the parks along San Juan and Trabuco Creeks, refer to Trip #12.

TRIP DESCRIPTION: **Trabuco Creek.** Ride south and turn right (west) on La Zanja Street. Follow the marked Class III route a short distance to Avenida De La Vista and turn left (south). Pedal about 0.2 mile through a residential neighborhood to a cul-de-sac (0.4). (Do not even think about those private swimming pools you see along the roadway!) Bike onto a small path that leads to the east side of Trabuco Creek. Follow the creek about 0.4 mile on a Class I path and exit at Del Obispo Street, heading right (southwest) (0.8).

    Del Obispo Street. Cruise on the Class II bike route through a residential area, passing Alipaz Street and Paseo Terraza (1.2). The roadway curves southward and follows a light upgrade just beyond. There are nearby hills with homes to the right (west), with residential below and the more distant hills, both to the left. This type of scenery continues for more than a mile. Pass the mammoth "Farm to Market" produce outlet (1.8), Via Del Avion (2.2), and Blue Fin Drive (2.6). The residential density increases on both sides of the street beyond this point.

    In 0.4 mile, bike across Stonehill Drive, passing a large shopping center. At (3.5), the route meets Quail Run, where there is a large condominium community across the road and an entry into Del Obispo Park just beyond. (This park has light shade, baseball diamonds, tennis courts, and a seasonal concession stand.) At (3.9) is the busy PCH intersection with its collection of small eateries.

    Dana Point Harbor. After crossing PCH, the road name becomes Dana Point Harbor Drive (also referred to as Harbor Drive). Pass the Doheny State Park main entrance (left) and the Street of the Park Lantern, with its steep road entry to Lantern Bay Park. Bike on Class II Harbor Drive and pass below the steep bluffs to the landward side of the road. Then turn left toward the harbor on the Street of the Golden Lantern (4.3). (Is this a great name or what?!) Proceed to the wharf area and eyeball the row-on-row of pleasure craft tied up there. A short tour to the westernmost edge of the wharf area leads to such places as Harpoon Harry's, a fun café with outdoor seating under sun umbrellas and a picture-postcard harbor view.

    Return to the boatslips and proceed west on the sidewalk alongside the harbor. Turn left onto Island Way (5.2) and bike on the bridge over to the central island in the harbor. At the island entrance is the statue of Richard Henry Dana, Jr., which sits in the middle of a long, thin park on the island's seaward side. The park has benches, grass, barbecue facilities, little roofed picnic shelters, water, and restrooms. Grab a bench and watch the boats sail the harbor.

    A tour to the east leads to The Beach House and the Harbor Patrol Building. There is a nice southward view from the eastern edge of the island (5.9). Heading back across Island Way to the western edge of the island, cyclists observe the fishermen on the breakwater as well as take in the super view west and north to the seaside bluffs (6.7). Next, bikers recross the harbor on Island Way and return to Harbor Drive at (7.3).

    Turn left and pass sand-strewn Heritage Park. It has all the amenities of the park on the island plus trees, recreation/play area, and a bona fide windsurfer area. Bicycling westward leads to Dana Cove and the foot of Cove Road (7.8). (A diversion on this sheer Class X road leads up to some great vista points on what becomes Scenic Drive. The view of Dana Point harbor from these heights is unparalleled!)

    Stay on Harbor Drive and pass the Ocean Institute (marine studies) within Dana Cove Park. Consider a sidetrack to the pedal tour and visit the old sailing ship docked there. The Harbor Drive route ends just beyond, at the beginning of the outer breakwater.

One can walk onto the breakwater or hike northward along the tight coves from this point.

Lantern Bay Park. Return to the Street of the Golden Lantern (9.0). At the northeast corner of the intersection, follow the short, steep Class I switchback trail up to Lantern Bay Park. There is a 360-degree view from the top of the bluff that takes in the hills to the east, harbor to the south, homes on the bluffs to the west (including a wedding chapel), and condomania to the north. The park has water, trees, picnic/barbecue facilities, and a children's playground. Continue along the south edge of the park on the bikeway/walkway to the Smyth Amphitheater (9.3). This is a mini-amphitheater with a great scenic view. There was a wedding here on the Saturday we passed through, complete with piccolo players in tuxedos!

San Juan Creek. Bike east to the Street of the Park Lantern and follow that steep roadway downhill past a restroom to the intersection with Harbor Boulevard. Cross the street into the Doheny State Beach/Park entrance and follow the path nearest the beach to the San Juan Creek outlet (9.8).

Stay to the west side of the creek and pedal north under PCH. (If this marshy area is flooded, take the diversion route described in Trip #12.) Pass the entrance to Del Obispo Park (10.3) and then cycle uninterrupted along San Juan Creek past the Mission Bell Park entrance (11.1). In another 1.2 miles, the path crosses a bike bridge over Trabuco Creek just south of the creek junction. Dead ahead is small Descanso Park with shade, water, restrooms, grass, and picnic benches/barbecues.

The bikepath branches at this juncture, left along Trabuco Creek, and right to stay on San Juan Creek. Take the right branch, pass under Camino Capistrano (12.6) and ride along a wide, green, natural riverbed on continued Class I bikeway. Pass under the

Dana Point Harbor from Dana Cove Park

San Diego Freeway and, in 0.4 mile from Camino Capistrano, meet the Paseo Triador cul-de-sac. Follow that road to Calle Arroyo and turn right onto a Class II bikepath.

Shift over to the Class I path along Calle Arroyo or take the small Class I walkway/ bikeway off to the right that runs through C. Russell Cook Park paralleling Calle Arroyo (13.2). The entry to the path is just beyond a large equestrian staging area and it stays near and parallel to San Juan Creek. There are trees, picnic benches, and barbecues scattered along this greenbelt. Pass Rancho Viejo Road (13.6), then bike along a more-developed recreation area which has restrooms, scattered trees, picnic tables, a children's playground, and sports fields and courts.

At the recreation area's eastern edge is La Novia Avenue where Cook Park's western edge ends. The path jogs to the left (north) and goes alongside Calle Arroyo, crosses La Novia Avenue, then continues as a Class I trail along the creek. To the north is heavy residential development, and to the south are open fields across the creek. There are horse trails which parallel the bikepath and several bike entry points in this area (13.8, 14.1). At (14.2), enter the unconnected east segment of C. Russell Cook Park, which has a small shady playground area. In 0.3 mile, skirt some athletic fields with restrooms and a water fountain near Via Solana. Return to Calle Arroyo at Via Estenaga, the main park entry at Cook Park's eastern edge. The bikeway next passes a large area of horse stables and ends at Avenida Siega (14.8). (The dirt road on the creekside of Avenida Siega may serve as a bikeway extension in the future.)

Mission San Juan Capistrano. Return to Rancho Viejo Road (16.0), turn right, and ride 0.3 mile to Ortega Highway. Go left and take a 0.4-mile Class X segment that requires careful biking because of fast-moving traffic. At Camino Capistrano, turn right (north) and pass Mission San Juan Capistrano. Stop and visit this venerable Spanish mission or continue biking another half mile to the parking area (17.2).

Excursions: Horno Creek Trail. At the Marbella Golf and Country Club entrance at Rancho Viejo Road, the Class I path along Golf Club Drive follows the rough contour of Horno Creek. The one-way distance is 1.2 miles. Admittance is a courtesy; the implicit understanding is that cyclists will respect the standard cycling rules of good conduct.

La Novia Avenue. A fun loop in the hills, bike across San Juan Creek from the Calle Arroyo/La Novia Avenue intersection, cross San Juan Creek Road and cycle on the wide-shouldered Class X road or pick up the Class I path on the street's east side. Pass Via Entrada (0.6) and begin a steep climb for 0.2 mile before the grade moderates. Enjoy the views eastward into San Juan Capistrano, up to and beyond the crest which is 0.25 mile beyond Via Cerro Rebal. The road transitions to a wide-shouldered Class X, passes the San Juan Hills Golf Course and continues downhill to Valle Road (2.0).

Turn right and bike 0.3 mile alongside the San Diego Freeway, then right again at San Juan Creek Road. Follow that Class II road 1.2 miles on the south side of San Juan Creek to La Novia Avenue, turn left and return to the excursion start point (3.7).

CONNECTING TRIPS: 1) Connection with the Doheny Bikeway (Trip #12) - at the Descanso Park junction, take the westernmost bike trail along Trabuco Creek; 2) connection with the Doheny/San Clemente Bike Route (Trip #14) - follow the roadway from the Doheny State Beach/Park entrance over San Juan Creek and link up with the bikeway heading south along the beach; 3) connection with the Arroyo Trabuco Loop (Trip #50) - at Ortega Highway and La Novia Avenue, go either direction on the former road.

TRIP #14 - DOHENY/SAN CLEMENTE BIKE ROUTE

GENERAL LOCATION: Dana Point-San Clemente

LEVEL OF DIFFICULTY: Loop - moderate
                                          Distance - 17.1 miles
                                          Elevation gain - periodic moderate grades in
                                                   San Clemente area

HIGHLIGHTS: This trip is a mix between a beach route and a city tour. The first half follows Pacific Coast Highway (PCH) and provides numerous views of surf and sand. The second half is a loop tour through the heart of San Clemente on El Camino Real (ECR). The return trip includes an alternate return leg on a number of connecting residential roadways.

Highlights of the tour are Doheny State Beach and Capistrano Beach Park near the trip origin, the San Clemente City tour in general, and the pleasant out-of-the-way beach at San Mateo Point at the trip's southernmost point. The route is a mix of Classes I, II, and III biking with a limited stretch of Class X. There are some moderate rolling hills in the San Clemente area and some segments of ECR where there is very limited bike room.

TRAILHEAD: From the San Diego Freeway, exit west on Camino Las Ramblas and continue until that roadway fuses with PCH. Continue about a quarter of a mile to Dana Point Harbor Drive (named Del Obispo Street at the northern end of the intersection) and turn left. Drive a short distance and turn left into Doheny State Beach Park. A free parking alternative is to motor up the hill across from the park's gate entrance and park at Lantern Bay Park. That roadway is named the Street of the Park Lantern.

Bring a moderate water supply. There are scattered public water sources as noted on the trip map, and other sources such as gas stations in the city proper.

TRIP DESCRIPTION: **Doheny State Beach.** Take the entrance road south which becomes a frontage road alongside PCH and pass over San Juan Creek. Follow the path to the right which passes alongside a camping area and then enters the north end of Doheny State Beach (0.3). This pleasant stretch has clear ocean views and passes directly alongside the sunbathing area (get our drift?). The Class I path parallels the beach, transits Capistrano Beach Park, and exits at Beach Road (1.1) where it then follows PCH on a Class II path. (Note that there is a restroom and water just south of Beach Road at Capistrano Beach Park.)

Pacific Coast Highway - El Camino Real. The next 1.7 miles is along a stretch of highway with low bluffs to the east and rows of bushes which block the sea view to the west. At this point, PCH meets Camino Capistrano where a nice ocean view opens back up. The road name becomes El Camino Real at this point. There is a small shopping center to the east and a snack bar on the beachfront (2.8). The route returns to the surrounding cliffs for another 0.6 mile, then enters the San Clemente City limits at Avenida Estacion.

The roadway changes to Class III at this juncture. Begin a long, steady upgrade through a heavy-trafficked commercial district (4.1). There are portions of the next two

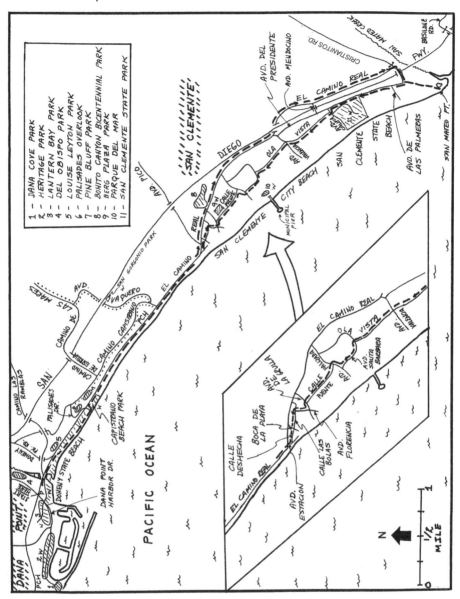

TRIP #14 - DOHENY/SAN CLEMENTE BIKE ROUTE

miles where bike room on ECR is very restricted. Pass the entry to Bonito Canyon Bicentennial Park at El Portal (tree shade, some facilities, but no water) (4.6), reach a level before Avenida Palizada and gain the crest near Avenida Del Mar (5.1). There is a view of the lovely hillside residential community from this area. After another more moderate upgrade, the route reaches its highest point near Paseo De Cristobal (5.7).

In 0.2 mile at Avenida Valencia, the road splits into ECR and Avenida Del Presidente. Our route forks left on ECR and passes under the San Diego Freeway onto a short, limited-shoulder, Class X section (6.0). Beyond here to the ECR terminus, the route is more residential, has lighter traffic, and offers more bike room. (If this is not your forte, use Avenida Del Presidente on both outgoing and return legs.) Parallel the freeway on small rolling hills with predominantly downhill riding. Pass Avenida Mendocino (6.5) and reach ECR's terminus at Cristianitos Road (8.0).

San Mateo Point. The trip route follows Cristianitos Road west over the San Diego Freeway. Just beyond the southbound on-ramp is a small path/roadway entrance that is blocked to automobiles. Follow that route south and downhill 0.3 mile and take the junction west at that point. (The southbound bikeway leads to the south gate of Camp Pendleton per Trip #16.) Pedal this junction path another 0.4 mile to a lovely and lightly used beach and an overlook/vista near San Mateo Point (8.7). If your timing is right, you may even see one of the high-speed AMTRAK passenger trains whiz by on the elevated railway near the beach.

Avenida Del Presidente. Return to Cristianitos Road and turn left (toward the ocean). This is the southern terminus (or origin) of Avenida Del Presidente (9.4). Follow the Class II roadway moderately and generally uphill past Avenida De Las Palmeras (9.7), the entry to a posh private residential area. Parallel the San Diego Freeway on the seaward side and head uphill past Avenida Vista De Oceano (9.9), then pass alongside the north edge of San Clemente State Park. There is a bike entry from this roadway into a large, pleasant, forested park (with campsites) (10.4). Our route stays along Avenida Del Presidente through rolling hills to Avenida Calafia.

San Vicente Residential Route. One option here is to pedal another 0.7 mile on Class II Avenida Del Presidente and turn south on Avenida Valencia. However, our reference route turns left (south) at Avenida Calafia and soon turns right at Ola Vista, a pleasant, quiet residential street through rolling hills. At Avenida Valencia, our tour mainly follows the old Pacific Coast Bicentennial Bike Route (11.3). The marked route (as shown on the detail map) follows in order: Ola Vista, left on Avenida Santa Barbara, right on Calle Seville, right on Avenida Palizada, left on Calle Puente, left and downhill on Avenida De La Grulla, right and downhill on Avenida Florencia, left on Calle Las Bolas, left on Boca De La Playa, right on Calle Deshecha, and right on Avenida Estacion, returning to ECR (13.7). Along the way is a market near Avenida Victoria and S. Ola Vista and the road access to the Municipal Pier on Avenida Del Mar near Calle Seville. Also there is a cozy rest and water stop at Max Berg Plaza Park along Calle Puente.

El Camino Real - Pacific Coast Highway. The return route is Class III along ECR until the automobile roadway narrows to one lane and the bike lane expands. It remains Class II until the left turn entry at Beach Road back into San Clemente Beach Park (16.0). From here the path reverses the outgoing route and returns to Doheny State Beach (17.1).

CONNECTING TRIPS: 1) Connection with the Doheny Bikeway (Trip #12) - from Doheny State Beach, bike to the outlet of San Juan Creek and follow the bikepath on the north side of that creek; 2) connection with the Del Obispo Bikeway (Trip #13) - return to the Doheny State Beach entrance, turn right (north) on Dana Point Harbor Drive and continue across PCH; 3) continuation with the San Clemente to San Diego ride (Trip #16) - continue south beyond the San Mateo Point turnoff discussed in this trip text; 4) connection with the Hillside San Clemente ride (Trip #40) - turn north at Camino Capistrano (Northern Loop) or Avenida Pico (Southern Loop).

TRIP #15 - NEWPORT BEACH/CORONA DEL MAR TOUR

GENERAL LOCATION: Newport Beach, Corona Del Mar

LEVEL OF DIFFICULTY: Loop - moderate
Distance - 10.1 miles
Elevation gain - periodic moderate grades

HIGHLIGHTS: This is a great coastal tour that provides a number of vistas and other scenic attractions. It is a mixed class route with a significant amount of Class X on relatively lightly traveled roadways. The outgoing bikepath travels Pacific Coast Highway (PCH) just north of Lower Newport Bay, then ducks inland to visit Ocean Boulevard on the bluffs above the Corona Del Mar beaches. The return leg is on Bayside Drive directly alongside the bay. There are numerous spur tours into the islands along the bay, the Newport Strand, or Upper Newport Bay.

TRAILHEAD: From PCH heading south, drive about half a mile beyond the Newport Boulevard overpass and turn left at Riverside Avenue. Bike a short, modest uphill to the southern junction with Cliff Drive and turn left to stay on Riverside Avenue. Turn left again at Cliff Drive (honest!) and find parking. Cliff Drive Park sports a grassy area with modest picnic facilities, a couple of palm trees, water, and a super view of the Newport Beach local area. From PCH northbound, go about one mile beyond Dover Road, turn right at Riverside Avenue and continue as described above.

Bring a light water supply. There is water at Irvine Terrace Park and on Ocean Boulevard near the trip midpoint.

TRIP DESCRIPTION: **Pacific Coast Highway/Lower Newport Bay.** Before starting the trip, take in the vista from Cliff Drive Park. Following this, bike back to PCH and turn left (east). The next half mile is Class X and best spent riding very carefully on PCH or using the wide sidewalks if the car traffic gets tough. The path soon becomes Class II. Pass the exclusive Balboa Bay Club (0.8) and enjoy the long-distance view of Fashion Island which opens up soon after. In 0.3 mile, cross Bayshore Drive and bike to the bridge over Newport Bay. There is a diversion under the bridge which takes riders to Dover Drive on the opposite side of PCH.

Cross the bridge on the sidewalk or on the Class II path on PCH. Stop and observe the boat traffic and the Pride of Newport (sternwheeler) floating restaurant/nautical museum, which is docked near the bridge on the east end. Next cross Bayside Drive (1.8) and start uphill. Near the crest is a grand view of Upper Newport Bay and Newport Dunes Waterfront Resort (2.2).

Pass private Promontory Drive, then Jamboree Road. In this tree-lined section of bikeway, there is a choice of using the marked sidewalk path or the Class II bikeway on PCH; this option continues for about half a mile. Cross Malabar Drive, which is one access to Irvine Terrace Park (restrooms, modest tree cover, barbecue facilities, sports fields, athletic courts, and children's playground) (3.0). In about 300 yards (near the

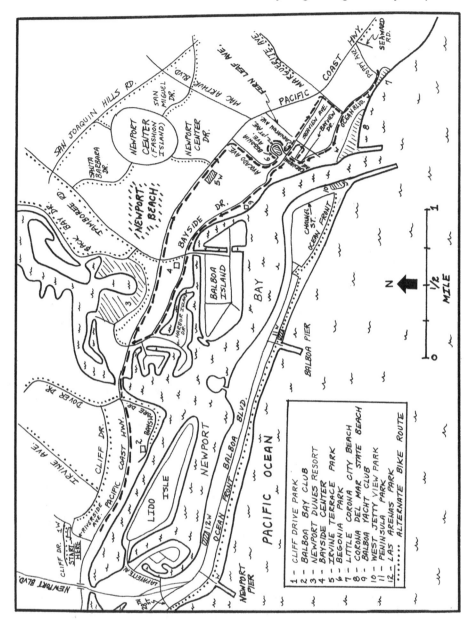

TRIP #15 - NEWPORT BEACH/CORONA DEL MAR TOUR

Newport Center Drive access to Fashion Island across PCH) is a gated entry to walled-off Irvine Terrace Park. Cycle another 0.2 mile and turn right (south) on Avocado Avenue. This is the beginning of a Class X segment on lightly traveled roadway; this will be typical of the biking conditions up to the loop return to PCH.

Corona Del Mar. In 0.2 mile, at the start of a small upgrade, cross the road and ride up the sidewalk in this short one-way section. The road curves left and becomes

Pacific Drive, proceeds a short distance, curves right and becomes Begonia Avenue (3.9). There is a park bench here and a captivating view down a small canyon to the ocean.

Soon the route swings around Begonia Park (Begonia Avenue, right on First Street, right on Carnation Avenue). Begonia Park appears to be the home of the Itsy-Bitsy Bathing Suit Frisbee Throwers Society (IBSFTS)! Coast downhill on Carnation Avenue and turn left (southwest) at Bayside Drive (4.1). To the right are bluffs and an overlook to be visited later. Pedal another half mile with some uphill through a residential neighborhood and turn right on Marguerite Avenue, then go 0.2 mile to Ocean Boulevard. This begins the highlight segment of the trip (4.8).

Ocean Boulevard. Turn left (southwest) on Ocean Boulevard and ride 0.2 mile to a small grassy vista point that has a fabulous overlook of Corona Del Mar State Beach, the Newport Harbor breakwater, and Catalina Island. There is a water fountain here. Bicycle another 0.2 mile to the end of Ocean Boulevard at Poppy Avenue. There is an equally fine view into Little Corona City Beach and southward.

Return to Marguerite Avenue (5.5) and cruise past Jasmine Avenue, the entry to the state beach. In another 0.1 mile is Heliotrope Avenue with a grassy overlook point which is directly above hillside residences. Just beyond is another mini-park (with water fountain) and vista point, this one with an excellent view down the breakwater and into Lower Newport Bay (5.8).

Ocean Boulevard soon fuses into Bayview Drive which turns right and becomes Carnation Avenue. Bike to the north end of this street for an interesting overlook of the harbor, Begonia Park, and lower Carnation Avenue (6.1). The two Carnation Avenue segments used to be at the same level until that "terrible quake of '38" (just kidding!). Backtrack to Seaview Avenue, turn left on Fern Leaf Avenue and follow a steep downhill to Bayside Drive (6.4).

Corona Del Mar State Beach from Ocean Boulevard

Bayside Drive. Turn left (northwest) and glide downhill a short distance on a tight roadway with the coastal bluffs to the right. The first view of the marina is at (7.1), followed by a transition back to a residential area (7.3), then a return to a marina setting near the classy looking Bahia Corinthian Yacht Club. The area returns to residential, now with bayside berths and classy boats, as the route passes Jamboree Road (7.7). Here is the Newport Beach Yacht Club and the Bayside Shopping Center, complete with a market and a classy restaurant at its western edge.

Pass alongside a canal with the lovely Balboa Island homes, each with its own boatslip, across the water. In 0.3 mile is the Balboa Yacht Basin road entry and at (8.5) the route returns to PCH. Bike across the bridge and carefully ride the narrow Class X segment back to Riverside Avenue and the trip starting point (10.1).

CONNECTING TRIPS: 1) Connection with the Sunset Beach to Newport Beach Strand tour (Trip #4) - continue northwest past Riverside Avenue on PCH and take the southside walkway up to Newport Boulevard. Cross the bridge and pedal to Ocean Front; 2) connection with the Upper Newport Bay ride and Newport Beach/Irvine Loop (Trips #6 and #7, respectively) - turn north on Jamboree Road and go a quarter of a mile to Backbay Drive; 3) connection with the Laguna Beach Tour (Trip #10) - follow the end of Ocean Boulevard as it curves north and becomes Poppy Drive, and bike 0.3 mile to PCH. Turn right (southeast) and go 0.15 mile to Seaward Road.

TRIP #16 - SAN CLEMENTE TO SAN DIEGO

GENERAL LOCATION: San Clemente, Camp Pendleton, Oceanside, Carlsbad, La Jolla, San Diego

LEVEL OF DIFFICULTY: One way - strenuous
Distance - 67.2 miles
Elevation gain - periodic moderate-to-steep grades; sheer grade at Torrey Pines Reserve

HIGHLIGHTS: Few trips that we've ridden have the variety and natural scenic beauty of this coastal classic. The entire tour described follows the Pacific Coast Bicentennial Bike Route, predominantly on Class I and Class II roadway. This classic visits the seaside bluffs of San Onofre State Beach, then the hilly roads through Camp Pendleton, and cruises along the beaches of cities from Oceanside to Del Mar. Next is a breathtaking scenic ride into the Torrey Pines State Beach area, followed by a breathtaking (huff-puff) sheer climb into the lovely woodlands of the Torrey Pines State Reserve. The trip winds up with a brief La Jolla City tour, then a pedal on the periphery of both Mission Bay and San Diego Bay, and ends near the Cruise Ship Terminal area of downtown San Diego.

An option is to start this trip from Santa Ana or Oceanside and take the AMTRAK train on the return leg. Refer to **The AMTRAK Option** at the end of the trip description.

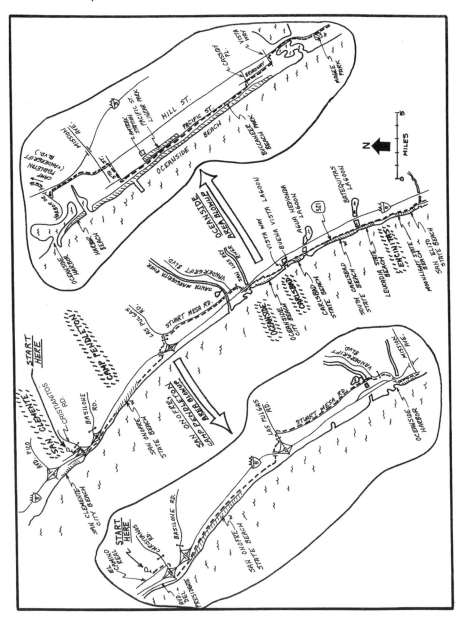

TRIP #16A - SAN CLEMENTE TO SAN DIEGO

TRAILHEAD: From the San Diego Freeway, exit at Cristianitos Road and drive north of the freeway to El Camino Real (ECR). Find parking subject to local traffic laws. If an overnight trip is planned, do not park on El Camino Real; an option is to park in a nearby residential area, subject to posted laws. AMTRAK riders can use the parking lots at or near the station. Bring a picture ID to enter Camp Pendleton.

Bring a couple of filled water bottles, particularly on hot days. There are public water sources at parks and commercial businesses scattered along the entire route.

TRIP DESCRIPTION: **San Onofre.** Return to Cristianitos Road and pedal to the Class I trail entry just west of the southbound freeway on-ramp. Follow the Class I road along the rolling terrain of the oceanside bluffs. In one mile, pass through a fence and follow a Class II frontage road, then cross over the northernmost Camp Pendleton entry at Basilone Road. Bike on a bridge over the railroad tracks (2.5), pass the main entrance of the San Onofre power generating station, and reach the entry to San Onofre State Beach (4.0).

For the next three miles, the bicycle path beelines through the park, passing RVs, tent campers, canyon hiking trails to the beach, and numerous water and restroom stops. If time permits, hike down one of the marked, scenic canyon trails. At the park's southern end, pass through the motorized vehicle barrier and ride on the Class I section of old Highway 1.

Camp Pendleton. Continue along the top of the ocean bluffs, pass below an automobile vista point and follow the path through a tunnel under the freeway (9.3). For the next 1.5 miles, the Class I roadway goes through flat and arid terrain, with the freeway fading in the distance. This stretch provides the feeling of real isolation (barring the numerous passing bikers). At trail's end, turn left at Las Pulgas Road and check in at the Camp Pendleton entrance gate (11.2). (Picture ID is required.) Just beyond the gate, turn right onto Stuart Mesa Road, pass Camp Flores (Boy Scouts of America) in one-half mile, and stay on Stuart Mesa Road by turning right.

The next three miles is on rolling hills with a particularly tough upgrade near the end of this stretch. In the middle section, the road passes the main Los Flores area at Nelson Drive. (Avoid the menacing tank parked there!)

Pass the road to the Cook overcrossing and stay to the right at the intersection with Hammond Road (16.1). Pedal past the large fields of cultivated flowers, continue alongside a canyon on a steep downgrade, pass the surrounding salt marshes, then pump an equally steep upgrade to the Stuart Mesa Road intersection with Vandergrift Boulevard (19.1). Turn right on the latter street and bike a one-mile upgrade of varying levels of steepness to Wire Mountain Road. Pass that street, exit the Camp Pendleton main gate, cross San Rafael Drive, and cycle under the freeway (20.7).

Oceanside. The street name is now Harbor Drive. At the first intersection, turn hard left and bike up to Class II Hill Street (the prettier but less direct route is to follow the winding Harbor Drive to Pacific Street and turn left), go 0.8 mile to 6th Street and cross the railroad tracks. Pedal to Pacific Street and turn left. Bike on that Class III road (including the southward jig-jog at 5th Street) through a coastal residential community. Pass above the Oceanside Pier and Pacific Street Linear Park (restrooms and The Strand) and enjoy the periodic views of the nearby beach. Next, pedal 1.25 miles to Morse Street and cozy little Buccaneer Beach Park, which has restrooms, limited shade, and a tiny snack stand.

Turn left on Cassidy Street, right on Broadway, left again on Vista Way (all are Class III), and right again on Class II Hill Street (25.1). This set of maneuvers occurs over a short 0.6-mile stretch but serves to avoid a busy Hill Street segment. This is the beginning of a 16-mile stretch on San Diego County Highway S21. Cross Buena Vista Lagoon, the first of several scenic lagoons on this trip segment, and enter Carlsbad.

Oceanside Beach

Carlsbad to Del Mar. Pass Magee Park (water and shade) and cruise an area with several popular but contrasting dining establishments, including venerable and posh Neimans. Nearby is the stately Carlsbad Inn and Hotel. Next is the entrance to Carlsbad State Beach (water). Pass Tamarack Avenue and Tamarack Surf Beach (water and a great surfer observation point), then enter an area with the fishermen working the Agua Hedionda Lagoon to the left and sunbathers and surfers doing their thing on the ocean side. The scenery in the southern Carlsbad area is exceptional, particularly because the bikeway is directly on the oceanfront.

The road passes Cannon Park at Cannon Road, then Palomar Airport Road, and stays alongside South Carlsbad State Beach (water, restrooms, campsites) for the next

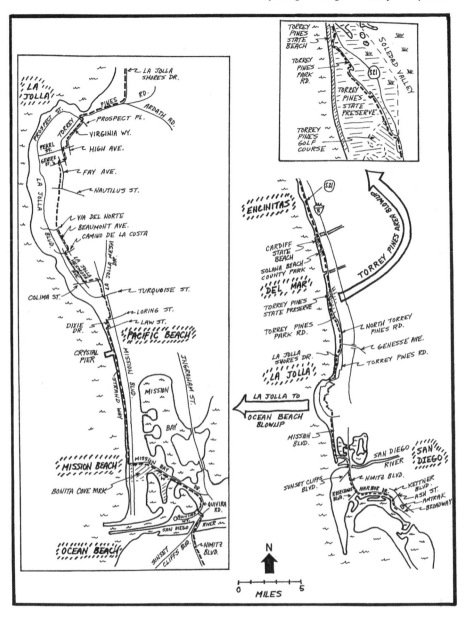

TRIP #16B - SAN CLEMENTE TO SAN DIEGO

2.5 miles. The main entry to this beautiful beach is at Poinsettia Lane. Pass over pictur-esque Batiquitos Lagoon and enter Leucadia as the tree-lined road turns inland. Cruise by a series of inviting lunch stops and delicatessens, Leucadia Boulevard (33.6), and Leucadia Park (with water), then enter Encinitas.

The Class II road passes the Moonlight State Beach entry at Encinitas Boulevard (water), the interesting Lumberyard shopping area, and the palatial Indian grounds of

Swamis City Park. Highway S21 returns to the beachfront and passes San Elijo State Beach (water) at Cardiff-by-the-Sea. There is an exceptional view of the coastal cliffs to the south from this area. The bikeway is two-way, Class II, although there is a Class I path on the opposite side of the street.

Bike on the bridge over the expansive San Elijo Lagoon with Cardiff State Beach on the opposite side. Follow a short upgrade away from the ocean to the city of Solana Beach. Stop at one of the cyclist-oriented eateries along the highway in this area. Menu choices include such goodies as "power sandwiches " and "energy drinks." Cross over the lagoon created by the San Dieguito River, take in the postcard view of the Del Mar Racetrack just inland, and enter the city of Del Mar (40.5).

Just past 27th Street, start a one-mile upgrade heading inland and enjoy the periodic views of the city below. The grade is steep for a quarter of a mile, then lessens to a steady, mild uphill. The road passes several posh inns and Del Mar Heights Road (42.7), then reaches its local high point just beyond.

Now all the work pays off! Follow a steep downgrade that opens up to one of the trip's premier spectacles, the view across Soledad Valley and the nearby small lagoon, and of the forested hills of the Torrey Pines State Preserve in the distance. Return to sea level at the gigantic seaside lagoon play area. Follow the bikeway into Torrey Pines State Beach. (An option is to stay on Highway S21 at this point; this option is faster, but far less scenic.)

Torrey Pines State Preserve. Follow a steep upgrade which gets even steeper beyond the first curve. In this segment there is some very difficult sustained biking, particularly after the prior 44-plus miles. In 0.6 mile of sheer upgrade is the North Grove area with several foot trails leading into the surrounding forest. Continue a steep uphill through the lovely forested preserve, then pass the ranger station and a fantastic overlook of La Jolla. Start another upgrade (with an elevation gain of 350 feet in the first mile) which soon flattens significantly. The path angles back towards the highway and offers some excellent inland views. Pedal along the Torrey Pines Memorial Golf Course and reach the top of this extended pull 1.9 miles from the beach. Return to S21 (North Torrey Pines Road) and follow the rolling hills along the golf course past Science Park Road and the Scripps Clinic, then reach Genesee Avenue (47.0).

La Jolla. Veer right and bike downhill on the Class II tree-lined road. Pass Torrey Pines Scenic Drive (the turnoff to the San Diego Glider Port and the Salk Institute), bike alongside the campus of the University of California, San Diego, and in 0.9 mile turn right again at La Jolla Shores Drive. In 0.6 mile on this Class III road, pass Horizon Way and begin a steep and winding downgrade on the lovely treed highway. There is a fine vista just beyond Horizon Way. Pass the Scripps Aquarium and Museum and in 0.3 mile reach a flat (49.7).

In 0.6 mile, turn right at Torrey Pines Road and follow a workout Class II uphill for 0.9 mile to the crest at Prospect Place. Turn left and bike a short, steep uphill to Virginia Way. (The route described for the next 2.6 miles is the low-traffic option.) The well-marked Class III route passes through a residential neighborhood and in succession turns left on High Avenue, right on Pearl Street, left on Girard Avenue, right on Genter Street, left on Fay Avenue, and right on Nautilus Street. Ride a short distance to a Class I path, cruise 0.75 mile on that rural bikeway and turn left at Beaumont Avenue. Pedal to Camino De La Costa, turn right and then left again on La Jolla Hermosa Avenue.

Torrey Pines State Preserve

Pacific Beach. To reach the beach, turn left on Colima Street, right at La Jolla Mesa Drive (which becomes Mission Boulevard), right on Loring Street, left on Dixie Drive, and right on Law Street. This places cyclists at the northern end of the Class I Strand Way on the ocean (56.4).

Bike south 1.9 miles to Ventura Place on this scenic and well-populated path. The strand bikeway passes Crystal Pier and cruises both the Pacific Beach and Mission Beach areas. There are numerous commercial stops in this stretch. A word of caution! On one trip, we arrived at 5 p.m. on Saturday night; we had to leave the super-crowded strand (walkers, bikers, skaters, skateboarders, windsurfers…okay, just kidding!) and followed the back alley known as Strand Way (58.8).

Mission Bay. Bike on Ventura Place past the amusement park and continue east on what is now Mission Bay Drive. Turn left into Bonita Cove Park (water, restrooms, shade, scenic harbor views) and pedal on the Class I trail that parallels Mission Bay Drive to a point just short of the bridge over Mission Bay Channel. Follow the small road up to the bridge. The scenic views from all bridges in this area are exceptional. Reenter the main road and follow the Class II route over the bridge, turning right into Quivira Road. Glide around Quivira Basin to the junction where the road becomes Quivira Way and turn left onto Sunset Cliffs Boulevard.

Ocean Beach to Point Loma. Bike on the bridge over the San Diego River and observe the myriad of bikepaths through the area (60.7). Stay with the fast-moving traffic for the few hundred yards needed to turn left at Nimitz Boulevard. (We found no easy or low traffic route to this intersection.)

Follow this Class II divided roadway about two miles through primarily residential territory, being very wary of cars entering and exiting Nimitz Boulevard north of Tennyson Street. The route turns sharply left at North Harbor Drive at the Nimitz Boulevard terminus.

San Diego Bay. Pedal on the sidewalk next to the Fleet Anti-Submarine Warfare School (where in Don's younger Navy days, he learned that, "A collision at sea can ruin a man's entire day"), then observe the cement-bound U.S.S. *Recruit* "floating" majestically along the north side of the highway. Pass over the bridge and on the opposite side, follow the Class I bikepath that meanders through the cozy mile-long thread of Spanish Landing Park. There are scattered water sources, restrooms, and tree shade, and benches from which to observe the comings and goings in the bay.

Proceed around the Sheraton Hotel (65.2) and cross Harbor Island Drive, returning to a Class I path along the harbor. Pedal alongside the San Diego International Airport, pass the U.S. Coast Guard Station, cross Laurel Street and take in the view of the San Diego City skyline. The bikeway rounds the bend of the harbor heading south, passes by the old windsailer, *Star of India* (now a museum), and reaches the trip's end point at the Cruise Ship Terminal (and a few eateries) just beyond (67.2).

Excursion: The AMTRAK Return Trip Option. Park at either the Santa Ana or Oceanside AMTRAK stations (these have baggage stops), bike to San Diego, and take the train on the return trip. The San Diego station is near the intersection of Kettner Boulevard and "C" Street. The biker's "special" presently leaves San Diego twice daily on the weekend (be there 45 minutes early). Call AMTRAK at 800-872-7245 for the latest information before starting the trip.

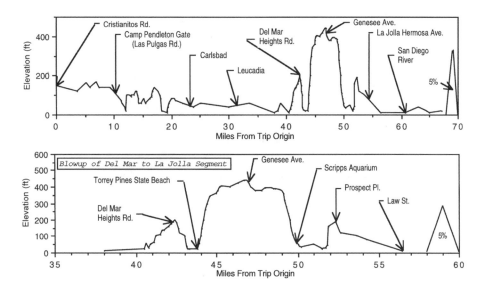

CONNECTING TRIPS: Continuation with the Doheny/San Clemente Bike Route (Trip #14) - at the trip origin, bike north on El Camino Real.

RIVER TRAILS

San Diego Creek Outlet to Upper Newport Bay

TRIPS #17A-#17C - SANTA ANA RIVER TRAIL

This moderate-to-strenuous level Santa Ana River trip from Prado Dam to Huntington Beach (61.5 strenuous miles round trip) is broken up into three sections. The general area map for the entire trip is provided below. Almost the entire route is Class I path with horse trails paralleling much of the bikeway. There are two places where the bikepath crosses the Santa Ana River bottom (Katella Avenue and 17th Street) and several areas where the path is very near the water (e.g., Orangewood Avenue). In high water level situations, the nominal route is blocked by locked fences. Cyclists must return to and cross highways, as necessary, in these instances.

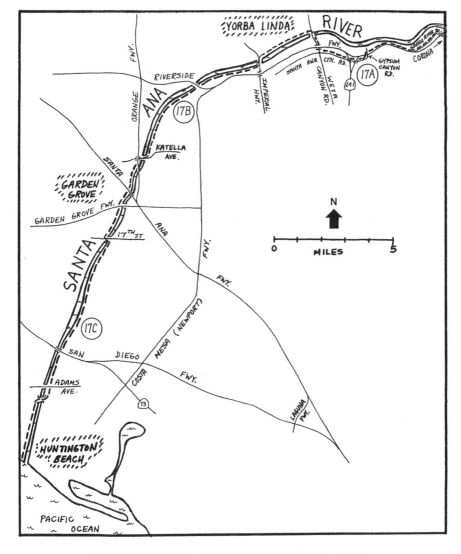

TRIPS #17A-#17C - SANTA ANA RIVER TRAIL

Trip #17A explores the most northerly section of the bikepath starting below Prado Dam, visiting Featherly Park and ending at Yorba Regional Park. Trip #17B starts at Yorba Regional Park, goes through a short, scenic treed section early in the route and terminates at Anaheim Stadium or El Camino Park. Trip #17C starts at El Camino Park, passes along Centennial Regional Park and the Mesa Verde Country Club and lets out at the Pacific Ocean in Huntington Beach.

TRIP #17A - SANTA ANA RIVER: GREEN RIVER ROAD TO YORBA PARK

GENERAL LOCATION: Prado Dam, Anaheim Hills, Yorba Linda

LEVEL OF DIFFICULTY: One way - moderate; up and back - moderate
Distance - 7.4 miles (one way)
Elevation gain - periodic moderate grades

HIGHLIGHTS: At the top end of the Santa Ana River Trail, this predominantly Class I route starts just south of the Prado Dam at Green River Road and ends at Yorba Regional Park. Along the way are a few rolling hills, a horse corral, a mini-motorcross area for children, inviting Featherly Regional Park, and a short tour of La Palma Avenue. Allow time for bicycle tours of Featherly and Yorba Regional Parks, which have an abundance of bikepaths or bikeable roadways. For cyclists interested in a more lengthy workout, the trip can be extended north along Green River Road toward the city of Corona (see Trip #17 Extension map) or continued south along the Santa Ana River (Trip #17B).

TRAILHEAD: From the Riverside Freeway, exit at Green River Road. Park north of the freeway where there are gas stations, a mini-market, restaurant, and fast-food outlets.
Bring a light water supply. There is water at Featherly Regional Park near the halfway point and Yorba Regional Park. If extending the trip north or south, bring additional water, as the nearest water supplies are several additional, exposed miles away.

TRIP DESCRIPTION: **Green River Country Club and Golf Course.** From the parking area, bike south on Class III Green River Road and begin an immediate moderate-to-steep downgrade. At 0.3 mile, the route begins a moderate uphill, passes a trailer park and reaches the crest near and at the level of the Riverside Freeway (0.7). The path meets the entrance to the Green River Country Club, a little road (taboo to bikers) heading right on a bridge over the river (1.0). Instead, ride straight ahead and to the right of the blocked freeway on-ramp to a Class I bikepath that travels directly alongside this very narrow stretch of the Santa Ana River. Further up the trail, stop and look back into a framed view of the Santa Ana Mountains. This stretch also provides some nice peeks into the Green River Golf Course.
Featherly Regional Park. Proceed up a moderate grade and reach Coal Canyon Road in 0.2 mile. To the right is a small ranch where there are several corrals with

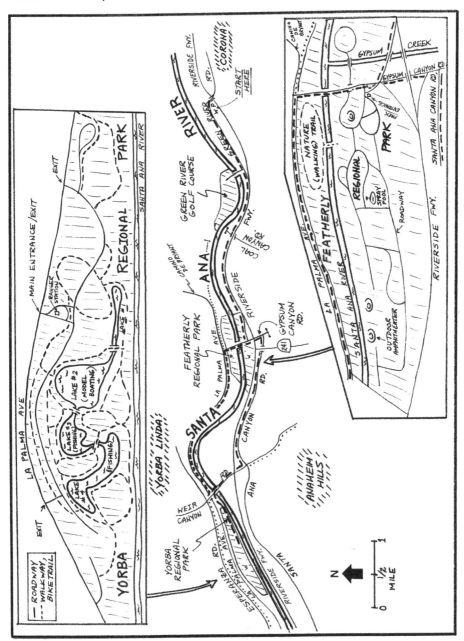

**TRIP #17A - SANTA ANA RIVER: GREEN RIVER ROAD
TO YORBA REGIONAL PARK**

a mix of horses and donkeys. Cycle directly south along the asphalt bikepath and pass
a mini-motorcross bicycle park in 0.3 mile (2.2).

For the next mile, the Class I path stays alongside trees, scrub, and a multitude of
other flora and fauna that indicate the river is nearby. At (3.2), the bikeway reaches the

fenced Featherly Regional Park boundary, and in another 0.2 mile it passes a lengthy tent and RV camping section of the park. At (3.6), the trail passes under Gypsum Canyon Road and swings toward the large Featherly entrance structure, below which is a water fountain. Look for the route signs near here.

The *Featherly Park* sign leads bikers to the park's main entrance, while the *River Trail East* sign just directs bikers back to the incoming route. Our route follows the *River Trail West* sign and climbs up to the west side of Gypsum Canyon Road.

One option here is to turn south, go under the freeway to Class II Santa Ana Canyon Road and follow that street east to Weir Canyon Road. (See Trip # 25.) However, the reference ride proceeds north on a Class I path over the Santa Ana River, a fine vantage point for viewing the gypsum mining in the hills to the southeast, the housing developments of Anaheim Hills, the San Joaquin Hills Transportation Corridor, and the classy homes in the hills to the north. Bike 0.3 mile to road's end (4.0).

La Palma Avenue and Yorba Regional Park. Turn left (west) and proceed on the Class I trail which is sandwiched between the river and La Palma Avenue. Enjoy the thick river flora while bicycling through a mix of residential, light commercial, and industrial sections for 3.1 uninterrupted miles to Yorba Linda Boulevard. Cross that street and pedal along the narrow walkway on the south side of La Palma Avenue for 0.3 mile. Take the first bike trail left into Yorba Regional Park, then ride around the park's east edge and return to a riverside portion of the Santa Ana River Bike Trail (7.4).

CONNECTING TRIPS: 1) Continuation with the middle segment of the Santa Ana River Trail (Trip #17B) - continue south past Yorba Regional Park and across Imperial

Near Yorba Regional Park

Highway to the south side of the river; 2) connection with the Santa Ana Canyon Road route (Trip #25) - continue west on Santa Ana Canyon Road at its intersection with Weir Canyon Road; 3) connection with the El Cajon Trail (Trip #22) - turn north on Weir Canyon Road at its intersection with La Palma Avenue. Cross the bridge, turn right on New River Road, then turn right again at Esperanza Road. Continue to the trail entry near Avenida Barcelona; 4) connection with the Yorba Linda Bits and Pieces Tour (Trip # 43) - from Yorba Regional Park, bike to La Palma Avenue and Yorba Linda Boulevard, going straight ahead or turning left, respectively.

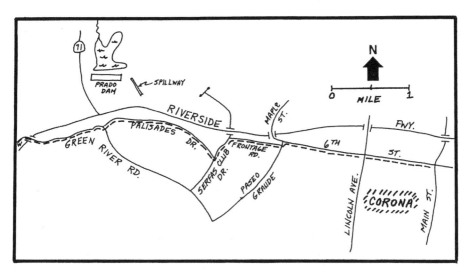

TRIP #17A EXTENSION: GREEN RIVER ROAD TO CORONA

TRIP #17B - SANTA ANA RIVER: YORBA TO EL CAMINO REAL PARK

GENERAL LOCATION: Yorba Linda, Placentia, Orange

LEVEL OF DIFFICULTY: One way - easy; up and back - moderate
Distance - 10.0 miles (one way)
Elevation gain - essentially flat

HIGHLIGHTS: This section of the river ride starts at Yorba Regional Park which, in itself, could serve as a nice area for a family biking excursion. The trip joins the Santa Ana River Trail at any one of several points from within the park, passes through a lovely area of trees and grassy knolls for several miles, and then transitions into an open and exposed route for the remainder of the ride. In the latter section are a gigantic

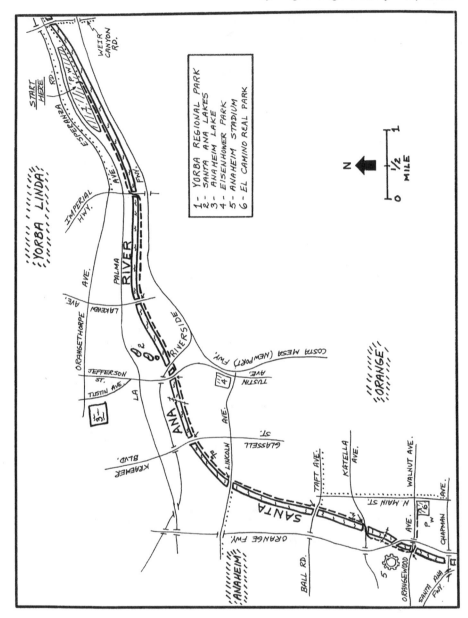

**TRIP #17B - SANTA ANA RIVER: YORBA REGIONAL PARK
TO EL CAMINO REAL PARK**

open mining pit, Anaheim Stadium, and the terminal point at shaded El Camino Real Park.

TRAILHEAD: From the Riverside Freeway, take the Imperial Highway exit and drive a quarter mile north to La Palma Avenue. Turn right (east) and travel about one mile to free parking at the baseball diamonds/soccer fields south of the roadway. Better yet, pay a small fee and park within Yorba Regional Park itself; the entrance is about another three quarters of a mile further northeast on La Palma Avenue.

Only a moderate water supply is needed. There are both water and restroom facilities at the beginning of the trip (at the park) and near the end (at a small restroom directly on the bikeway). There is also a small market stop along the way.

TRIP DESCRIPTION: **Yorba Regional Park to "The Rest Stop."** There are bikepaths around the lakes and throughout Yorba Regional Park (see the detailed map accompanying the prior ride). Follow the park bikepath nearest the river and take one of the many paved or direct paths across to the river trail. Within the first mile from the main parking area within the park, there is marshland along the river with many birds.

Bicycle along the natural riverbed and cross from the north to the south levee at Imperial Highway (2.1). Pass through a pleasant area with grassy knolls, trees, bushes, a few joggers, and even a few horseback riders (on a paralleling path). At (3.9), pass under Lakeview Avenue and at (4.9) the Riverside Freeway. Stop and check out the manmade water holding basins in the riverbed; they're cleverly constructed. At (5.1), pass an exit through a fence which leads to a little market that has soft drinks and other "stuff" on ice. Do the entire Santa Ana River and you will know why we call this "The Rest Stop!"

Anaheim Stadium and El Camino Real Park. The river bends in a more southerly direction in this area. Pass under Glassell Street (6.2) and ride alongside a gigantic open mining pit in another 0.3 mile. Next the path crosses under Lincoln Avenue (7.0) and Ball Road (8.3) while traveling through an industrial area.

At (9.1), there is a small restroom stop (with water) alongside the bike trail. Soon the route crosses the river bottom at Katella Avenue (9.3). Shortly after, the bikepath travels alongside Anaheim Stadium and under the Orange Freeway (9.7). In 0.3 mile is Orangewood Avenue; a nearby exit to the north and a right turn at Stadium Way will lead to Anaheim Stadium. For our reference trip, however, an exit to the south and an additional 0.4-mile pedal leads to El Camino Real Park. (See Trip #17C for a discussion of park facilities.)

CONNECTING TRIPS: 1) Connection/continuation with Trips #17A or #17C along the Santa Ana River Trail - follow the described route to the Santa Ana River and turn north (Trip #17A) or continue south from the trip terminus (Trip #17C); 2) connection with the Santa Ana Canyon tour (Trip #25) - at the trip origin, ride to Weir Canyon Road (east) or Imperial Highway (south) on the Santa Ana River Trail - cross the Riverside Freeway and head in either direction on Santa Ana Canyon Road; 3) connection with the Anaheim Hills ride (Trip #44) - exit the river at Lincoln Avenue and bike east across the river to Santiago Boulevard.

TRIP #17C - SANTA ANA RIVER: EL CAMINO PARK TO PACIFIC OCEAN

GENERAL LOCATION: Orange, Garden Grove, Costa Mesa, Huntington Beach

LEVEL OF DIFFICULTY: One way - easy; up and back - moderate
Distance - 13.4 miles (one way)
Elevation gain - essentially flat

HIGHLIGHTS: Initially, this Santa Ana River Bike Trail segment is a tree-lined route along a portion of the riverbed that is lush meadowland. The Class I bikeway passes near several golf courses, as well as a couple of small parks and the large and pretty Centennial Regional Park. In between some of these lovely sights is a lot of concrete and industry backed up along the river. The trip lets out at a pleasant stretch of beach at the southern end of Huntington State Beach.

TRAILHEAD: From the Santa Ana Freeway, exit at Katella Avenue and head east 0.75 mile to State College Boulevard. Turn right (south) and make a left turn in 0.4 mile at Orangewood Avenue, then continue one mile to El Camino Real Park. The park has water, limited shade, a children's play area, and varied sports facilities. There is parking closer to the river on the side streets off Orangewood Avenue; however, read the parking signs carefully if you park here. From the Orange Freeway, exit at Orangewood Avenue and proceed east about half a mile. From the Garden Grove Freeway, exit at Main Street, proceed north about 1.75 mile to Orangewood Avenue and turn left.

Fill a water bottle at the park. There are facilities at a couple of nearby stops along the trip south, or travel one mile north (see Trip #17B) where there is a restroom and water along the bikeway.

TRIP DESCRIPTION: **Lower Santa Ana River Meadowland.** From El Camino Real Park, bike 0.4 mile west on Orangewood Avenue to the entrance point on the west side of the river. Cruise south and pass Chapman Avenue (1.0), the Santa Ana Freeway, and the Garden Grove Freeway (1.8).

Just beyond this point is one of the most refreshing stretches of the trip. The river bottom is a rich meadowland for the next one to two miles and the bikepath meanders through a surrounding mini-forest. Pass Garden Grove Boulevard, which is an exit to luscious River View Golf Course (2.2). Soon after is Alona Park with a children's play area, barbecue facilities, and a biker's rest stop (water, restroom).

Centennial Regional Park. At 17th Street, the bikepath crosses the river bottom (3.4). From this point to the ocean, the river is one long concrete waterway. Pass under Fairview Street (3.8), 5th Street, McFadden Avenue, and Edinger Avenue (6.0). Shortly after Edinger Avenue and about 200 yards off the bikepath is inviting Centennial Regional Park with its little lakes, birds, and shady gazebos. There is a maze of bikeways/walkways throughout the park, as well as restroom facilities. (The park circuit by itself might serve as a grand locale for a family bike outing.)

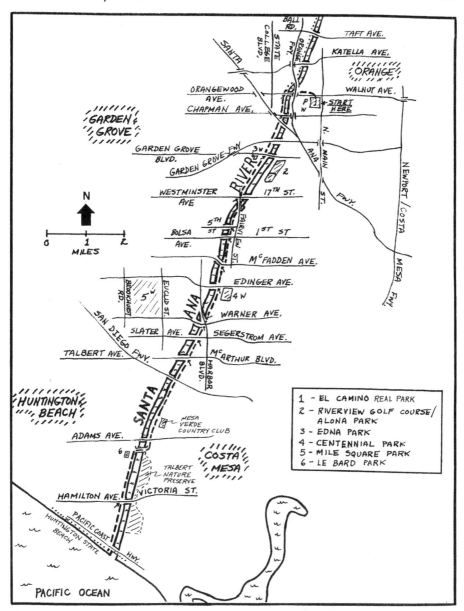

TRIP #17C - SANTA ANA RIVER: EL CAMINO PARK TO PACIFIC OCEAN

Cycle south past Harbor Boulevard (6.9) and Warner Avenue, then pass one of the steepest underpasses of the river bikeway system at Slater Avenue (7.6). Cross under Talbert Avenue; at (8.1), traverse a tunnel under the San Diego Freeway (be watchful for broken glass) and pass a grassy rest area next to the path. The route becomes more scenic as it cruises alongside the Mesa Verde Country Club (9.4) and passes under Adams Street and by the site of Fairview Regional Park (10.7).

The Coast. In about a mile, follow the wooden bike bridge across the river to the west side; there is a small park/playground a few hundred yards beyond the crossing and off the trail at Le Bard Park (water) (10.9). Across the river is the Talbert Nature Preserve. Proceed south and pass Victoria Street/Hamilton Avenue (11.9), the "fragrant" Orange County Sanitation Treatment Plant (12.9), and a small bridge over a separate channel just north of Pacific Coast Highway (PCH) (13.3). In another tenth of a mile, pass under PCH and enter Huntington State Beach at the junction with the Sunset Beach-Newport Beach Strand bikepath.

CONNECTING TRIPS: 1) Continuation with the Sunset Beach-Newport Beach Strand route (Trip #2) - at the terminus of the Santa Ana River Trail, turn south and pass over the bridge/bikeway toward Newport Beach or turn north and head towards Sunset Beach; 2) connection with Mile Square Regional Park (Trip #5) - turn west at Edinger Avenue or Warner Avenue and turn into the park in about one mile at Euclid Street.

Near the Warner Avenue Overpass

TRIP #18 - SAN DIEGO CREEK

GENERAL LOCATION: Newport Beach, Irvine

LEVEL OF DIFFICULTY: One way - easy; up and back - moderate
Distance - 9.9 miles (one way)
Elevation gain - generally flat; periodic light grades
in Yale Loop area

HIGHLIGHTS: This pleasant trip follows San Diego Creek upstream, starting from the creek's confluence with upper Newport Bay. The creek is soil-lined for the most part and contains marshes, water pools, and mud flats at low water, particularly along the lower creek segment. The route passes near a state wildlife preserve, the Irvine campus of the University of California, two parks, and the attractively developed Yale Loop residential area. The 2.1-mile end segment beyond Jeffrey Road transits less-developed territory, terminating at the Laguna Freeway. There are numerous spur trips off the main route. The trip is nearly 100 percent Class I on well-maintained bike surfaces.

TRAILHEAD: From the intersection of Pacific Coast Highway (PCH) and Jamboree Road in Newport Beach, drive north on Jamboree Road for 1.5 miles to Eastbluff Drive. Turn left, proceed 0.75 mile to Vista Del Sol and turn left again. At Vista Del Oro, the next street, find parking subject to local traffic laws. From the San Diego Freeway, take the Highway 73 exit in Costa Mesa and continue to the S. Bristol Street turnoff. Follow this one-way street a quarter of a mile further to Jamboree Road, turn right (south) and drive half a mile to Eastbluff Drive. Turn right on Eastbluff Drive, then head up the hill 0.75 mile to Vista Del Sol and find parking as described above. From the Costa Mesa Freeway, exit southeast at State Highway 73 and continue as described above.

Bring a moderate water supply. There are well-placed public water stops near the bikeway up to Jeffrey Road. The remaining 2.1-mile segment is waterless.

TRIP DESCRIPTION: **Upper Newport Bay to University of California, Irvine.** From the intersection of Eastbluff Drive and Jamboree Road, follow the bikepath on the west side of Jamboree Road down to San Diego Creek. Follow the trail sharply right and parallel to the creek on its south bank, passing under Jamboree Road (0.3). Proceed into the quiet, open, natural area above the soil-lined riverbed and go over a small wooden bridge (0.5). Pass an outlet to the University Drive/S. Bristol Street intersection (see the **Bonita Creek Trail Excursion** below) and bike under the San Joaquin Hills Transportation Corridor. In another 0.1 mile is the MacArthur Trail junction which leads to MacArthur Boulevard. There is a sign with a map of the local streets and trails, one of several along the route.

Cycle under MacArthur Boulevard and then meet the California Road junction (1.1). To the left, on the other side of the creek bank, are the manmade ponds of the State Wildlife Preserve. To the right is the California Road entry along the periphery of the campus of the University of California, Irvine. Our reference route passes under Campus Drive (1.6) and begins a slow turn to the north away from University Drive. There is a junction off to the right which leads to the William R. Mason Regional Park.

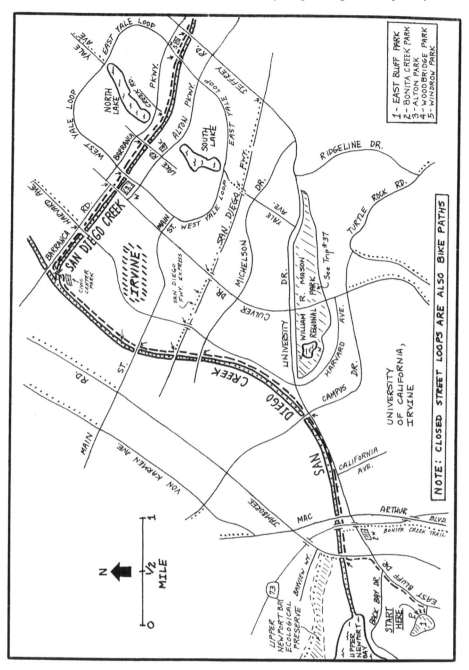

TRIP #18 - SAN DIEGO CREEK: JAMBOREE ROAD TO JEFFREY ROAD

The Marshlands to Peters Canyon Channel. On the San Diego Creek route, there is a marshy area that seems to be a favorite for a variety of birds and even a few ducks (1.8). Cycle alongside the Rancho San Joaquin Country Club/Golf Course and then jig-jog on a bridge over a small wash (2.8). Pedal under Michelson Drive, the San Diego Freeway, and Main Street (3.5) through some of the more open territory of the trip. There are trail exits from each of these undercrossings, with the exit along the San Diego Freeway described in the **San Diego Freeway Express** Excursion in Trip #8.

In a mile from Main Street, the bike trail skirts the Irvine Civic Center, passes through Civic Center Park (sports fields and a water fountain), then crosses a bridge to the opposite side of San Diego Creek (4.4). The waterway heading north is the Peters Canyon Channel, while our route takes us right (east) paralleling Barranca Parkway. The gigantic airship hangers at the now-closed U.S. Marine Corps Air Facility are to the northeast.

Alton Park. In about 0.7 mile, cross Harvard Avenue at the signal, then return along the channel. There is a steep undercrossing at Culver Drive (may be flooded during storms) and another in 0.2 mile at West Yale Loop (5.9). To the right (south) is little Alton Park with restrooms, a water fountain, trees, and baseball fields. Nearby and accessible West and East Yale are part of a four-mile-plus circular bike loop. (Refer to Trip #8.)

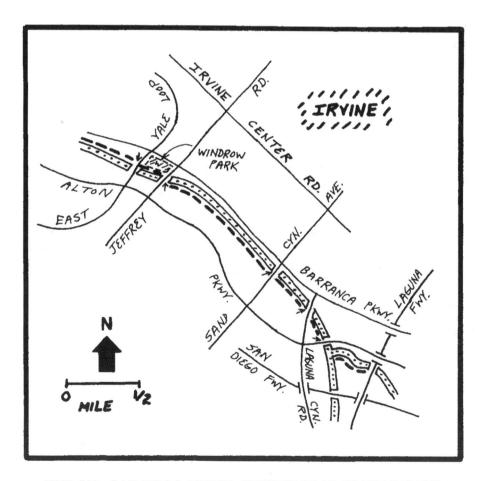

TRIP #18 - SAN DIEGO CREEK: JEFFREY ROAD TO TRAIL'S END

Condomania to Jeffrey Road. Cruise through an area where condominiums are built up alongside the creek with a lovely church across the water (6.2). In 0.2 mile, cross under Lake Road (a short spur takes bikers to North Lake) and enter another condo area alongside the creek. Next, pass under Creek Road (6.8), pedal along a pleasant eucalyptus-lined stretch, pass the East Yale Loop bikepath, and go under Jeffrey Road through a small tunnel (7.8). (The tunnel floods during rainy periods and collects a layer of dirt afterwards. If it is impassable, bike to Barranca Parkway or Alton Parkway and cross at the light.)

Jeffrey Road to the Laguna Freeway. Turn right and bike to the south creek levee. (Though paved, the north side has road crossings at Valley Oak Drive, Sand Canyon Avenue, and Laguna Canyon Road.) The initial section is surrounded by residences up to the place where the cement-block-lined creek creeps up beside Barranca Parkway. Beyond Sand Canyon Avenue, trees lining the bikeway hide Barranca Parkway and filter out many of the industrial complexes on the south side (8.9). The creekbed transitions to a natural bottom.

Follow the tree-lined path under Laguna Canyon Road (9.2) and Alton Parkway (9.5), noting that these under-road sections can flood during winter rains. Beyond Alton Parkway, the trail leaves the creek levee, passes next to a modern industrial complex and becomes the Alton Regional Bikeway. Return to creekside in a short distance and cruise to the trail terminus (both north and south side paths) in half a mile from Alton Parkway. At this point are the steep berms that support the fenced-off Laguna Freeway (9.9).

Alternate Return Routes. There are many ways for completing the return trip. The fastest return to Windrow Park is via Alton Parkway southbound, then north at

Windrow Park

Jeffrey Road. After a return to the creek, there are options to divert south on East Yale Loop and ride to Main Street or to exit the loop at Alton Parkway and bike west. The sneakiest and fastest return is to bike south from Windrow Park on Jeffrey Road and take the Class I path just to the north side of the San Diego Freeway 1.9 miles to the creek. (See the Trip #8 **San Diego Freeway Express** spur trip.)

Excursion: Bonita Creek Trail. Leave the San Diego Creek and bike to the University Drive/S. Bristol Street intersection. Cross the street and look for the Class I trail on the left (east) bank of brush- and tree-strewn Bonita Creek. Parallel the San Joaquin Transportation Corridor on a mild, steady upgrade 0.7 mile and turn right at its end. In about 20 yards there is a junction. Biking south leads to the end of the separated trail at Bison Avenue and MacArthur Boulevard in another half mile. Taking the junction westbound across the creek leads to a Class I trail which returns downhill alongside Bonita Creek Park. The park, whose entry is at Milano Drive and La Salud, has restrooms, limited shade, snack shop, recreation fields, sports courts, and a children's playground. Bypassing the entry leads back to University Drive. The round-trip distance from San Diego Creek to Bison Avenue is 2.8 miles.

CONNECTING TRIPS: 1) Connection with the Upper Newport Bay route (Trip #6) and the Newport Beach/Irvine Loop (Trip #7) - these trips share a common segment on Eastbluff Drive; 2) connection with the Irvine Bikeway (Trip #8) - exit the creek trail at either West or East Yale Loop; 3) connection with the Laguna Canyon Road tour (Trip # 9) - use the creek outlet at Laguna Canyon Road; 4) connection with the Turtle Rock Road ride (Trip #36) leave the creek at Campus Drive and bike west to street's end; 5) connection with the William R. Mason Regional Park ride (Trip #37) - leave the creek at Campus Drive, turn northeast at University Drive and cycle half a mile to the park's main entrance.

TRIPS #19A-#19E - SAN GABRIEL RIVER TRAIL

The San Gabriel River Trail is probably the premier single river trail in this book. It is heavily plied by bikers from both Orange and Los Angeles Counties, since it starts from the border between the two. The route captures southern California from the sea through the inland valley to the mountains, all in one continuous 39-mile shot. Taken in the winter after a cold storm, this trip is one of the best in every sense. The general area map is provided on the following page.

The first segment (#19A) explores the river outlet near Seal Beach, then a wildlife area to the north, and ends at super El Dorado Park. The connection segment (#19B) visits no less than five parks and finishes at Wilderness Park in Downey. The next northerly segment (#19C) leaves Wilderness Park, travels alongside some fine San Gabriel River bottom and ends at one of the tour high-points, the Whittier Narrows Recreation Area. Trip #19D starts at that fabulous recreation area and ends at another, the Santa Fe Dam Recreation Area. The most northerly segment (#19E) leaves from that dam and ends in the foothills at the entrance to San Gabriel Canyon.

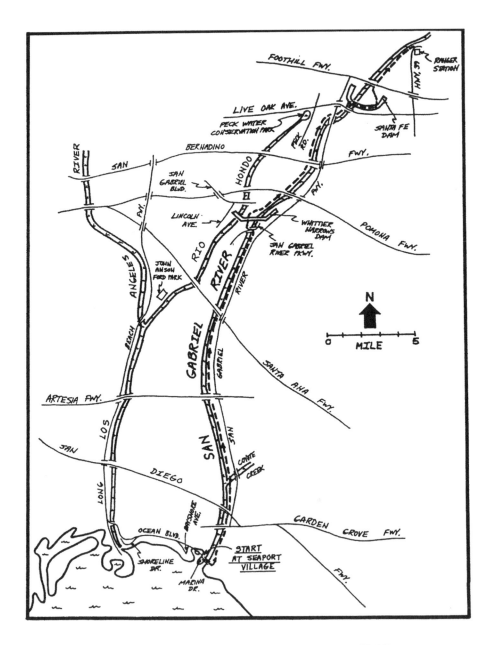

TRIPS #19A-#19E - SAN GABRIEL RIVER TRAIL

TRIP #19A - SAN GABRIEL RIVER: SEAL BEACH TO EL DORADO PARK

GENERAL LOCATION: Seal Beach - Long Beach

LEVEL OF DIFFICULTY: Up and back - easy
Distance - distance - 5.6 miles (one way)
Elevation gain - essentially flat

HIGHLIGHTS: This is the starting segment of one of the most varied and interesting trips in this book. This is a completely Class I bike route that starts at the scenic lower section of the Gabriel River Trail near the Long Beach Marina and winds up at El Dorado Park. The early part of the trip provides a look at "recreation city," with water, boats, water-skiers, and jet-skiers. The trip transitions into a nature area rich in wildlife and ends in a park that is so inviting that it could serve as a separate family excursion.

TRAILHEAD: Free public parking is available at the Long Beach Marina along Marina Drive in Naples or along First Street in Seal Beach. From Pacific Coast Highway (PCH) in Seal Beach, turn west on Marina Drive (2-3 blocks from Main Street in Seal Beach) and drive roughly half a mile to First Street. In 0.25 mile, cross the San Gabriel River and continue a short distance into the marina near Seaport Village for parking. The trailhead is at Marina Drive at the east end (Seal Beach side) of the bridge over the San Gabriel River.

Coyote Creek Bridge Crossing

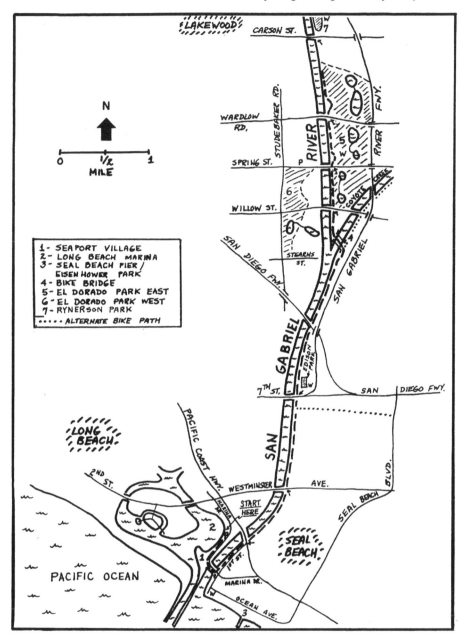

TRIP #19A - SAN GABRIEL RIVER: SEAL BEACH TO EL DORADO PARK

Only a light water supply is needed for this short trip. There are public water sources at the trip origin and terminus.

TRIP DESCRIPTION: **The Scenic Lower River Segment.** The first part of the trip provides views of boaters, water-skiers, and an interestingly developed shoreline.

The natural river basin passes PCH (0.4), the Westminster Avenue access, and the Haynes Steam Plant (electricity generation). At (2.2), a small alternate Class I bikepath leads off to the east along a 1.2-mile shaded route to Seal Beach Boulevard. In this stretch of the river, up to the concrete portion (3.5), cyclists have views of the large bird population that includes pelicans, egrets, and the ever-present seagulls. The bikeway passes under the Garden Grove Freeway (2.3); just beyond is an exit which takes cyclists to College Park Drive and Edison Park. Next is the San Diego Freeway undercrossing (3.5). In this part of the bikepath are many "freeway orchards," those freeway-locked areas under the power poles filled with containerized plants.

The Creek Crossing and El Dorado Park. In 0.4 mile, take the signed bikeway/walkway bridge across the river. Do not miss the bridge unless you've decided to change plans and see Coyote Creek (Trip #20). Once over the bridge, there are views across the river to the El Dorado Golf Course and El Dorado Park West. At 0.7 mile from the bridge crossing, reach Willow Street and skirt the edge of the Nature Study Area which is the south end of El Dorado Park East (5.0). Shortly afterward, the bikepath reaches Spring Street and the entry to Areas I and II of the park (5.6).

The park has a myriad of bike trails. This portion of the trip is worth a good exploration effort in itself, particularly for family riding.

CONNECTING TRIPS: 1) Continuation with the San Gabriel River Trail (Trip #19B) - bike north beyond El Dorado Park toward Wilderness Park; 2) continuation with the Seal Beach/Sunset Beach tour (Trip #1) - at the trip origin, bike east on Marina Drive; 3) connection with the Coyote Creek Trail (Trip #20) - at the eastern end of the bike bridge across the San Gabriel River, stay on the eastern river bank.

TRIP #19B - SAN GABRIEL RIVER: EL DORADO PARK TO WILDERNESS PARK

GENERAL LOCATION: Long Beach, Lakewood, Cerritos, Norwalk, Downey

LEVEL OF DIFFICULTY: One way - easy; up and back - moderate
Distance - 9.7 miles (one way)
Elevation gain - essentially flat

HIGHLIGHTS: This segment of the Class I San Gabriel River Trail has direct access to five major parks. In particular, this trip should not be completed without a tour of El Dorado Park. Rynerson Park provides a pleasant diversion from the river route, and Wilderness Park is a fine rest stop with a small pond/lagoon to dip the toes into before returning to the trip origin. There are horse corrals and equestrian trails beside the bike route in some sections. This is a good workout section, as the bike and foot traffic is relatively light.

TRAILHEAD: From the San Diego Freeway, turn north on Palo Verde Avenue and drive 0.9 mile to Spring Street. Turn right (east) and continue about 0.8 mile to free

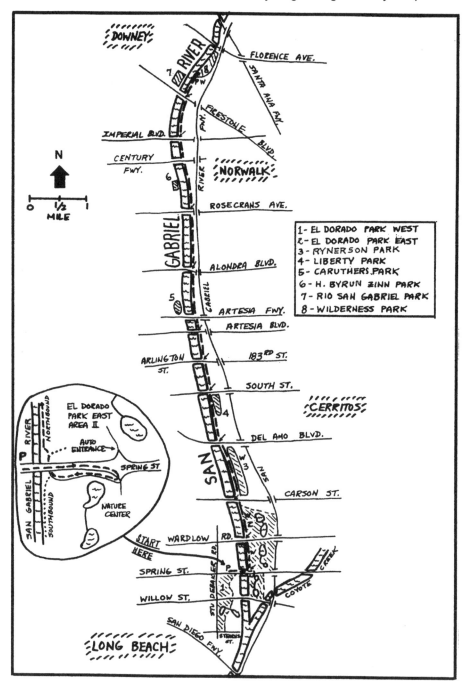

**TRIP #19B - SAN GABRIEL RIVER: EL DORADO PARK TO
WILDERNESS PARK**

parking along Spring Street, just west of the bridge over the San Gabriel River. Other
options are to head over the bridge and park in the Nature Center parking area (turn

south at the park entrance), or to drive up Spring Street, make a U-turn and return to the Area II park entrance to the north (right). The latter two options are pay parking.

From the San Gabriel Freeway, turn west on Willow Street (Katella Avenue in Orange County), continue about one mile to Studebaker Road and turn right (north). Drive 0.3 mile to Spring Street and turn right. Follow the parking instructions above. For direct entry at Area II (pay parking) from the southbound freeway, exit at Spring Street and turn right at the park entrance.

Bring a light water supply. Parks along the way have water and restroom facilities. El Dorado Park is a particular delight! Bring some food for the barbecue and enjoy munchies at the park after a "tough" bike ride.

TRIP DESCRIPTION: El Dorado Park. From the parking area on Spring Street, ride over the bridge and turn right (south) at the Nature Center entrance. Make another sharp right and pedal parallel to Spring Street (but in the opposite direction) along the Nature Center roadway. Bike 0.2 mile to the fence along the San Gabriel River Bike Route. Rather than passing through the fence entry, follow the roadway as it turns to the right and passes under Spring Street. The road enters Park Area II.

Stay to the left rather than bike into El Dorado Park. Pass through the fence and head right (north) along the San Gabriel River Trail (0.6). The first part of the trip parallels Park Area II. The path leaves the river again and follows the roadway under Wardlow Road (1.1). Again, stay to the left and pass through a fence which returns to the river trail. (The other option is to bike through Park Area III and rejoin the trail one-half mile later.) The path stays beside a stand of trees and passes the end of Park Area III (1.6) near the weapons firing range.

Rynerson Park. Pass a pedestrian bridge (a diversion route which crosses over to De Mille Junior High School) and then pass Carson Street (2.0). For the next 0.7 mile, cruise alongside fun River Park, which boasts tree cover, horse stalls and corrals, horse trails, a little footbridge leading to a connecting alternate bike trail (which reconnects near Del Amo Boulevard), baseball diamonds, and water (near the baseball fields). The shady park area ends near Del Amo Boulevard (3.0).

The Middle Trip Section. For the next half mile, the trip highlight is the clever (and in some cases not so clever) graffiti on the concrete river walls. In 0.8 mile, reach little Liberty Park which is effectively a grassy rest area. Just beyond the park is South Street (3.8), followed by a passage below 183rd Street through a narrow tunnel (4.5). (Reduce speed and keep an eye "peeled" for oncoming bikers.) The route then passes more horse stalls.

The path dips down into the riverbed to cross under Artesia Boulevard (4.9). If you miss the marked route, you can walk (crouch) under the roadway. There is a short section where bikes must be walked across a railroad crossing, followed by passage under the Artesia Freeway (5.3). The first of many river spillways is near this junction.

Pass the Cerritos Ironwood Golf Course; nearby is the pedestrian bridge across the river that leads to Caruthers Park (5.6). Our reference path stays on the east levee. Beyond Alondra Boulevard, enter a pleasant residential stretch, several miles long, where there are horses in many of the backyards (we even spotted a llama). Pass Rosecrans Avenue (7.0) and another walk bridge over the river, then bike under a bridge that is part of the Century Freeway (7.8). In 0.3 mile, the path reaches Imperial Highway and later dips down nearer the river, passing below a railroad trestle (8.7).

Wilderness Park. At (9.0), the bike trail passes Firestone Boulevard, then reaches the transition to a natural river bottom after 11 solid miles of concrete. Rio San Gabriel Park is across the river and a small spillway graces the river bottom. There is some excellent river bottomland north of this area (see Trips #19C and #19D). In about 0.7 mile, the tour reaches a refreshing terminus at Wilderness Park. This is a half-mile strip of park that offers water, restrooms, shade trees, sports and recreation areas, playgrounds, a small pond, and a lovely decorative water fountain.

CONNECTING TRIPS: 1) Continuation with the San Gabriel River Trail south to Seal Beach (Trip #19A) from the trip origin, or north to the Whittier Narrows (Trip #19C) from the trip terminus.

TRIP #19C - SAN GABRIEL RIVER: WILDERNESS PARK TO LEGG LAKE

GENERAL LOCATION: Downey, Santa Fe Springs, Whittier, Pico Rivera

LEVEL OF DIFFICULTY: One way - easy; up and back - moderate
Distance - 7.7 miles (one way)
Elevation gain - essentially flat (single steep grade
at Whittier Narrows Dam)

HIGHLIGHTS: This is a pleasant segment of the San Gabriel River Trail that starts at Wilderness Park, visits Santa Fe Springs Park and ends at the trip highlight in the Whittier Narrows Recreation Area. A short diversion at Whittier Boulevard leads to Pio Pico State Historical Park. The Whittier Narrows area sports a ride on the dam levee, a visit to a wildlife refuge area, and a trip at the end to relaxing Legg Lake. This is one of the few river segments that is predominantly natural river bottom and there are some lush areas that beckon for rest stops. This is 99 percent Class I trail (two street crossings) with light bike traffic south of the Whittier Narrows Dam.

TRAILHEAD: From the San Gabriel River Freeway, exit west on Florence Avenue. A short distance west of the freeway, turn left (south) on Little Lake Road. This road also leads back onto the southbound freeway; therefore, in a few hundred feet, turn right onto Little Lake Road proper. Continue on this roadway to the free parking area at Wilderness Park. From the Santa Ana Freeway, exit west on Florence Avenue. Pass under the San Gabriel Freeway and follow the directions above.

Bring a moderate water supply. There is no water supply en route between Santa Fe Springs Park and the Whittier Narrows Recreation Area. (Water sources near the recreation area are at Legg Lake and the Nature Center.)

TRIP DESCRIPTION: **Wilderness Park to Santa Fe Springs Park.** From the south end of the parking lot, skirt the south edge of Wilderness Park and follow the path

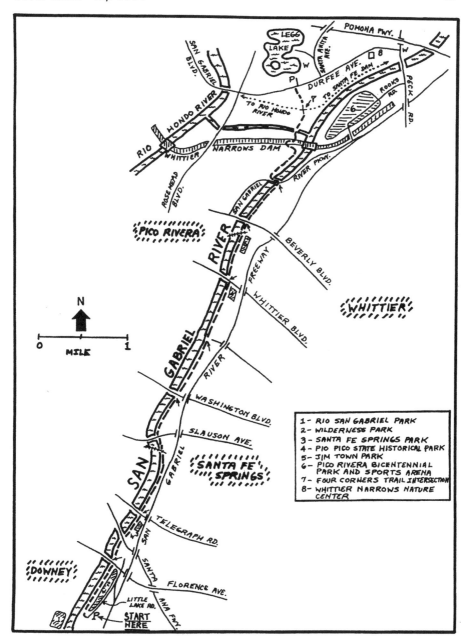

TRIP #19C - SAN GABRIEL RIVER: WILDERNESS PARK TO LEGG LAKE

to the river entry. Turn right (north) and bike past Florence Avenue (0.2) and the first of many spillways 0.2 mile further. There are scattered trees and a great deal of brush along the path. The riverbed is built up into holding basins. At (0.7), reach Santa Fe Springs Park where there are play areas, shade, recreation fields, and restrooms. Fill up with water here if you are running low.

The Railroad Route and Pio Pico Historical Park. About 0.4 mile from the park, cross Telegraph Road. At (1.4), the bikeway passes the highest spillway (about six feet high) on this segment of the river. In this area there is a stand of eucalyptus trees, and a collection of horse stalls is tucked between the river and the San Gabriel Freeway. At (2.1), pass under a railroad trestle. Soon after, another railroad track comes in from the east and parallels the bike route for several miles. There is a high likelihood of having a train for company on this stretch.

Shortly, pass under another railroad trestle; it lies below the highly elevated Slauson Avenue overpass (2.3). The riverbed and greenery in the riverbed continue, while brush and railroad tracks are to the right. At (3.0) is Washington Boulevard and the beginning of a long, exposed stretch of bikeway. In about 0.6 mile is the biker/pedestrian entry at Dunlap Crossing Road. At (4.7), the path meets Whittier Boulevard; it is a 0.2-mile diversion to the right (east) to visit Pio Pico Historical Park and the Pio Pico Museum.

Our route transits a short tunnel under Whittier Boulevard and passes alongside dense brush on the right. At (5.3), the path heads under another railroad trestle; the paralleling railroad tracks fuse and the merged track leaves the river heading east. In 0.2 mile is Beverly Boulevard. Further north is a spillway with a collecting basin large enough to support a flock of young water frolickers. There is a view into Rose Hills to the east.

Whittier Narrows Dam. The trip reaches a junction where the trail changes from asphalt to dirt at San Gabriel River Parkway (6.1). The dam can be seen at this point. Continue ahead if you have a wide-tire bike and a desire to see Pico Rivera Bicentennial Park and Sports Area. Our reference route follows the parkway and crosses the river to the west side. Pedal north and observe the lush tree-filled river bottom. Pass the Pico Rivera Golf Course (6.7) and make a hard left at the dam base. From this point there is a short, steep path to the top of the dam (6.9). Stop and take in some of the excellent sights that are viewable here.

Whittier Narrows Recreation Area. (See the Whittier Narrows Recreation Area Detail Map.) Cruise down the meandering concrete bikeway on the backside of the dam, cross a water runoff channel and reach the marked Four Corners Trail Intersection (7.2). Bike straight ahead and pedal about 0.3 mile to a junction near another water channel. Turn left and cross over the channel, then bike a couple hundred yards through the lush bottomland to Durfee Avenue and pass through the gate. Turn right (east) and cruise a few hundred feet to the Legg Lake parking area entry within the Whittier Narrows Recreation Area (7.7).

Excursions: Legg Lake. (See Whittier Narrows Recreation Area Detail Map.) The entire lake trip is on well-compacted dirt and is easy to ride with any type of bike. However, some care is needed in a couple of fine-gravel and wet areas. Leave the parking lot and head north toward the lake. Veer right for the counterclockwise tour. Pass a roofed picnic area, then a little spillway into the lake, and visit a giant sandy play area with a ten-foot-high cement octopus (0.2).

Shortly the route passes a food stand and boat rental area. There are numerous ducks and geese in the area. Further on is a "rocket" playground and some lovely shaded picnic sites situated at the lake edge (0.4). Just beyond is a trail junction. Diverting to the left leads to a bridge crossing between the northernmost lake and the main lake. The reference trip heads right and passes around the north lake through the green, natural, tree-covered surroundings. On this southbound segment the path meets

Four Corners Trail Intersection (Susan Cohen Photo)

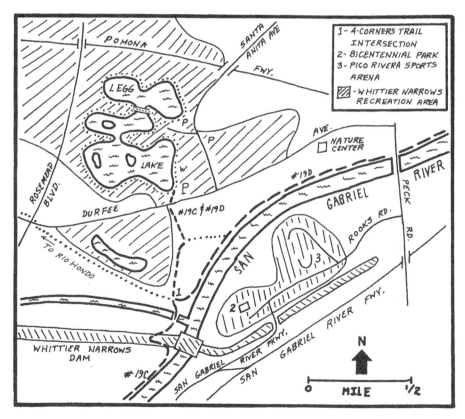

WHITTIER NARROWS RECREATION AREA DETAIL MAP

the other end of the junction route between the lakes at (1.6). This area is one of the fishermen's favorites.

In 0.1 mile, pass a spillway near the western end of the lake, one of the few lake areas where motor traffic is visible. We passed a group of ducks sleeping on the grass six feet away from a busy fisherman near here. The route turns eastward later and roughly parallels Durfee Avenue (2.1). The final stretch continues to wind along the lake edge and returns to the trip origin in another half mile (2.6).

Upper Rio Hondo and Lario River Trails. Exit the parking lot and cross Durfee Avenue a few hundred feet to the west. Pass through the signed gate and retrace the incoming route back to the Four Corners Trail Intersection (0.5). The route to the left (east) goes to the San Gabriel River and heads north, while the route dead ahead (south) heads back toward the dam and returns to the southerly San Gabriel River segment (the incoming route). Our tour goes right (west) and roughly parallels the dam, passing alongside some striking vine-covered trees. In 0.5 mile is a view back into Rose Hills (1.0). Cross a small footbridge over a wash and reach Durfee Avenue in 0.1 mile. Pedal on Class I road and go 0.2 mile to the intersection of Rosemead Boulevard and Durfee Avenue/San Gabriel Boulevard (1.3). Cross the intersection to the north side and bike on Class I San Gabriel Boulevard until reaching the bike entry to the Rio Hondo river (just before the bridge and on the east levee) (1.5). This is a key junction point.

Upper Rio Hondo Trail (northbound). Drop down from the road and ride along a pleasant, natural, tree- and brush-lined stretch of the river. The growth is so dense that the river view does not open up for 0.25 mile or so. Pass under the Pomona Freeway (3.3), veer to the right, then parallel the freeway at road level for 0.6 mile before reaching the northern recreation area (Recreation Area "A") entrance.

Whittier Narrows Recreation Area "A." The bike entrance to the park is at its south end. Cyclists can cruise both the bikeways and slow-moving, lightly traveled roads within the recreation area. The park dimensions are roughly half a mile, north-south, and a quarter mile, east-west, providing plenty of room to roam. It is a moderately treed park with restrooms, water, picnic areas, recreation fields, and model car racing and model airplane flying areas. This Los Angeles County recreation area, combined with Legg Lake, is certainly on par with recreation/biking areas such as Mile Square, William R. Mason, and Irvine Regional Parks.

Upper Rio Hondo and Lario Trails (southbound). At the key junction point mentioned above, proceed over the river 0.1 mile to Lincoln Avenue (1.6). Turn left and make another immediate left turn onto an asphalt road blocked to cars. The trail follows above and at some distance from the Rio Hondo's west bank. This section has scrub brush, an oil well pump or two, and eroded low hills to the west.

The trail pulls away from the river at about 0.2 mile from the Lincoln Avenue entrance and comes within close view of that street. Just beyond are the first views of the backside of the Whittier Narrows Dam. In 0.2 mile, follow a steep trail up the backside of this dam to the summit of the west levee of the dam (2.1). As noted by the sign near the levee entry, this is the start of the Lario Trail.

For the detailed discussion and maps associated with the Upper Rio Hondo and Lario Trails, the Los Angeles River, and the "Big Banana" ride which connects them all to the San Gabriel River, see B-D Enterprises' publication, *Bicycle Rides: Los Angeles County.*

CONNECTING TRIPS: 1) Continuation with the San Gabriel River Trail south to El Dorado Park (Trip #19B) - from the trip origin, bike south; 2) continuation with the San Gabriel River Trail north to Santa Fe Dam (Trip #19D) - from the Four Corners Trail Intersection, turn right (east) at the junction.

TRIP #19D - SAN GABRIEL RIVER: LEGG LAKE TO SANTA FE DAM

GENERAL LOCATION: Whittier Narrows, El Monte, Baldwin Park, Irwindale

LEVEL OF DIFFICULTY: One way - easy; up and back - moderate
Distance - 11.4 miles (one way)
Elevation gain - essentially flat (short, steep grades at Santa Fe Dam and at Whittier Narrows Dam for up-and-back ride)

HIGHLIGHTS: This is one of our favorite segments of the river trips. The San Gabriel River in the Whittier Narrows region is river stomping at its best. There are trees, thickets, clear running water, and readily visible wildlife in all. The Whittier Narrows Recreation Area offers a wildlife sanctuary, Legg Lake, vista points from the top of the dam, and a diversion trip to the Pico Rivera Bicentennial Park and Sports Area. The Santa Fe Dam Recreation Area offers an expansive, pleasant picnic and recreation area at the edge of the lake, as well as superb lookout points from the top of the dam. Set aside a few hours and fully explore these territories. The best time to take this trip is within several days of a cold winter storm when the snow level in the nearby mountains is low. The route is nearly 100 percent Class I (one street crossing).

There are also some excellent trip excursions in the Santa Fe Dam area, such as: on-road explorations to the west of the San Gabriel River Freeway; and on the west levee, some fat-tire bike meandering in the flood control basin behind the dam.

TRAILHEAD: From the Pomona Freeway, exit at Rosemead Boulevard south, travel about 0.8 mile to San Gabriel Boulevard/Durfee Boulevard and turn left. Drive on Durfee Avenue 0.6 mile and turn left into the pay parking area at Legg Lake. Find a tree under which to park your car. Bring four quarters for the parking area fee.

Bring a moderate water supply. There are rest and water stops directly on the route and at the Santa Fe Recreation Area terminus.

TRIP DESCRIPTION: **Whittier Narrows Recreation Area.** (See the Whittier Narrows Recreation Area Detail Map in Trip #19C.) Leave the parking area and cross Durfee Avenue a few hundred feet west of the parking area. Pass through the signed gate and pedal down a small asphalt road through an area surrounded by bushes, plants, trees, and brush. In a short distance there is a junction just beyond a small water channel. The path left leads toward (but bypasses) the Whittier Narrows Nature Center.

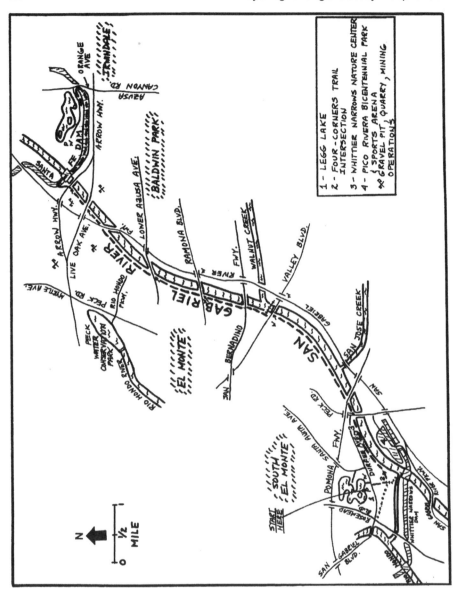

TRIP #19D - SAN GABRIEL RIVER: LEGG LAKE TO SANTA FE DAM

However, our route proceeds to the right and meets the Four Corners Trail Intersection in 0.3 mile (0.5). There is a nice view into the backside of the Whittier Narrows Dam from this area.

Turn left (east) and follow the path as it turns northward and rejoins the San Gabriel River (0.7). There are permanent horse trails to the left (west) and also "find-your-way" paths in the lush riverbed; both are well used by horse riders, the latter accompanying our path for the next couple of miles. This area has excellent views of Rose Hills to the east.

The Unofficial Recreation Area/San Jose Creek Confluence. Pass the first of many spillways that stair-step their way up the river (1.4). Small children slide down the rounded portion of the spillway into a holding basin below, and even a swimming dog might be seen. In 0.4 mile is Peck Road and a second spillway with a large pool backed up behind it. (There are gas stations and restaurants not too far from the river at this exit.)

The trail passes under the Pomona Freeway (2.0) and reaches the third spillway, which usually has some fishermen and a few swimmers using the upstream water pool. In 0.3 mile is the confluence with San Jose Creek and one of the most well-used of the unofficial recreation spots on the river. There are inner-tube riders, swimmers, fishermen, horses with riders crossing the river, and even some off-road bicycling.

The Middle Segment. At (2.7), there is a small rodeo ring where bikers have a free chance to watch the trainers work with horses or, with luck, to watch a mini-rodeo. Just beyond is one of the highest spillways (about ten feet high) on the river, with a holding basin stretched across the river on the downstream side. Cycle alongside residential areas, pass the Mountain View High School athletic field (3.9) and reach Valley Boulevard (4.1). There is a small bike rest stop here with a simple pipe water fountain. On a clear day there is a striking view into the San Gabriel Mountains from this point.

Travel under a railroad bridge and later meet the Walnut Creek junction (4.3). From this point north, the water level drops significantly and the riverbed is much less interesting. At this junction, to the left (west) of the trail, there is a corral that holds Brahma bulls and a buffalo. Continuing onward, the bikeway passes the San Bernardino Freeway (4.7) and then meets another biker rest area at Ramona Boulevard (5.6).

The Gravel Pits. At (6.5), pass the first of several large gravel dredging operations (to the right). In another 0.2 mile, reach Lower Azusa Road. There is a large, open, water-filled gravel pit to the left (west) (5.9), followed by a "granddaddy" gravel pit across the river to the right (6.4). Also there are several highly visible above-ground mining operations.

Santa Fe Dam. At (7.5), cross under the San Gabriel River Freeway and stare directly into the Santa Fe Dam face. Pass a power station (7.0), then Live Oak Avenue, and bike to an apparent dead-end at Arrow Highway (8.8). Cross that street, follow the signed path left and bike to the base of the dam. Pass through the walker/biker entry opening in the fence and pump a short, steep grade to the top of the dam (9.2).

From the top of the dam in winter there are views into the San Gabriel Mountains that are awe-inspiring, along with views into the San Jose Hills to the southeast and Puente Hills to the south. The cities of the foothills are spread out all the way to the western horizon.

There is a paved trail to the left (northwest) that ends just below the west levee terminus. (See the last of the "Santa Fe Dam Excursions" below.) However, our route goes to the right and continues another 1.9 miles along the top of the dam, providing other fine views, including those down into the Santa Fe Recreational Area. The dam trail descends and then ends at the bike trail access gate. Proceed 0.2 mile further to the auto access road into the recreation area (Orange Avenue which is named Azusa Canyon Road south of Arrow Highway). The mileage at this point is (11.4).

Santa Fe Dam Recreation Area. The recreation area behind the dam is a charmer. To get there, make a hard left onto the automobile roadway access just downhill of the auto pay gate. There are bikepaths and a low-speed-limit, lightly traveled,

Atop Santa Fe Dam with Recreation Area below

paved road that can be linked into a couple more miles of biking. The entire park is built alongside a lake and comes equipped with water and restrooms, picnic areas, a swimming area with a sand beach, playgrounds, fire pits, shaded pagodas (group area at the western end of the lake), boat rental, and a snack bar.

There are also bicycle roadways beyond the west end of the lake. In periods of low water, fat-tire bikes can be ridden through this maze of dirt trails to the westside dam levee access. (See the last of the "Santa Fe Dam Side Trips" below.)

Excursions: Santa Fe Dam Side Trips. At the west base of the dam, just before beginning the climb to the top, there is a trail heading north and west to a tunnel under the San Gabriel River Freeway. On the west side of the freeway is a "T"-junction. The south fork transitions to dirt in half a mile and follows the Buena Vista Channel west almost to Buena Vista Street, but a fence prevents access to that street. The north fork climbs a small levee in 0.8 mile to San Gabriel Freeway level, then drops down to the Santa Fe Dam Flying Area (model airplanes). Climbing to the opposite levee leads to a ride extension of half a mile, paralleling Duarte Road, to the levee's terminus. At the terminus, the packed-dirt road leading west towards Duarte Road is blocked by the City of Duarte Maintenance Yard, while the eastern path leads into the dirt areas of the main flood control basin. The path south runs parallel to the freeway and loops back to the incoming route in half a mile. The north fork route totals three miles, round trip.

Another choice, once on top of the Santa Fe Dam, is to bike northwest and explore the levee, a mile west, which parallels the San Gabriel River Freeway. The outlet is a downhill into the main flood control basin behind the dam. There are dirt paths winding over the entire basin, including routes leading across to the lakeside recreation area or under the San Gabriel River Freeway and Foothill Freeway. (Do not attempt to bike in this area during rainy periods!)

CONNECTING TRIPS: 1) Continuation with the southbound San Gabriel River Trail to Wilderness Park (Trip #19C) - from the Four Corners Trail Intersection, head south and over the Whittier Narrows Dam; 2) continuation with the northbound San Gabriel River Trail to the San Gabriel River Canyon (Trip #19E) - at the recreation area auto access, bike north (nearly straight ahead). Follow the trail signs.

TRIP #19E - SAN GABRIEL RIVER: SANTA FE DAM TO SAN GABRIEL CANYON

GENERAL LOCATION: Irwindale, Azusa

LEVEL OF DIFFICULTY: One way - easy; up and back - moderate
Distance - 7.5 miles (one way)
Elevation gain - essentially flat (single short,
    steep grade at Santa Fe Dam)

HIGHLIGHTS: This 100 percent Class I trip starts downstream of the Santa Fe Dam, then climbs onto and follows the dam levee. The route cruises from the dam upstream to the end of the San Gabriel River Trail near the Angeles National Forest Ranger Station at the entrance to San Gabriel Canyon. Along the way, the path traverses the Santa Fe Dam Nature Area which has a natural river-bottom cactus garden. There are spectacular close-up views of the foothills and surrounding mountains. These views are absolutely great after a cold winter storm. The stretch north of the dam is little used and makes a good workout trip.

TRAILHEAD: From the San Gabriel River Freeway, exit east on Live Oak Avenue. Go 0.9 mile to the junction with Arrow Highway, making a U-turn onto Arrow Highway. Drive in the reverse direction about 0.8 mile to free parking near the dam outlet.

An option is to use pay parking in the Santa Fe Dam Recreation Area. This is particularly useful if you wish to avoid riding up onto the dam and want to start from the recreation area. Exit on Live Oak Avenue (east) as above, but continue one mile past the junction of Live Oak and Arrow Highway. Turn left (north) at the Recreation Park entrance at Orange Avenue (named Azusa Canyon Road to the south).

TRIP DESCRIPTION: **Santa Fe Dam.** From the free parking area on Arrow Highway, pedal to the bike entry through the fence (to the west of the spillway near the dam base). Follow the bike trail signs and pump the steep roadway to the top of the dam (0.2). At the top is a great 360-degree view. Most prominent are the San Gabriel Mountains to the north and the San Jose Hills and Puente Hills to the southeast and south, respectively. The view into the mountains is a real "heart grabber" when the snow level is down to low elevations and the sky is clear.

There is a paved trail to the left (northwest) that ends just below the west levee terminus. (See the last of the "Santa Fe Dam Excursions" in Trip #19D.) However, our

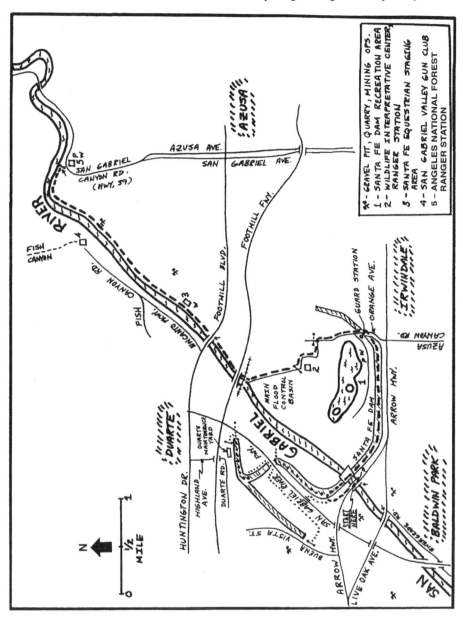

**TRIP #19E - SAN GABRIEL RIVER: SANTA FE DAM TO
SAN GABRIEL CANYON**

route goes to the right and continues another 1.9 miles along the top of the dam, providing other fine views, including those down into the Santa Fe Recreational Area. The dam trail descends, ending at the bike trail access gate. The route proceeds 0.2 mile further to the auto access road into the recreation area (Orange Avenue which is named Azusa Canyon Road south of Arrow Highway). The mileage at this point is (2.3).

Head downhill and turn sharply left below the pay gate to visit the developed park (southern) section of the Santa Fe Dam Recreation Area (see Trip #19D). Our reference route follows the signed bikeway and keeps straight ahead.

Northern Santa Fe Dam Recreation Area. Follow the road to the dead-end at a little walled parklike area (2.8). Turn left and continue tracking the well-marked road 0.2 mile until it turns right (north) again. In 0.2 mile, reach the Wildlife Interpretive Center which has both picnic and tent camping areas near the roadway intersection (3.2). Turn left again and pedal a few hundred feet to the ranger station. There are two bike route options at this point, plus marked walking/nature trails which tour the wildlife area. All routes head west and shortly meet an old north-south asphalt road. Follow the bike trail marker and turn right (north) on that old road.

The roadway passes through an interesting ecological area which is surrounded by a wide variety of cactus. At (3.8), reach the top of a small rise from which there is a nice view, including a good look at the surrounding bottomland, the backside of the Santa Fe Dam, and a view north to the Foothill Freeway. In 0.4 mile the path returns to the San Gabriel River and passes under the Foothill Freeway just beyond (4.3).

The Gravel Pits. At (4.8), pass a trans-river passenger cable car. In 0.1 mile, pass Huntington Drive/Foothill Boulevard. Next is the Santa Fe Equestrian Staging Area which has restrooms and water (5.2). There is a large above-ground gravel mining/processing works in the background. The riverbed is boulder- and brush-filled with a low spillway breaking the continuity of the scene every half mile or more.

At (5.5), the path goes by an old closed-off railroad bridge. There is a residential area across the river, with the homes continuing up into the nearby foothills. There are more gravel operations along the roadway to the right (east), with one sand and gravel operation lying right next to the trail (6.1). The route also passes a large water-filled gravel pit (6.5).

San Gabriel Canyon Entrance. The trail heads into a progressively more well-defined canyon environment. At (6.8), pass Fish Canyon in the hills to the left (west). There is an exquisite series of waterfalls (in wintertime) several miles back into the canyon called Fish Falls. (Sorry, this is hiking country only.) At this point on the bike trail there is also a firing range, the San Gabriel Valley Gun Club. The hills echo the sounds, providing a "Gunfight at the O.K. Corral" aura.

Just beyond, the trail dead-ends at a fence (7.5). A small trail to the right leads to Highway 39 and the Angeles National Forest Ranger Station at the entrance to San Gabriel Canyon. There is water and parking here if you want to start from this direction or to use this as a pickup or turnaround point.

CONNECTING TRIPS: 1) Continuation with the San Gabriel River Trail south to Whittier Narrows (Trip #19D) - cross Arrow Highway and bike east a few hundred feet (in front of the spillway); 2) continuation with a very strenuous Class X "gut-buster" up San Gabriel Canyon Road - we observed a few hearty bikers working their way up the several miles of continuous steep grade.

TRIP #20 - COYOTE CREEK TRAIL

GENERAL LOCATION: Long Beach, Seal Beach, Cerritos, Santa Fe Springs

LEVEL OF DIFFICULTY: One way - easy; up and back - moderate
Distance - 14.0 miles (one way)
Elevation gain - essentially flat

HIGHLIGHTS: Another of the river trails, this is a 99.44 percent pure Class I route. It starts at the scenic lower section of the San Gabriel River outlet near the Long Beach Marina and proceeds to the Coyote Creek junction. The Coyote Creek path is well maintained but lightly used. The 10.1-mile Coyote Creek section is not highly scenic, unless one enjoys "window shopping" into backyards of the adjoining homes and apartments. It is a fine workout bikeway, however. The trip passes alongside Cerritos Regional County Park, which is a convenient and pleasant rest point near the center of the Coyote Creek segment. Beyond the Artesia Freeway is the 2.5-mile (most recent) extension through commercial area to a terminus at Foster Road. A short ride from here leads to shaded Frontier Park.

TRAILHEAD: Free public parking is available on Marina Drive in Long Beach or along First Street in Seal Beach. From Pacific Coast Highway (PCH) in Seal Beach, turn west on Marina Drive (2 to 3 blocks from Main Street in Seal Beach) and continue roughly half a mile to First Street. In another quarter of a mile, cross the San Gabriel River and continue a short distance along the marina for parking. The trailhead is located at Marina Drive at the east end of the bridge over the San Gabriel River (across from Seaport Village).

An alternate start point is Edison Park, which starts cyclists much nearer to the Coyote Creek/San Gabriel River junction. From Studebaker Road in eastern Long Beach, turn east on E. 9th Street and right (south) immediately after. Continue on that unnamed road to its end at College Park Drive, cross the San Gabriel River, then turn left, just beyond, into the park. Carefully observe posted parking signs.

Bikers should have a filled water bottle since the trip is waterless up to Cerritos Regional Park. Riders starting at Seal Beach can cycle south about 0.3 mile from the trailhead to use restrooms at the beach. The side trip may also serve as a very pleasant scenic diversion. After the ride, Seaport Village at the edge of the marina may serve as a nice dining spot, watering hole, or place to shop.

TRIP DESCRIPTION: **The Scenic Lower Segment.** (See Trip #19A for a map of this segment.) The first part of the trip provides views of boaters, water-skiers, and an interestingly developed shoreline. The natural river basin then passes the PCH access, the Westminster Avenue entry (1.2), and the Haynes Steam Plant (electricity generation). At (2.2), a small diversion Class I path leads off to the east along a 1.2-mile shaded route to Seal Beach Boulevard. In this stretch of the river, up to the concrete portion at about (3.5), cyclists have views of a large bird population that includes pelicans, egrets, and the ever-present seagulls. The path goes under the Garden Grove

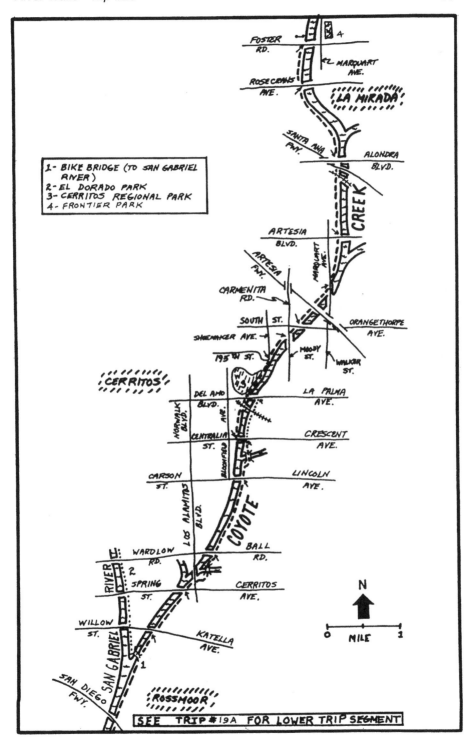

TRIP #20 - COYOTE CREEK

Freeway (2.3), passes Edison Park, then ducks below the San Diego Freeway (3.5). In this portion of the path are many "freeway orchards," those freeway-locked areas under the power poles which are used for growing containerized plants.

Coyote Creek. At (3.9), a marked bridge over the river takes bikers to the connecting portion of the San Gabriel River Bike Trail (Trip #19A). However, at this junction, our route continues along the east side (stay to the right) of the channel and passes the Katella Avenue entry, the San Gabriel River Freeway, and the Cerritos Avenue access (5.2). Nearby, the channel junctions to the north (no easy access at this junction was found), although our reference route stays along the east side of the channel. Two additional small channel junctions to the east are encountered at (5.6) and (7.3). However, both junctions are closed off by locked gates, and the main Coyote Creek path crosses those junctions via small overpasses. The Los Alamitos access is at about (5.6). Pass Ball Road, a small walking-only bridge across the creek (6.3), and Lincoln Avenue, then bike to Crescent Avenue/Centralia Street.

Exit the bikeway and cross to the west bank. Continue half a mile to La Palma Avenue/Del Amo Boulevard and pass alongside Cerritos County Regional Park. There is water within sight of the bikeway plus a park complete with restrooms, recreational fields, and a limited amount of shade. Pedal along a residential area and pass under Moody Street/Carmenita Road, then South Street/Orangethorpe Avenue. There are fast-food establishments and gas stations to the west (9.2).

In a short distance, bike under the Artesia Freeway and pass alongside residential developments (with scattered shade trees), then cycle past Walker Street/Marquart Avenue. The path veers left (due north) along the La Cañada Verde Creek fork (the main Coyote Creek fork branches northeast) and continues another 0.4 mile to Artesia Boulevard. The channel dips under the Santa Ana Freeway and Alondra Boulevard on the most recently opened 2.5-mile path extension through a strictly commercial zone. The bikeway passes alongside the Santa Fe Springs Drive-in Theater (12.3), then it beelines 1.7 miles to its end at Foster Road.

A short ride east on Foster Road leads to Marquart Avenue and Frontier Park. The park has shade (a rare commodity on the ride), water, restrooms, a children's play area, and barbecue facilities.

CONNECTING TRIPS: 1) Continuation/connection to lower and middle portions of the San Gabriel River tour (Trips #19A and #19B) - take major access streets west and cross the San Gabriel River Freeway, noting that the distance between Coyote Creek and the San Gabriel River increases as cyclists go further north on Coyote Creek; 2) connection with the Cypress tour (Trip #21) - bike east from any exit street between Katella Avenue and La Palma Avenue; 3) connectors to the lower portion of this trip along the San Gabriel River are described in Trip #19A.

INLAND

Lake Forest

TRIP #21 - CYPRESS TOUR

GENERAL LOCATION: Cypress, La Palma, Buena Park

LEVEL OF DIFFICULTY: Loop - easy to moderate
Distance - 14.9 miles
Elevation gain - essentially flat

HIGHLIGHTS: This is a pleasant cruise primarily on Class II city streets that explores several inland Orange County cities. The tour leaves pleasant and tiny Eucalyptus Park and follows a lightly traveled loop through mostly residential and some light industrial areas. There are two enjoyable Class I loops within the larger tour. Other highlights are Cypress College, El Rancho Verde Park and Bicycle Path, and the numerous exceptional parks spread throughout. The route described can be linked with numerous other Class II and III routes in the area.

TRAILHEAD: From the Garden Grove Freeway, exit north on Valley View Street and drive 1.75 miles to Orangewood Avenue. Turn left and motor a short distance to Eucalyptus Park. From the San Gabriel River Freeway, exit east at Katella Avenue/Willow Street. Continue east three miles to Valley View Street, turn right and drive one-half mile to Orangewood Avenue. Turn right again and continue to the park.

Bring a light water supply. There are numerous well-placed water sources scattered along the way.

TRIP DESCRIPTION: Northbound. Leave the park and bike east on Orangewood Avenue. Once across Valley View Street, pass Maplegrove Parks North and South (athletic courts, grass, shade, water) and in another 0.4 mile go past Manzanita Park (water fountain, trees, athletic courts, children's play area). Turn left (north) at Knott Avenue and bike 0.3 mile to the end of the housing tract. Turn left and bike 1.0 mile along a wash on the Class I path, returning to Valley View Street (2.5).

Turn right and cruise north on the sidewalk one-half mile to Cerritos Avenue, turn left onto the Class II street, turn right shortly on Walker Street (the eastern edge of the Los Alamitos Race Course) and left again on Class II Ball Road. There are small shopping complexes and a gas station at this intersection (3.9). Cycle west on Ball Road to Moody Street and begin a pleasant, sporadically shaded, 1.5-mile Class I partial loop on the large sidewalk. Along this stretch is Veteran's Park with restrooms, recreation fields, extensive lawns, and a children's play area. The path turns right at Denni Street and right again at Orange Avenue, passing Willow Park with restrooms, tree shade, picnic facilities, grass, and a duckpond. The path then returns to Moody Street (5.4); bike north on that street for 1.8 miles. (Just south of Lincoln Avenue on this stretch is Evergreen Park with restrooms, modest tree cover, benches, and a children's play area.) Turn right just past Sharon Drive onto the Class I bikepath below the power poles.

This is the westernmost edge of the El Rancho Verde Park and Bicycle Path, a laid-back two-mile stretch of mixed Class I path/grass, the last one mile (east of Valley View Street) for wide-tread tires only. Our reference route follows the (lighted) first mile;

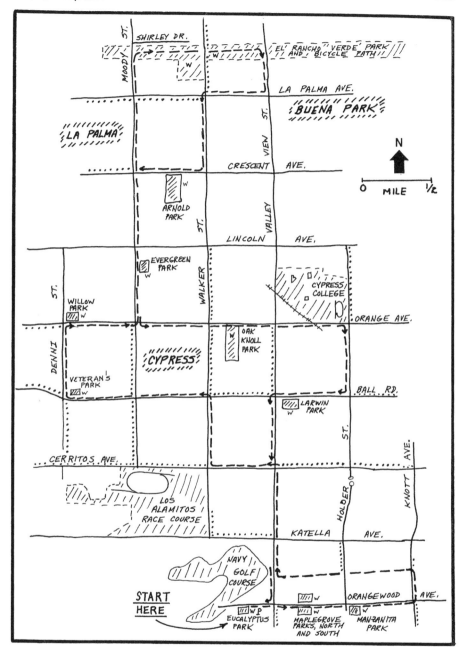

TRIP #21 - CYPRESS TOUR

water fountains are along the path at the baseball field near the halfway point and just across Walker Street. Cruise to the end of the Class I path at Valley View Street (8.2).

Southbound. Follow Class X Valley View Avenue a short distance to La Palma Avenue and the La Palma Center (shopping). Turn right (west), left on Walker Street then right on Crescent Avenue. All streets in this short, 1.8-mile zigzag stretch are

Class II. Stay on Crescent Avenue between the tennis courts to the right (north) and the sports complex of Arnold Park/Cypress Park to the left. (This fine park has stately trees, restrooms, barbecue facilities, park benches, and a children's playground.) At Moody Street, turn left (south) (10.0).

Return on Moody Street to Orange Avenue and turn left, passing the Cypress Community Center/Oak Knoll Park with its recreation field, water, and restrooms. At 1.5 miles from the Moody Street/Orange Avenue intersection, pass the expansive lawns of the Cypress College campus and turn right on Holder Street. Follow Holder Street one-half mile to Ball Road, turn right, pass Larwin Park (water fountain, scattered tree cover, benches, children's play area) and return to Valley View Street (13.5). Bike 1.4 miles south, turn right at Orangewood Avenue and return to Eucalyptus Park (14.9).

CONNECTING TRIPS: 1) Connection with the Western Orange County Loop (Trip #33) - at La Palma Avenue and Valley View Street, bike east on the former street to Western Avenue; 2) connection with the Coyote Creek ride (Trip #20) - bike west on Lincoln Avenue, Crescent Avenue, or La Palma Avenue at the intersection with Moody Street and continue to the creek.

TRIP #22 - EL CAJON TRAIL

GENERAL LOCATION: Yorba Linda

LEVEL OF DIFFICULTY: One way - easy; up and back - moderate
Distance - 8.2 miles (one way)
Elevation gain - periodic moderate grades

HIGHLIGHTS: This delightful trip roams through some of the most pleasant residential neighborhoods in Orange County, particularly for bikers who are horse lovers. The primarily Class I route meanders along the general route of the old El Cajon Canal (now the Anaheim Union Canal). The trip is segmented as follows: 1) 3.6 miles through a rural residential setting (several road crossings required); 2) a diversion onto a Class X roadway on Sunmist Drive, followed by a Class I passage through the Yorba Linda Country Club; 3) a climb to Lindafair Lane, Class X downhill on Fairlynn Boulevard and return to Class I on Esperanza Drive; and 4) a final 1.8-mile Class I trailway through a rural residential neighborhood, ending near Yorba Linda Boulevard and Esperanza Road. This is a particularly fine trip for nosy people who like to peek into backyards.

TRAILHEAD: From the Orange Freeway, exit east at Yorba Linda Boulevard. Continue about 2.2 miles and turn left on Rose Drive. Continue 0.6 mile, just past Verna Lane (on the right-hand side only), and look for the asphalt bike trail. If you pass Bastanchury Road, you've gone too far. Find parking near the trailhead, subject to local parking laws. From the Riverside Freeway, exit north at Tustin Avenue. Continue 3.5 miles as Tustin Avenue becomes Rose Drive and meets Verna Lane. Park as described above.

Bring a moderate water supply. There are two water fountains that we found along the western bikeway segment and one on the east side.

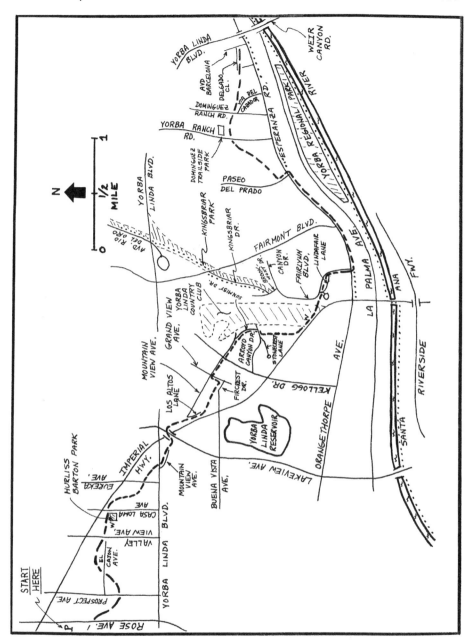

TRIP #22 - EL CAJON TRAIL

TRIP DESCRIPTION: **Trailhead to Hurliss Burton Park.** The trail has a short
spur to the west of Rose Drive but our route starts from the east side. Proceed along a
eucalyptus-lined path and a mini-orange grove through a pleasant residential neighborhood. Cross Prospect Avenue (0.3) and enjoy a quarter mile of "pure" horse country
(both sights and smells). Transit El Cajon Avenue (0.6) and continue through a fenced

trail area that borders many residential backyards. (We saw a wedding reception and also some young children jumping from the roof into a swimming pool in this stretch!) Make your way across Valley View Avenue (1.0), pass a small tank farm, then cross Casa Loma Avenue (1.3). Small, shaded Hurliss Barton Park is located just to the right at the crossing which has water.

Hurliss Barton Park to the Imperial Highway Crossing. Parallel Imperial Highway for a short distance, then loop back away from the roadway and pass over the canal on a little wooden bridge (1.6). Cruise along a eucalyptus-lined section, cross Eureka Avenue (1.9) and enjoy the transition to a colorful oleander-lined section. Work across Yorba Linda Boulevard and parallel Mountain View Avenue, climbing to a small, scenic crest (2.3). Next is the Lakeview Avenue undercrossing; half a mile south (right) from here is the Yorba Linda Reservoir with several miles of jogging, equestrian, and wide-tire bike trails.

However, our reference route crosses under Lakeview Avenue, turns right and passes on a bridge over Imperial Highway (2.5). Once across, follow the fenced trail (a short distance and to the right) downhill, then level off near a residential area at Los Altos Lane (2.8). The path winds above and around Buena Vista Equestrian Park, then passes a small commercial zone near Fircrest Drive. At (3.0), cross Grand View Avenue, turn left, proceed one block and continue right along Mountain View Avenue (3.4).

Yorba Linda Country Club and Golf Course. In 0.2 mile, the Class I path ends at Kellogg Drive. Proceed across that roadway onto a short, testy grade to Sunmist Drive and turn right. Follow that road on a milder grade through a plush neighborhood to its terminus at Arroyo Cajon Drive (4.1). Turn right and look for the little asphalt continuation trail in a short distance. Follow the path downhill while taking in the views of the Anaheim Hills and the Santa Ana River floodplain. At 0.3 mile from Arroyo Cajon Drive, the path reaches a point above Imperial Highway (4.3), then continues downhill to the Yorba Linda Golf Course and Country Club. Traverse the golf course near the fence, cross a small golf cart path (with a nearby water fountain) and pass over the canal on a little concrete strip.

There is a trail junction just beyond this point (4.8). The tree-shaded trail, left, for golf carts, travels along the golf course's western edge. Our route goes straight ahead up a short, steep hill, with an expansive view to the south and southeast at the top of the grade. The trail winds around the hill, passes through a fence, then meets little Lindafair Lane. Cross that street and continue on the Class I trail 0.2 mile to Fairlynn Boulevard.

Esperanza Road. Bike 0.3 mile downhill on Fairlynn Boulevard to Esperanza Road and turn left. Follow that Class I roadway 1.2 miles to Paseo Del Prado and turn left. Climb a short grade and, in about two blocks, turn right onto a perpendicular asphalt bikepath (6.9). In another 0.2 mile, the trail travels along a cactus-lined hillside, followed by a cruise alongside the backyards of numerous residences.

At (7.6), cross Yorba Ranch Road, travel along a stately tree-lined section, pass through Dominguez Trailside Park (restrooms, water, swimming pool, tennis courts, children's playground) and soon reach Dominguez Ranch Road (7.8). Cross it and follow the Class I trail through this residential neighborhood, passing in succession Via Del Conejo, Via Del Bisconte, Avenida Antigua, and the trail terminus at Avenida Barcelona, just above Avenida Granada (just north and west of the junction of Yorba Linda Boulevard and Esperanza Road) (8.2). If time permits, backtrack and try a freewheeling tour through the well-laid-out residential community.

Near the Yorba Linda Golf Course

Return Options. Round-trip bicyclists can modify the return route slightly by biking south to Esperanza Road, then pedaling 2.2 miles west on that Class I route back to Fairlynn Boulevard. From this point, retrace the incoming route.

Excursion: Kingsbriar Park. For up-and-back cyclists, start from the park's south end at Kingsbriar Drive and Brookmont Drive, thereby doing most of the mild uphill on the outgoing leg. Bike north 0.7 mile on the quiet Class III road, alongside the park and its small creek, to Fairmont Boulevard. Cross this busy street (no traffic signal) and look for the start of a Class I trail. Follow the trail through a treed section just behind a row of residences and bike 0.8 mile to Avenida Rio Del Oro. A short pedal to Yorba Linda Boulevard completes the signed tour (1.6).

The trip can be extended, but is not on a signed bikeway. Cross Yorba Linda Boulevard at the traffic signal and continue along the park's northern reaches on a lightly treed walkway. Cross neighborhood street Puesta Del Sol and bicycle another 0.35 mile to the greenbelt's end at Avenida Del Este. The total one-way distance is 2.1 miles.

CONNECTING TRIPS: 1) Connection with the Santa Ana River Trail (Trip #17A north or Trip #17B south) - continue east on Class I Esperanza Road under the Weir Canyon Road overpass, walk your bike across the open field to the right (south) to La Palma Avenue, turn right and continue to Yorba Regional Park; 2) connection with the Fullerton Tour/Craig Park route (Trip #24) - continue from the trip origin three miles west on Bastanchury Road, turn right (north) and proceed one mile to the Craig Park entrance - this road is on a Class X roadway with some sections having very narrow shoulder; 3) connection with the Carbon Canyon Workout (Trip #23) - at the trip origin, bike north 1.5 miles on Rose Drive to Valencia Avenue, turn right and continue 0.4 mile to Carbon Canyon Road; 4) connection with the Yorba Linda Bits and Pieces tour (Trip #43) - the trips share a common segment on Esperanza Road east of Fairmont Connector.

TRIP #23 - CHINO HILLS LOOP

GENERAL LOCATION: Carbon Canyon, Chino Hills, Diamond Bar, Brea

LEVEL OF DIFFICULTY: Round trip - strenuous
Distance - 23.3 miles
Elevation gain - long moderate-to-steep grades on Car-
bon Canyon Road and Grand Avenue in Chino Hills

HIGHLIGHTS: This three-county tour is for experienced bikers in excellent condition. Initially, cyclists pump a rugged uphill which starts from Carbon Canyon Park
and proceeds to the Carbon Canyon Road summit, with an elevation gain of nearly 700
feet in 5.5 miles. This segment is a canyon-watcher's delight with nice unobstructed
views (which also means that there is little in the way of surrounding tree cover). A
lengthy, sinuous, and scenic downhill dumps bicyclists into the developing city of Chino
Hills with its myriad of parks. Once onto Grand Avenue, bikers climb to a second
scenic summit near Summitridge Drive, then essentially coast through Diamond Bar,
Brea Canyon, and the city of Brea. The finale is a nearly flat four miles on State College Boulevard and Lambert Road.

TRAILHEAD: Exit the Orange Freeway eastbound at Lambert Road, drive two miles
and cross Valencia Avenue on what is now Carbon Canyon Road. Continue one mile
further to the Carbon Canyon Regional Park marked entry. There is an entry fee.
   Bring a couple of quarts of water, particularly important for hot days. There are
commercial stops on the rugged Carbon Canyon Road climb, if needed, plus numerous
parks in the Chino Hills area and at the Grand Avenue summit (Summitridge Park). No
on-route public water sources were found for the remaining (mostly downhill or flat)
twelve miles of the trip, although there are commercial stops in Diamond Bar and Brea.

TRIP DESCRIPTION: Before leaving the park, explore the general area by using the
roughly two miles of bikepath/roadway within. Families might consider using the park
itself as a self-contained bike tour. There are also scenic hiking and equestrian trails in
the area, with the most lengthy trail exploring the redwood tree stand at the southwest-
ern park edge. The park has numerous water and restroom facilities, tree shade, playgrounds, sports grounds, tennis courts, and picnic facilities.
   Carbon Canyon Park to Olinda Village. Leave the park and turn right, immediately beginning a workout upgrade on a two-lane road with a modest biking shoulder. Pass through a pleasant forested area in this early segment, cycle by a large citrus
grove and enter an area where the grade steepens (0.6). In 0.2 mile is an impressive canyon view looking north. The winding uphill road goes past a horse grazing area and
reaches a flat at 1.4 tough miles from the trip start. The vegetation transitions from lightly forested to more of a high desert appearance as the road climbs and heads further
back into the canyon. Just beyond is Olinda Village with a restaurant and small market.
   Olinda Village to Sleepy Hollow. Follow the steep downgrade which levels and passes La Vida Mineral Springs (with resort). Pedal another winding upgrade

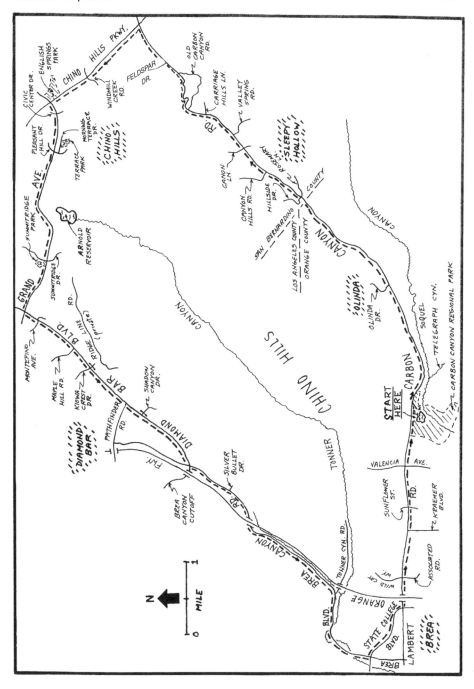

TRIP #23 - CHINO HILLS LOOP

through this short treed segment before reaching another flat (3.0). Proceed up again, cross the San Bernardino County Line, and soon reach the community of Sleepy Hollow.

At Hillside Drive is the "Party House," featuring liquid refreshments and a shaded terrace, as well as a grocery store (3.7).

Sleepy Hollow to the Carbon Canyon Road Summit. Continue on another difficult uphill on a 0.4-mile pull with scattered tree cover. (We didn't say that this was a picnic route!) Not far beyond the flat is Canyon Hills Road and Canyon Hills Stables (4.3). Bike alongside the Western Hills Golf Course, pass Valley Spring Road (5.0) and sweat out the quarter-mile-steep upgrade to a plateau. Pedal another 0.4 mile on the plateau, pass Carriage Hills Lane and reach a crest at (5.6).

Summit to Summit. Carbon Canyon Road presents a dynamite S-curve almost immediately. The canyon vista below is gorgeous, as is the distant look at the eastern edge of the San Gabriel Mountains, provided you stop and take a look! Just beyond Old Carbon Canyon Road, the shoulder opens to a marked Class II bikeway (6.2). The curves moderate and the grade lessens as cyclists pass Feldspar Drive (6.4) and coast another mile into residential environs and meet Chino Hills Parkway. Cucamonga Peak sits above the nearby homes to the distant north.

Turn left (northwest) onto the wide four-lane and pass a series of parks, each of which has water and restrooms but very limited or no shade. Pass a shopping center just beyond Eucalyptus Avenue (7.7), continue coasting to Windmill Creek Road and climb mildly another 0.3 mile to a steeper uphill near Grand Avenue (8.9).

A left here leads bikers along another wide four-lane road on a 2.4-mile, 300-foot upgrade to a crest at Summitridge Drive. On the climb through the surrounding residential area are Civic Center Drive, Pleasant Hill Drive, and Grand Avenue Park (9.8). Entering a relatively undeveloped area, cyclists are treated to a short downhill in another 0.4 mile, then more heavy-breathing uphill past the Arnold Reservoir (10.7). Longview Drive, just beyond the county border, is the beginning of a marked Class III in Diamond Bar. In 0.3 mile, reach Summitridge Drive and Summitridge Park, which has water, restrooms, shade, an abundance of grass, picnic and sports facilities, and a killer view west into the residence-filled canyon below (11.3).

Downhill into Brea. Life is good! The next eight miles into Brea is predominantly downhill. A steep downgrade leads to Diamond Bar Boulevard and a cluster of shopping centers in 0.9 mile. Turn left (south) and coast on a Class II roadway past shopping centers near Montefino Avenue (12.5) and Shadow Canyon Drive (14.4), taking in the estates on the ridge to the left and above (Ridge Line Road). In another mile, reach Brea Canyon Road and a bevy of gas stations.

Turn left onto a Class X road with a narrowing shoulder and cross Silver Bullet Road (15.9). The next two-plus miles travel through a currently undeveloped section of Los Angeles County. Pass under the Orange Freeway at (16.2) and enter Brea Canyon proper. Just beyond the Orange County reentry (17.4), the road straightens on what is now Brea Boulevard, passes Tonner Canyon Road (18.0), then takes a sweeping turn south. Canyon Country Road appears (19.1) and the road leaves the canyon, reaching State College Boulevard/Central Avenue in the city of Brea in another 0.3 mile.

The Final Lap. The return to dense residential area and the immediate array of shopping centers is a mild shock. Turn left onto State College Boulevard, bike a short uphill on a wide four-lane Class II road and reach Lambert Road in 0.8 mile (20.2). Make the final left turn of the trip (east) onto this wide Class X street and pedal back under the Orange Freeway in 0.2 mile. Pass a large shopping complex on the left and enter an area with a mix of open residential areas and gated communities. The road

Brea Canyon

skinnies down to two lanes and takes some of the bike shoulder with it at (21.6). Pass a limited tree-lined stretch beyond Sunflower Street and reach Valencia Avenue at (22.3). The development thins as trip-hardened cyclists cruise the final mile to the Carbon Canyon Regional Park entry.

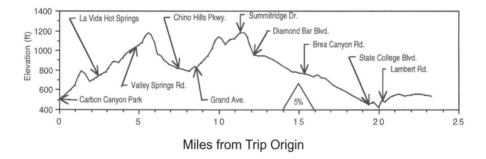

Miles from Trip Origin

CONNECTING TRIPS: 1) Connection with the El Cajon Trail (Trip #22) - return to Valencia Avenue and turn left (south), continue 0.4 mile to Rose Drive, turn left and follow that road 1.5 miles to the trip origin; 2) connection with the Fullerton Tour/ Craig Park (Trip #24) - from the trip origin, bike west on Carbon Canyon Road (Lambert Road beyond Valencia Avenue) about four miles to State College Boulevard, turn south and cycle three quarters of a mile to Imperial Highway.

TRIP #24 - FULLERTON TOUR/CRAIG PARK

GENERAL LOCATION: Fullerton, Placentia, Brea

LEVEL OF DIFFICULTY: Full loop - moderate to strenuous
Distance - 15.4 miles (full loop)
Elevation gain - periodic moderate-to-steep grades

HIGHLIGHTS: This trip tours the hilly rural portions of Fullerton and takes in pleasant Craig Park as well. Craig Park could serve as a family bike outing on its own. This tour has everything from Class I to Class X bike routes, but is mostly on signed motor vehicle roadways (Class III). The general area is scenic and the interspersed hill climbs provide a little extra variety. Well-stocked Ralph B. Clark Regional Park is an added bonus. Finally, a small family tour at Tri-City Park in Placentia is included.

TRAILHEAD: From the Artesia Freeway (Riverside Freeway) take Harbor Boulevard north into Fullerton. Drive about three miles to Valencia Mesa Drive and turn left (west). Find parking near the intersection, but be sure to comply with the local parking regulations.

Bring a moderate water supply. The primary watering holes are in the shopping area near the starting point and at Ralph B. Clark and Craig Regional Parks. The latter two points are strategically located at the westernmost and easternmost ends of the trip, respectively. Although there are numerous parks with excellent grounds and facilities along the way, we found few which had a source of drinking water.

TRIP DESCRIPTION: **Clark Park Loop.** The trip starts southwest on Valencia Mesa Drive, traveling along a tree-lined route onto a moderate upgrade, then crossing over a small bridge near the crest (0.2). The route is Class III. For the next mile, cruise through a peaceful, rural residential neighborhood. The route crosses Euclid Street (0.9) and later follows a steep downhill to Bastanchury Road (1.5). A hard right, 0.2 mile of pedaling, and a left turn on Parks Road lead bikers past Edward White Park (1.8) along an upgrade through a residential area.

The upgrade continues to Rosecrans Avenue (2.4) where the tour heads left (west) and stays on an uphill. In this area, there is little biking room on the Class III roadway; an option is to use the narrow path along the fence that surrounds the neighborhood. The route crests at Gilbert Street (3.2), where there is a pleasant rest spot around the northeast corner at Coyote Hills Park.

Glide downhill 1.2 miles to significantly larger Ralph B. Clark Regional Park. There are restrooms, water, shade, an array of walkway/bikeways, picnic areas, barbecues, a small lake, recreation fields, and playgrounds. The park could serve as a nice base of operations for a family bike ride. On departing the park, note the interesting formations of the East Coyote Hills to the north.

Return east on Rosecrans Avenue 0.5 mile to Sunny Ridge Drive (4.7) and turn right (south). Follow a pleasant Class III path downhill through a residential neighborhood to Pioneer Avenue and turn right (6.2). Bike a short distance and follow the road

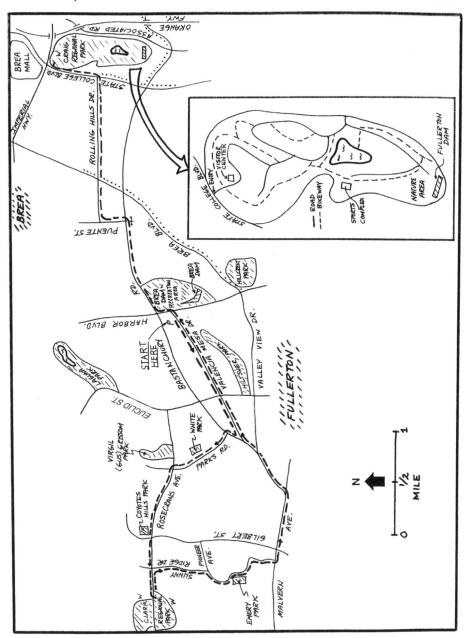

TRIP #24 - FULLERTON TOUR/CRAIG PARK

as it turns left, passes little Emery Park (5.6), and suddenly recaptures its old name, Sunny Ridge Drive. The route winds downhill from this point to meet with Malvern Boulevard (6.0). Turn left (east) and go 0.8 mile on a Class III roadway to Bastanchury Road, then turn left again. Cruise 0.5 mile to Valencia Mesa Drive (7.3), then head up the steep grade and return to the starting point (8.8). This loop, by itself, is a moderate trip on a 100 percent Class III route.

On To Craig Park. One option is to pack up the bikes and drive to Craig Park. The other is to turn left (north) on Harbor Boulevard, proceed 0.2 mile and turn right on Bastanchury Road (9.0). Now comes a Class X route (with wide shoulder) through some moderate-to-steep hills past the Fullerton Municipal Golf Course and an area with a view into the backside of Brea Dam. The dam drainage is virtually dry and is now Brea Dam Recreation Area.

Bike along the reservoir drainage area and, in 0.6 mile from Harbor Boulevard, turn left on Puente Street and ride 0.2 mile to Rolling Hills Drive (10.1). Turn right and pump uphill on a Class II roadway through a residential area. At Woodline Avenue (10.4), the route heads downhill then back uphill to a crest 0.5 mile from that intersection. Shortly, Rolling Hills Drive ends at State College Boulevard (11.5). Head left and downhill and turn right at Rosalia Drive to enter Craig Park (12.1). The return trip to the car from this point is 3.3 miles, making the "full loop" a 15.4-mile ride.

Craig Park Tour. There are numerous ways to tour Craig Park. There are over two miles of Class I bike trails which make this an attractive family option. When the bike trails are hooked up with the slow-moving, lightly traveled roads within the park, the number of potential bike routes is multiplied several times. The park also has picnic areas, shaded pavilions, hiking and equestrian trails, a natural amphitheater, lakes, and turfed play areas. This park rivals some of the other larger parks visited in our travels, such as Mile Square Park (Trip #5), Irvine Regional Park (Trip #26), and El Dorado Regional Park (Los Angeles County).

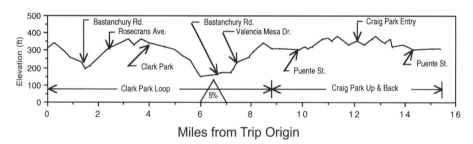

Miles from Trip Origin

Excursion: Tri-City Park. So called because it is near the borders of Fullerton, Placentia, and Brea, this excellent park is off the basic Fullerton/Craig Park tour, but is close by and has some great family biking possibilities. It is about 1.5 miles east of Craig Park on Kraemer Boulevard, with an entry from Golden Avenue. The park's dimensions are one-fourth mile by one-fourth mile. The main walkway/bikeway circuits the large central lake and is connected to other spurs. In addition, the park has water, a restroom, trees, shaded picnic/barbecue areas, and a children's playground.

CONNECTING TRIPS: 1) Connection with the El Cajon Trail (Trip #22) - from Craig Park, bike south 0.9 mile to Bastanchury Road, turn left (east) and continue 2.7 miles on mild Class X and Class II bikeways to the Anaheim Union Canal (about half a mile east of Valencia Avenue; 2) connection with the Chino Hills Loop (Trip # 23) - at Imperial Highway, bike north on State College Boulevard for one mile, turn east at Lambert Road and cycle three miles to Carbon Canyon Regional Park; 3) connection with the Western Orange County Loop (Trip #33) - at Bastanchury Road and Malvern Avenue, continue east on the latter road.

TRIP #25 - SANTA ANA CANYON ROAD

<u>GENERAL LOCATION</u>: Santa Ana Canyon, Anaheim Hills

<u>LEVEL OF DIFFICULTY</u>:   One way - easy; up and back - moderate
Distance - 7.6 miles (one way)
Elevation gain - periodic moderate grades

<u>HIGHLIGHTS</u>: This is a fine workout trip on a Class II bikeway that traverses one seg-
ment of Santa Ana Canyon. It starts near Eisenhower Park in Orange and ends at the entry
to Featherly Regional Park in eastern Yorba Linda. On clear days there are excellent views
north into the Chino Hills and east further into the canyon. The route traverses the base
of the Anaheim Hills and parallels the Santa Ana River for most of the trip. The greater
portion of the trip is unshaded and can be rather hot in the summer, particularly on the
eastern segment. A particular joy of this ride is the limited number of stoplights.

<u>TRAILHEAD</u>: From the Costa Mesa Freeway southbound, use the Lincoln Avenue/
Nohl Ranch Road exit which lets out at Tustin Boulevard across from Eisenhower
Park/The Brickyard. Go south, cross Lincoln Avenue and turn right into the Park and
Ride area just beyond. Northbound traffic should use the same exit, which puts traffic
onto Santiago Boulevard. Go north a few hundred feet and turn left onto Lincoln Ave-
nue, then left again onto Tustin Avenue and enter the Park and Ride area.

An option is to start the ride from Eisenhower Park. There is parking to the west
(Lincoln Avenue to Ocean View Avenue and right on Main Street) and north (Lincoln
Avenue to Ocean View Avenue and right on Bixby Avenue). This is a pleasant, shaded
little park with a small lake, picnic benches, play areas, a mini-barnyard, and a bikepath to boot! The park sits right next to The Brickyard, a shopping plaza. There is an
excellent restaurant in the plaza with a verandah area that looks out over the lake; it's a
great place to end the trip.

Bikers should come prepared with a moderate water supply. Though several public
water sources are easily accessible on the west side, the single public source east of Quintana Road (the Eucalyptus Park entry) is at Featherly Regional Park at the trip terminus.

<u>TRIP DESCRIPTION</u>: **Trailhead to Peralta Canyon Park.** Exit the Park and
Ride area and head north a short distance to Lincoln Avenue. Turn right (east) and bike
under the Costa Mesa Freeway. Turn left on Santa Ana Canyon Road (0.2). Note that
both streets change names at the intersection: Lincoln Avenue/Nohl Ranch Road and
Santiago Boulevard/Santa Ana Canyon Road. The route starts with the hills to the right
and the freeway to the left and passes through a eucalyptus-lined flat stretch.

At Lakeview Avenue, the path pulls away from the Riverside Freeway and starts a
moderate upgrade (2.2). In 0.2 mile is the crest with a nice view into the Santa Ana
River Canyon. Bicycling through small rolling hills, pass Pinney Drive (south)/Royal
Oak Road (north) (1.9). A short 0.1-mile detour on Pinney Drive leads to Peralta Canyon Park, a sports and recreation paradise. The park has restrooms, large grassy grounds,
tree cover, both covered and open picnic tables with barbecues, sports fields, and a large
children's playground.

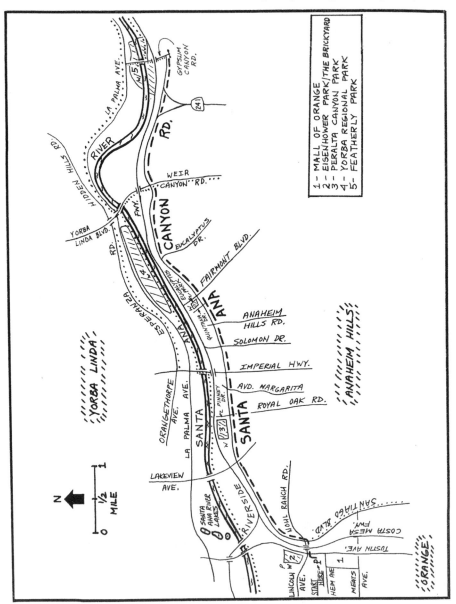

TRIP #25 - SANTA ANA CANYON ROAD

Anaheim Hills Proper. At Avenida Margarita, there are shopping centers along both sides of the roadway (2.4). There are also nice views into the Peralta Hills (south) and across the canyon into the Chino Hills. The tour passes another tree-lined section of town with more shopping centers at Imperial Highway (2.6). Beyond this intersection, ten years ago, the surroundings became significantly more rural, but not so now.

Bike on a flat Class II bikeway past Anaheim Hills Road (3.2), Quintana Road (entry to Eucalyptus park, with a restroom, water fountain, light tree cover, full picnic facilities, a children's play area, and a baseball diamond) (3.5), and a small shopping center to the left (3.6), and reach Fairmont Boulevard in another 0.1 mile. There are more excellent views across the canyon near this junction. The bikepath heads uphill in another 0.4 mile and crests in a short distance (4.3). The route returns near the freeway at this location and has a nice view further eastward into the canyon.

The Less-Developed Spaces. The remainder of the trip is more exposed and certainly has some isolated stretches. The bikeway heads up a 0.2-mile steep upgrade and crests near an area with some large open fields (4.7). Pass the Anaheim Hills Festival (shopping center) and newer housing developments near Roosevelt Road (5.5) and Weir Canyon Road (5.7), and in 0.2 mile reach an area with an excellent view further into the Santa Ana Canyon. Soon the route narrows to one lane and passes under a hillside housing development (6.1), then enters dry dusty brushland and goes under the spans of the Eastern Transportation Corridor (State Highway 241) starting at (7.0). In another 0.6 mile is the road terminus at Gypsum Canyon Road. (To the left is Featherly Regional Park while to the right is a private mining operation.)

CONNECTING TRIPS: 1) Continuation with the Santa Ana River Trail (Trip #17A) - at the terminus, continue west on Gypsum Canyon Road toward Featherly Regional Park, then turn right onto the Class I trail just before entering the park (also see Trip #17A for a loop connection with the Class I trail on the north bank of the Santa Ana River); 2) connection with the Orange/Irvine Regional Park Loop (Trip #26) - near the trip origin, turn south on Santiago Boulevard from Lincoln Avenue and bike two miles on a Class II bikeway to Villa Park Road; 3) connection with the Yorba Linda Bits and Pieces tour (Trip #43) - at Weir Canyon Road (becomes Yorba Linda Boulevard) or Gypsum Canyon Road, bicycle north across the Santa Ana River to La Palma Avenue; 4) connection with the Anaheim Hills tour (Trip # 44) - at Nohl Ranch Road and Santiago Boulevard, go east on the former street.

TRIP #26 - ORANGE/IRVINE PARK LOOP

GENERAL LOCATION: Orange

LEVEL OF DIFFICULTY: City of Orange Loop - moderate
                                  Distance - 10.2 miles
                                  Elevation gain - periodic moderate-to-steep grades

HIGHLIGHTS: A predominantly Class II loop through a rural section of Orange County, this route works its way through some pleasant, lightly trafficked residential areas after leaving Irvine Regional Park. There is a short challenging grade on Chapman Avenue and a longer workout on Santiago Canyon Road, while the remainder of the tour is downhill or on light grades. There are several spurs off the primary route, with Orange Park Boulevard being the most rural and scenic, and Cannon Street being the most challenging. The park section is primarily Class I and could serve as a family trip in itself.

The park has several miles of paved and dirt bikeway, as well as bike rentals, picnic areas, pony rides, a small zoo, mini-train rides, a lovely lagoon, and other attractions.

TRAILHEAD: From the Orange Freeway or Costa Mesa Freeway, take the Chapman Avenue turnoff east. The distances to the Jamboree Road intersection are 4.5 miles and 7.5 miles, respectively. Turn left (north), get into the right-hand lane and go one-third mile to the signed Irvine Regional Park entrance at Irvine Park Road. From the Eastern Transportation Corridor, exit at Chapman Avenue/Santiago Canyon Road and drive west one mile to Jamboree Road. Turn right and go one-third mile to the park entrance.

Pay the entry fee and enjoy the park after the ride. (See the detailed map provided for park facilities.) An alternative is to start at Santiago Hills Park off of Trail's End Lane. The park has water, restrooms, walkway/bikeways, scattered tree cover, sheltered picnic/barbecue facilities, and a children's playground.

Bring a filled water bottle. This is a relatively exposed trip and there are no on-route public water stops after leaving the park. There is a concession stand at the park which might be a nice place to visit at the end of the ride.

TRIP DESCRIPTION: City of Orange Loop. Leave the park and return to Class II Jamboree Road, turning left. (Note there is also a paralleling Class I bikepath.) Bike to Class II Chapman Avenue and turn right (west), passing a shopping complex across the street. Observe the stately homes built high on the hillsides to the left while coasting to Newport Boulevard and another shopping center. Parallel a horse trail on the right which passes into an oak-shaded area next to a residential community, then pump a gritty climb for 0.8 mile to a crest near Cliffway Drive (1.8). Just before the crest is Orange Hill Terrace and a sheer trip up to the Orange Hill Restaurant with a spectacular view of the local Orange Country area.

There is an outstanding view into the canyon and back into the residential areas at this point. Cruise downhill past Cannon Street/Crawford Canyon Road, where the Class II section ends (2.6). Then coast on a moderating grade another 0.6 mile to Hewes Street. Pedal on this quiet residential Class X street to another at Spring Street and turn left (west). Cycle another half mile to Prospect Street, turning right onto a Class II route, as it will remain for most of the trip's remainder. Bicycle on this curving roadway, taking a short Class I diversion alongside the Santiago Creek flood control basin. Across the street is an entry to the Class I bike trail along the creek. (See the **Santiago Creek Spur Trip** described below.)

A right on Class I Wanda Road (5.0) is followed by another right in half a mile onto Class II Villa Park Road (Katella Avenue to the west). Bike through a tree-lined residential section to Lemon Street where hillside views open directly ahead. Climb modestly and cross Santiago Creek, then pass Cannon Street (7.1), where the road name is now Santiago Canyon Road. In another challenging uphill 0.7 mile is Orange Park Boulevard; Windes Drive, the entry to Santiago Oaks Park, follows shortly.

Continue climbing past Angel View Terrace and reach the northern edge of the well-manicured lawns that are a part of the Holy Sepulcher Cemetery. Reach a crest near Amapola Avenue (9.2) and enjoy the striking hillside views to the left. Coast past Newport Boulevard and reach Jamboree Road in half a mile. Turn left, then return to Irvine Park and look forward to your post-ride picnic (10.2).

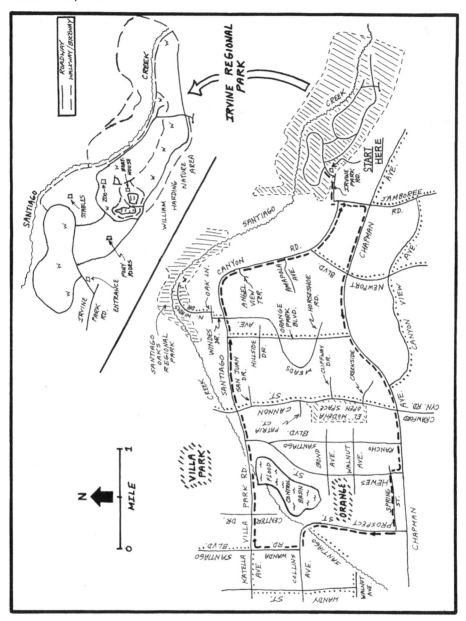

TRIP #26 - ORANGE/IRVINE PARK LOOP

Irvine Park. There is a multitude of ways to tour this park, which rivals Mile Square Park (Trip #5) and El Dorado Park (Los Angeles County) and which is certainly more in its natural state. Our tour started with a 1.9-mile ride around the bikepaths at the park boundaries and included a 2.0-mile interior tour.

The outside tour includes the route across (north of) Santiago Creek, a swing-by of open expanses of the easternmost picnic and kite flying areas, and a pass-by of the

Ocean Park Boulevard

William Harding Nature Area. The interior tour includes the Santiago Creek parallel path, the middle park path through the playgrounds and group picnic areas, and a pedal around the lagoon and zoo areas. In addition there is an equal amount of roads through the area that are lightly traveled and serve as excellent bikepath options for all but the most inexperienced bikers. In itself the Irvine Park tour could serve as part of an all-day family picnic and biking outing.

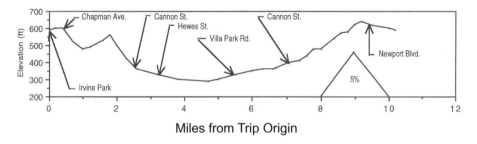

Miles from Trip Origin

Excursions: **Orange Park Boulevard and Cannon Street Options.** The tour of Orange can be extended by connecting the reference tour with either or both of these roadways. Class II Orange Park Boulevard meanders through a rural residential area for 1.3 miles between Santiago Road and Chapman Avenue. This moderate segment has horse trails, scattered tall trees, and upscale homes. Cannon Street is a 1.6-mile, mostly Class II roadway with a Class I segment along the El Modena Open Space. There is a very steep (0.7-mile, 300-foot) climb from the south and a steep (0.9-mile, 240-foot) pump from the north; these bump the overall ride to the moderate-to-strenuous category. The crest is near Cliffway Drive.

Canyon View Avenue. From Chapman Avenue, turn south on this lightly developed residential street and pedal a Class II roadway on a 0.1-mile flat before taking a gritty 0.8-mile climb to a crest near Outrider Street. There are neck-bending views of the ridgetop homes to the left and some great vistas into distant Santiago Canyon beyond the crest. Coast past Newport Boulevard and reach Jamboree Road in two miles from Chapman Avenue. Another 0.6 mile north on Jamboree Road returns bikers to Chapman Avenue.

Santiago Creek Trail. From Prospect Street, this south side Class I path was open for about 0.6 mile, ending at a turnaround. This might eventually become part of a trail which extends from Irvine Lake to near the Santa Ana Freeway, provided rights-of-way and other issues can be resolved.

Santiago Oaks Park. At Meads Avenue/Windes Drive, turn north and take a right at Oak Lane to remain on rural two-lane Windes Drive. Ride to Lewis Drive and turn right. In a short distance is the ranger station and the Santiago Oaks Park entry kiosk. The oak-studded park has interesting flora, water, both hiking and horse trails, and limited on-road biking areas. The distance from Santiago Canyon Road to the park entry is about half a mile.

CONNECTING TRIPS: 1) Connection with the Santiago Canyon Road route (Trip #27) - the two tours share a common segment on Jamboree Road just outside the Irvine Park entrance; 2) connection with the Anaheim Hills tour (Trip #44) - at Katella Avenue and Santiago Boulevard, go north on the latter street.

TRIP #27 - SANTIAGO CANYON ROAD

GENERAL LOCATION: Santiago Canyon

LEVEL OF DIFFICULTY: One way - strenuous; up and back - strenuous
Distance - 12.6 miles (one way)
Elevation gain - continuous moderate-to-steep
grade to the summit

HIGHLIGHTS: This is an excellent workout trip through a scenic, but highly sun-exposed canyon. It is one of the most popular for serious bikers training against the clock. The tour is 12.6 Class III miles (rides like a Class II) in rolling hills with a near-continuous moderate-to-steep six-mile grade to the summit. On a hot day, this is a strenuous one-way trip. The route has several scenic points, passes near Irvine Lake, and ends near Cook's Corner at a rustic restaurant/bar. Just beyond this terminus is stately Saint Michael's Abbey. This trip also links up with three alternate canyon routes for the more adventurous: Silverado Canyon Road, Modjeska Canyon Road, and Live Oak Canyon Road, all described as separate tours.

TRAILHEAD: From the Orange Freeway or Costa Mesa Freeway, take the Chapman Avenue turnoff east. The distances to the Jamboree Road intersection are 4.5 miles and

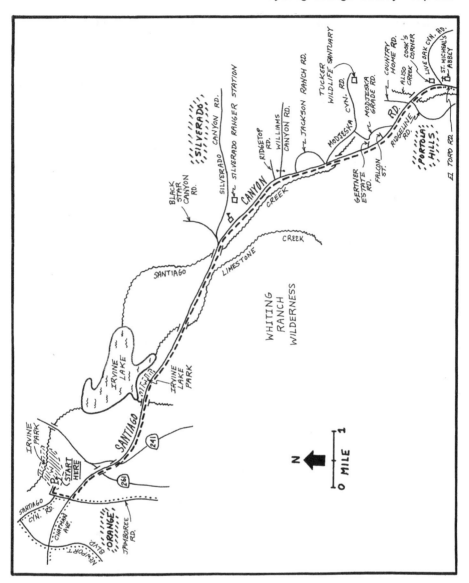

TRIP #27 - SANTIAGO CANYON ROAD

7.5 miles, respectively. Turn left (north), get into the right-hand lane and go one-third mile to the Irvine Regional Park entrance. From the Eastern Transportation Corridor, exit at Chapman Avenue/Santiago Canyon Road and drive west one mile to Jamboree Road. Turn right and motor one-third mile to the park entrance.

Pay the entry fee and enjoy the park after the ride. (See Trip #26 for detailed park information.) A nonpaying alternative is to start at the shopping center at the southwest corner of the Chapman Avenue/Jamboree Road intersection.

Bring a conservative supply of water (two filled water bottles) and munchies. There is water at Irvine Lake Park, although this is a diversion off the main course. The next convenient stop is at Cook's Corner at the trip's end or turnaround point.

TRIP DESCRIPTION: Trailhead to Irvine Lake Park. Leave the park and take Jamboree Road to Chapman Avenue. Turn left onto a four-lane Class III roadway (with spaced signs asking truck drivers to stay out of the bike lane) and cycle into an open, flat area. Begin a steady moderate climb, then pass over the Eastern Transportation Corridor (State Highway 241) at (1.3). Parallel the corridor, then climb to a local summit and observe the toll road's bend to the south.

Coast on a long downgrade which flattens near a viewpoint above the Irvine Lake area. The roadway proceeds modestly uphill again for about 0.4 mile, leveling out just before the Irvine Lake turnoff (3.7). There are rental boats, swimming, shady picnic areas, athletic fields, and water at Irvine Lake Park. Better yet, there is a little restaurant/bar here. If you have doubts by now, this might be a fine spot to rest and ponder turning back.

Irvine Lake Park to Silverado Canyon Road. Beyond the turnoff, cycle a moderate uphill and reach the top of the grade where there is a lightly treed area and the wide Limestone Canyon creekbed to the right. Bike through lightly rolling (mostly uphill) terrain along the creek in an area with a superb view of Mount Saddleback (5.5). This is the first half mile of a sweaty six-mile climb. In another half mile is the first view into the Santiago Creek watershed and a bridge crossing not far beyond (6.6). In a tenth of a mile is the Silverado Canyon turnoff. The Silverado Forest Station is about three quarters of a mile further up that road.

East Santiago Canyon Road

Silverado Canyon Road to Cook's Corner. Stay near Santiago Creek and pass a small school (7.0). Pump another mile-plus upgrade and reach a local crest at Ridgetop Road. Soon after, pedal the moderated uphill under some high-tension lines (8.3), then pass William's Canyon Road (8.7) and Jackson Ranch Road North (8.9) in a scattered residential area. Cross Modjeska Canyon Road (9.6), make the last crossing over Santiago Creek and pump a very steep grade which lets up near Gertner Estate Road (10.6). (The residents in the homes on the ridge overlooking the climb probably have a field day watching cyclists climbing this segment.)

Now all the hard uphill work pays off! First is a scenic turnout with a view of the surrounding canyonland and a "peek" southward into Portola Hills and Mission Viejo. Next is a long downhill, an Aliso Creek crossing, Ridgeline Road (12.0), and the route terminus at the Live Oak Canyon Road junction at Cook's Corner (12.6). Stop and take a well-deserved break at the rustic restaurant/bar located there.

Excursion: Saint Michael's Abbey. A neat side trip is to examine the grounds of Saint Michael's Abbey, reached by turning east a few hundred feet down the main highway (now named El Toro Road) from Cook's Corner. The interesting atmosphere includes little rolling hills, abundant overhanging tree cover, the interesting abbey, and other buildings on the grounds.

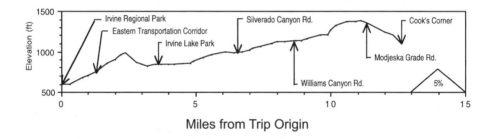

Miles from Trip Origin

CONNECTING TRIPS: 1) Continuation with the Aliso Creek Trail (Trip #29A) - continue south on El Toro Road beyond the trip terminus; 2) connection with the Orange/Irvine Park Loop (Trip #26) - the two tours share a common segment on Jamboree Road just outside the park entrance; 3) connection with the Cities and Canyons tour (Trip # 47) - the trips share a common segment on El Toro Road below Cook's Corner; 4) connection with the Silverado Canyon ride (Trip #48) - at the 7.6-mile point, turn north onto Silverado Canyon Road; 5) connection with the Modjeska Canyon ride (Trip #49) - at either Modjeska Canyon Road or Modjeska Grade Road, turn east.

TRIP #28 - O'NEILL REGIONAL PARK

GENERAL LOCATION: Trabuco Canyon, Rancho Santa Margarita

LEVEL OF DIFFICULTY: Up and back - easy
Distance - 7.4 miles
Elevation gain - moderate grades in Mesa
day-use area

HIGHLIGHTS: The focus of this trip is O'Neill Regional Park with over four miles of bikeway on roads within an oak forest. The trip is a winner for families, as it is contained within an enticing natural environment well removed from high-traffic streets. The park roadway/bikeway visits the central picnic area and nature center, crosses Trabuco Creek, cruises the elevated Mesa day-use area, visits the equestrian camping area, then ends with a countryside ride north, paralleling Live Oak Canyon Road.

TRAILHEAD: From the intersection of El Toro Road and Santiago Canyon Road at Cook's Corner, turn east onto Live Oak Canyon Road and drive about three scenic and hilly miles to the park. From Rancho Santa Margarita, follow Plano Trabuco north to where it turns sharply west and becomes Trabuco Road. In about 1.6 mile, on a road now named Trabuco Canyon Road, is the park entrance.

Only a light water supply is needed. There are scattered sources within the park.

Family Outing near Oak Grove

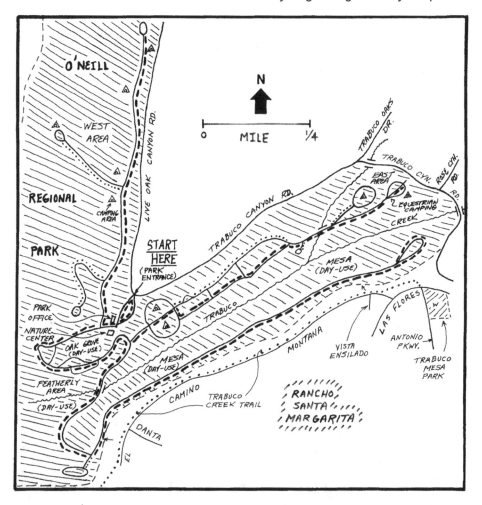

TRIP #28 - O'NEILL REGIONAL PARK

TRIP DESCRIPTION: Minors must accompany adults, and a minimum traveling party of two is required, as there are limited inherent dangers such as mountain lions, rattlesnakes, poison oak, and rugged terrain in the park. This is particularly applicable for off-road hiking and biking.

From the park entry area, first cruise the (Oak Grove) day-use picnic area. Pass the gate to the north camping area near the park entrance and the nature center (spring and summer interpretive programs) near the end of the picnic area. There are picnic facilities, turf play area, a softball diamond, playground, water, and restrooms in this part of the park.

Leave the picnic area (0.5) and follow the curving road to the right. Cross Trabuco Creek, bike to the intersection with the parking loop (0.9) and follow hard left, pedaling on a short, steep upgrade. Note that there is a hiking trail below which parallels Trabuco Creek. Pedal a more modest incline along the southern park boundary on the

Plano Trabuco and pass the Mesa day-use area. This is prime territory for nature view-
ers. At the end of the line is a parking/turnaround loop (2.0).

Return across Trabuco Creek to the park office area (4.0) and bear to the right,
following the flat roadway past the group camping area and turning right again just
beyond. Stay to the right (south) at each junction until reaching a single roadway which
veers right (4.55). Cross a feeder creek in a tenth of a mile, then bear right at the next
major junction to reach the Equestrian Camping area (4.9). (We expected to see horses
bedded down in sleeping bags!)

Retrace the route back to the park office area (5.8) and turn north just beyond. Pass
through the gate and follow that tree-covered road as it passes alongside (but remains
fenced from) Live Oak Canyon Road. Note the abundance of hiking and off-road biking trails to the left all along this section. There are two westside spurs off the main
route for those who want to explore every "nook and cranny" of this beautiful park,
with a group camping cluster near the second. Near road's end is a series of group
campsites and a turnaround area at the terminus (6.6). Now, simply return to the park
entrance (7.4)!

Excursion: Rancho Santa Margarita. From the Mesa area, there are exits from
the park onto Class I Camino Montana. This Trabuco Creek Trail goes three quarters of
a mile from the Danta exit to Antonio Parkway's end.

CONNECTING TRIPS: 1) Connection with the Aliso Creek Trail (Ride #29A) - ride
west three miles on Live Oak Canyon Road to El Toro Road; 2) connection with the
Cities and Canyons ride (Trip #47) - exit the park and turn in either direction.

TRIPS #29A & #29B - ALISO CREEK TRAIL

The moderate-level Aliso Creek Trail from Cook's Corner to the terminus in Laguna
Niguel (a round trip of 31.8 miles) is broken up into two sections. The general area map
for the entire trip is provided on the following page. The ride is entirely Class I.

The upper segment (Trip #29A) leaves from the foothills above El Toro, winds its
way downhill and southward along Aliso Creek and ends at El Toro Park. The lower
segment (Trip #29B) leaves the park and continues the creekside cruise, except for a
short Class I on-road stint in the Laguna Woods area.

The subsequent creek revisit ends near the Orange County Natural History Museum; it is followed by a tour of Laguna Niguel Park/Sulphur Creek Reservoir and ends
at Crown Valley Community Park.

There are sections of the trail near El Toro Park and further downstream of Laguna
Hills Drive where the trail may be flooded during winter storms. Plan ahead for route
alternates if trips are scheduled under adverse weather conditions.

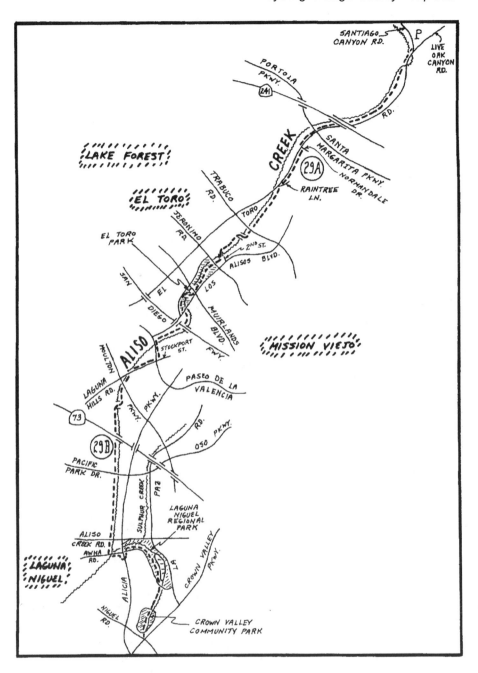

TRIPS #28A & #28B - ALISO CREEK TRAIL

TRIP #29A - ALISO CREEK TRAIL (Northern Segment)

GENERAL LOCATION: El Toro, Lake Forest

LEVEL OF DIFFICULTY: One way - easy; up and back - easy to moderate
Distance - 7.7 miles (one way)
Elevation gain - periodic moderate grades

HIGHLIGHTS: The upper segment starts in the foothills above El Toro, winds its way downhill and southward along Aliso Creek and terminates at El Toro I Park. One of the most pleasant rides in Orange County, this route explores significant stretches of relatively unspoiled bottomland in the middle of high-density residential areas. The upper portion of the trip segment takes cyclists through lightly developed high-desert terrain, while the lower portion winds through the developed cities of El Toro and Lake Forest below, all on Class I bikeway. Inviting, shaded El Toro Park at segment's end is a delightful end point or a fine rest stop for bikers continuing on to the southern trip segment. Portions of this route may be flooded during storms.

TRAILHEAD: From the San Diego Freeway, exit north at El Toro Road and continue about eight miles north to the road junction at Oak Canyon Road. Park in the lot at the junction at Cook's Corner. From the Foothill Transportation Corridor (State Highway 241), exit south at Portola Parkway and go half a mile to El Toro Road. Turn left (east) and drive 2.75 miles to Cook's Corner. From the Costa Mesa Freeway, exit east at Katella Avenue/Villa Park Road. Follow that roadway, which becomes Santiago Canyon Road, roughly eight miles to Cook's Corner. This option is presented since the route is scenic.
Bring a filled water bottle. There are few reliable and available water stops directly along the path. The single public water stops that we found are at the baseball diamonds in El Toro II Park and at the tennis courts at the southern end of El Toro I Park.

TRIP DESCRIPTION: **Cactus Country to Raintree Lane.** From Cook's Corner, pedal south just past Ridgeline Road (about a quarter of a mile) on El Toro Road and follow a signed small asphalt path leading diagonally away from the main roadway (on the right-hand or west side). (Note that there is also an entry on the east side of the road, just south of Saint Michael's Abbey.) Observe the Portola Hills ridgeline homes high up to the right while transiting lightly developed Whiting Ranch Wilderness Park.
Pass the McFadden Ranch House and Interpretive Center and observe the jumble of natural foliage near the trail. Pass the first exit and go under Glenn Ranch Road (1.1), staying parallel to and below El Toro Road while continuing through high-desert terrain. The path swings toward the west and steepens, passing an area with an abundance of cactus (1.5). Contrast this with the developments on the ridges to the left (east) and the huge monolith that is the Foothill Transportation Corridor in another 0.3 mile.
Just south of the Marguerite Parkway (2.0) undercrossing is an alternate entry to the trail. In a short distance, pass alongside an extended eucalyptus grove that is next to

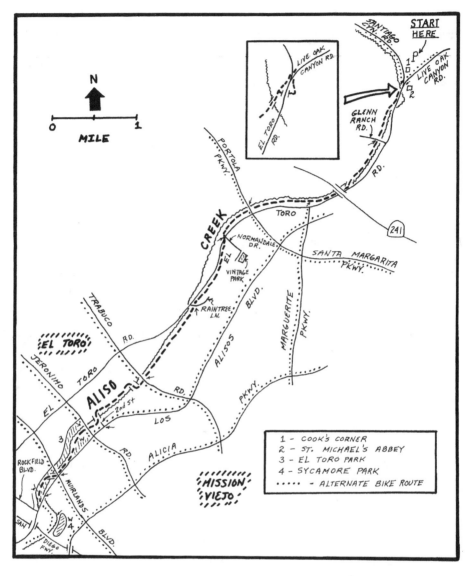

TRIP #29A - ALISO CREEK TRAIL (Northern Segment)

El Toro Road. Cross additional bike entries and exit the eucalyptus-lined portion of the route, remaining next to El Toro Road. Next is the Santa Margarita exit followed by an undercrossing which dips to near creek level (it floods during rainy periods). The trail leaves the eucalyptus stand and meets the Normandale Drive undercrossing at (3.3). Exit the creekside trail at the traffic signal, cross over to the east side of El Toro Road and bike on the sidewalk/bikeway. (The Class I path does continue on the west side, but there are no convenient street crossings prior to Raintree Lane.)

Raintree Lane to El Toro Park. Bike 0.9 mile further through this higher-density residential area to Raintree Lane (4.2). At the southeast corner of that intersection, follow the Class I path beyond the trail sign. Just beyond Raintree Lane, Aliso Creek shifts to the southeast side of El Toro Road. The bikepath transits a pleasant, treed, rural setting alongside the creek through a residential community for the next two miles.

In one-half mile the bikeway follows a moderate downhill past Creekside, then spends the next 0.7 mile alongside a mini-forest. The trail goes under Trabuco Road (5.9), crosses the creek to the west side on a wooden bridge for walking/biking and soon follows between the creek and Cherry Avenue alongside stands of fragrant eucalyptus and other trees. Near the end of 2nd Street, the path recrosses the creek to the west side on another bikeway/walkway (6.6). In this section the creekbed is concrete and there are residences on both sides.

The path returns to near creek level (this may flood during storms as may the undercrossings at Muirlands Boulevard and Los Aliso Boulevard) and crosses under Jeronimo Road. It comes up on the opposite side at El Toro II Park with its baseball diamonds and water fountain. (Just up the park pathway to Jeronimo Road is a restroom.) Follow the signed route on the periphery of the baseball diamonds and make a wide arc to the left, passing under a railroad trestle (7.0). Another sharper sweep to the left takes cyclists along the edge of the Lake Forest Golf and Practice Center.

Next the trail takes a wide turn to the right (southwest), climbing to and paralleling Los Alisos Boulevard at road level (7.4), then ducks back down near creek level below Muirlands Boulevard. It comes up on the opposite side into the most scenic part of the park (7.6), named El Toro I Park. It has abundant tree shade, water near the tennis courts along Larkwood Lane, picnic benches and barbecues, a children's play area, and a maze of crisscrossing bikeway/walkways. The park's southern edge and trip terminus is just north of Rockfield Boulevard where Aliso Creek turns east and crosses below Los Alisos Boulevard (7.7).

CONNECTING TRIPS: 1) Continuation with the lower Aliso Creek segment (Trip #29B) - bike east underneath Los Alisos Boulevard; 2) continuation with the Santiago Canyon Road trip (Trip #27) - ride north from the trip origin on Santiago Canyon Road; 3) connection with the Mission Viejo Bikeway (Trip #30) - at Los Alisos Boulevard and Jeronimo Road, turn north onto Los Alisos Boulevard - there are numerous other connection points (refer to Trip #30 map); 4) connection with the O'Neill Regional Park tour (Trip #28) - at Cook's Corner, turn east on Live Oak Canyon Drive; 5) connection with the Cities and Canyons ride (Trip #47) - the trips have a common segment on El Toro Road south of Cook's Corner; 6) connection with the Arroyo Trabuco Loop (Trip #50) - at El Toro Road and Santa Margarita Parkway, go east on the latter roadway to Alicia Parkway.

TRIP #29B - ALISO CREEK TRAIL (Southern Segment)

GENERAL LOCATION: Lake Forest, Laguna Hills, Laguna Niguel

LEVEL OF DIFFICULTY: Up and back - easy
Distance - 8.2 miles (one way)
Elevation gain - periodic light grades

HIGHLIGHTS: This Class I trip segment is the southern connector for the Aliso Creek Trail. The route starts at El Toro I Park, proceeds 1.5 miles along Aliso Creek, plies the trail along surface streets for one-plus miles, then returns to the creek all the way to the Aliso Creek Trail terminus. Next the tour enters Laguna Niguel Regional Park and follows a scenic and interesting trail from this park to the trip terminus at Crown Valley Community Park. The trip highlight is Laguna Niguel Park with its plentiful facilities, offerings of several interesting family mini-tours, and a lake to explore.

TRAILHEAD: From the San Diego Freeway, exit north on El Toro Road and drive about a quarter of a mile to Rockfield Boulevard. Turn right and go 0.6 mile to Larkwood Lane (the street just before Los Alisos Boulevard). Turn left and find parking next to El Toro I Park. From the San Joaquin Hills Transportation Corridor (State Highway 73), exit north at El Toro Road and head 3.25 miles to the San Diego Freeway undercrossing, then continue as above. From the Foothill Transportation Corridor (State Highway 241), exit south at Portola Parkway/Rancho Santa Margarita Parkway and drive half a mile to El Toro Road. Turn right and go 4.5 miles to Rockfield Boulevard, turn left and motor 0.6 mile to Larkwood Lane, turning left again.

Bring a light water supply. This is a short trip with strategically placed public water sources.

TRIP DESCRIPTION: El Toro I Park to Sheep Hills Park. Follow the bikepath nearest Los Alisos Boulevard and look for an entry trail into the creekbed. (This may be inaccessible in rainy weather.) Dip down into the concrete bottom and cross the creek over a metal plate. Just beyond, pass under Los Alisos Boulevard and turn east. Climb out of the creekbed almost immediately; soon after, the trailway opens up in the vicinity of Sycamore Park across the creek (0.3). This bridge-accessible park has a water fountain, shade trees, walking/biking trails, picnic benches, and barbecues.

In 0.2 mile there is a small concrete crossover trail leading to Sycamore Park, immediately followed by a passage under the San Diego Freeway. (This also may be flooded during or after storms.) There is a trail junction here; turn left. A quarter-mile pedal leads alongside the Alicia Parkway turnoff from the San Diego Freeway to the Laguna Hills Plaza.

Our route heads right and proceeds up a short grade past the commemorative Juan Avila Adobe marker, skirts below the local residences, then heads back down into a more open canyon area. The creek bottom supports natural growth in contrast to some of the concrete stretches to the north. Note the dirt trail across the creek; this is part of the equestrian trailway that will parallel the paved Aliso Creek Trail to its current

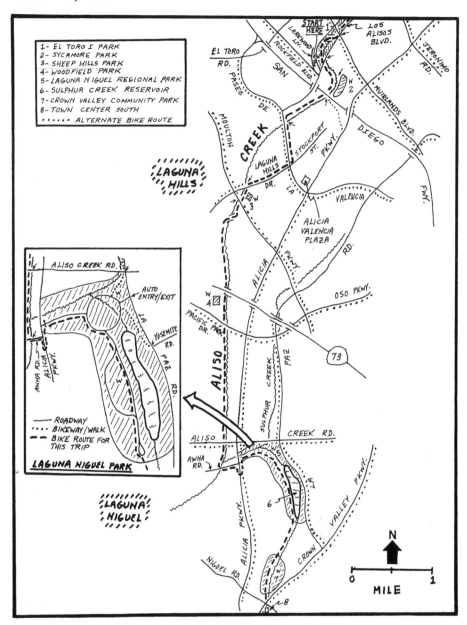

TRIP #29B - ALISO CREEK TRAIL (Southern Segment)

terminus. In 0.3 mile there is a four-way junction. Two legs travel a short distance and die out at local roadways. Take the middle leg which has a trail marker for bikers coming from the opposite direction (0.7). This trail climbs just below the walls of nearby residences and heads south.

Shortly, bikers reach Paseo De Valencia and the bike trail leaves the creek. Turn left (southeast) on Paseo De Valencia (stay on the north side of the street) and follow the signed Class I trail uphill past Kennington Drive (1.1) and Beckenham Street (1.3) to a crest near Stockport Street (1.5). Cross the street at the stoplight and ride on the westside Class I path on what is now Laguna Hills Drive. Coast a steepening downgrade, pass Indian Hills Lane and bottom out at the bridge over Aliso Creek in 0.6 mile.

From the northeast side of the bridge, drop down near creek level on the signed Class I path and turn left, passing under Laguna Hills Drive. Almost immediately, reach Sheep Hills Park which offers scattered tree cover, a water fountain, porta-potty, baseball diamond, soccer field, picnic tables, barbecues, and several interior walkway/ bikeways.

Sheep Hills Park to Laguna Niguel Park. Skirt the park, pass under Moulton Parkway and enter one of several segments of Aliso and Wood Canyons Regional Park. Cross to the creek's west side and begin a broad sweep, skirting some school grounds. Continue along the natural creek bottom, taking time to look into the hillside residences which pepper the route's landscape. Pedal under the San Joaquin Hills Transportation Corridor (3.0), pass cozy Woodfield Park to the right (water fountain, baseball fields) and go under Pacific Park Drive (3.8).

Pass another school, Foxborough Park (many facilities but no water), and the lengthy Aliso Niguel High School campus. To the left is the mammoth, hard-to-miss Hollyfield Federal Building. Pass waterless pocket-sized Hillview Park (4.8), go under Aliso Creek Road in another 0.3 mile and reach a "T"-intersection at Awma Road (5.3). As per the directional signs here, turn left (east), bike to Alicia Parkway and cross the street at the walker/biker stoplight just to the south. Return north a short way and look for a Class I path into Laguna Niguel Park.

Sulphur Creek Reservoir

Laguna Niguel Park. Bike east on park roadway next to Sulphur Creek. Pass covered and open, family and group picnic sites (some of the latter with running water), restrooms, park maintenance facilities, children's play areas, and tennis courts before reaching a road fork (5.8). Turn right and bike the semicircle past a volleyball court, more picnic facilities, and restrooms, to another junction in a quarter of a mile. Turn right again and bike up a short steep roadway which crests near the north end of the Sulphur Creek Reservoir (6.2).

Bring a fishing pole; this reservoir is an inviting spot for a short biking diversion. There are numerous great fishing spots spread along the edge of the reservoir, and numerous waterfowl share the territory. The road passes the Laguna Niguel Lake concession and boat rental (6.7) and runs near the tree-lined southern end of the reservoir in 0.3 mile. That area is reached by crossing a small bridge over the outlet creek.

Laguna Niguel Park to Crown Community Park. The bike route reaches a parking lot cul-de-sac. Just beyond is a small trail heading south that parallels the outlet creek, passes a small water treatment plant (7.3) and enters a wide-open canyon. There are views of hillside residences, and the first glances at Crown Valley Parkway. At (7.9), the trail passes between the Crown Valley Community Park and a gymnasium/pool. A small footbridge leads over to the park, a putting green, and restrooms.

Continue along the path across a road access to the park's parking lot. There are small picnic/barbecue spots here. The bikeway passes through a shaded corridor along the creek and ends soon near Niguel Road and Crown Valley Parkway (8.2).

CONNECTING TRIPS: 1) Continuation with the upper Aliso Creek Trail segment (Trip #29A) - from the trip origin, bike north along Los Alisos Boulevard; 2) connection with the Laguna Niguel Bikeway (Trip #11) - at the trip's end at Niguel Road, proceed in either direction on Crown Valley Parkway; 3) connection with the Mission Viejo Bikeway (Trip #30) - at Paseo De Valencia and Stockport Street, continue southeast on the former roadway - there are numerous other connection points (refer to Trip #30 map); 4) connection with the Aliso Viejo Figure "8" (Trip #46) - at Aliso Creek Road or Pacific Park Drive, exit the creek path.

TRIP #30 - MISSION VIEJO BIKEWAY

GENERAL LOCATION: Mission Viejo, El Toro, Laguna Hills

LEVEL OF DIFFICULTY: Loop - moderate to strenuous Distance - 15.6 miles
Elevation gain - frequent moderate grades;
periodic moderate-to-steep grades

HIGHLIGHTS: A loop trip that tours a part of the Mission Viejo Bikeway System, this route is primarily a mixed Class I/II adventure that hits several of the local highlights. The trip is hilly with moderate mileage and provides a wide variety of natural and manmade scenery.

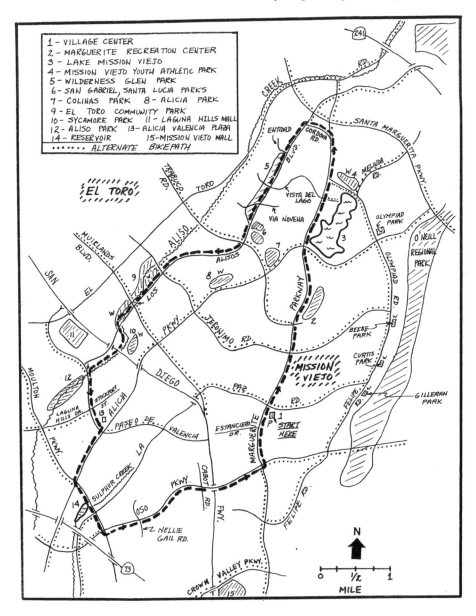

TRIP #30 - MISSION VIEJO BIKEWAY

The tour leaves the Village Center and passes near the Marguerite Recreation Center, Lake Mission Viejo, and Mission Viejo Youth Center, then cruises through Wilderness Glen Park and picks up a segment of the Aliso Creek Trail that goes through El Toro I and II Parks. The northern and middle portions of the route are in established residential environs, while the southernmost portion is in the more recently developed hillside areas.

TRAILHEAD: From the San Diego Freeway, exit east at La Paz Road and continue about 1.25 miles to Marguerite Parkway. Cross that street, turn right and find parking under a tree in the Village Center parking area. From the San Joaquin Hills Transportation Corridor (State Highway 73), exit east on La Paz Road and drive one mile to Marguerite Parkway, then continue as described above. From the Foothill Transportation Corridor (State Highway 241), exit west at Oso Parkway and go 3.25 miles to Marguerite Parkway. Turn right (north) and motor two miles to Village Center. If you prefer to start at a park, the best on-route options are El Toro I and II Parks.

Bring a filled water bottle for hot days and refill at the public water sources at El Toro I Park, El Toro II Park, or Sycamore Park, each located near the trip midpoint. No other on-route public sources were found.

TRIP DESCRIPTION: **Village Center to Marguerite Recreation Center.** Exit the Village Center and bike north on Class II Marguerite Parkway. The surrounding area is residential with some tree cover and a developed hillside above the roadway to the left (west). Much of the northern segment of the trip is on hillside-surrounded roadways. Pass Via Florecer (0.3) and head into a steady, light upgrade past Jeronimo Road (0.7) to a crest near Trabuco Road (1.1). Just across the intersection is a shopping center to the west and the Marguerite Recreation Center to the east. The center has accommodations for a wide variety of sports activities, including an Olympic-size aquatic center.

Lake Mission Viejo. In half a mile the path is alongside the Casta Del Sol Golf Course. There is a view of the hills to the west from this point into what we labeled "Condo Canyon" (1.6). The bike route begins another steady upgrade and reaches Alicia Parkway in 0.6 mile and the crest 0.1 mile further. There is a magnificent view into the local mountains from this area. Bike to Vista Del Lago, turn right (east) and ride 0.2 mile past the Market On The Lake shopping center to a great overlook of Lake Mission Viejo.

Lake Mission Viejo

Cordova Road. Return to Marguerite Parkway (3.1) and continue the hilly route 0.3 mile further to Olympiad Road. Check out the over-the-shoulder Mission Viejo views in the next mile before reaching the Cordova Road/Mustang Run trip summit. Turn left and cycle 0.3 mile further to Los Alisos Boulevard (4.6). The Portola Plaza shopping center is just to the north.

Wilderness Glen Park. Turn left again and start south and downhill on a Class I path. Bike through this residential area with a high hillside and homes to the left (east). Pass a school and recreation field and reach Entidad at (5.1). There is a maze of trails below this street along English Creek, allowing bikers and walkers to pass under Entidad. This style of "through route" is the same at Vista Del Lago and Via Novena.

Cruise on the Class I sidewalk/bikeway along the north edge of Wilderness Glen Park (5.4). There are trees and a forested creekbed with some canyonlike areas for the next mile, as well as some off-road bicycle paths scattered through the park. Cycle downhill past Vista Del Lago to Via Noveno (5.8); stop and look back at the line of condos resembling a castle on a hill. In 0.4 mile, head steeply downhill and pass a particularly well-forested section of the park. The roadway levels and passes Via Santa Lucia across the street. In a short distance the park ends and soon the path meets Trabuco Road (6.2). There are some eateries and a small shopping center at this intersection.

El Toro Park. Cross the intersection and bike through a residential area, passing Vallejo (6.5), Madero (7.4), and then Jeronimo Road in another 0.35 mile. There is a shopping center at this intersection. Shift over to the sidewalk; in a quarter of mile, join the Class I trail coming up from El Toro II Park. Pedal another quarter mile and follow the bikepath under Muirlands Boulevard near creek level (see the discussion on flood warnings from Trip #29A). Come back up on the opposite side into the northern edge of the popular and scenic part of El Toro I Park (8.3). There is a water fountain near the tennis courts, reached via a wooden bridge over Aliso Creek.

El Toro Park to The Aliso Creek Trail Exit. The reference route follows the bikepath nearest Los Alisos Boulevard, where there is an entry trail into the creekbed. (This may be inaccessible in rainy weather.) Dip down into the concrete bottom and cross the creek over a metal plate. Just beyond, pass under Los Alisos Boulevard and turn east. Climb out of the creekbed almost immediately; soon after, the trailway opens up in 0.3 mile in the vicinity of Sycamore Park across the creek. This bridge-accessible park has a water fountain, shade trees, walking/biking trails, picnic benches, and barbecues. (Note that no public water sources were identified between here and the trip's end.)

In another 0.2 mile is a small concrete crossover trail leading to Sycamore Park, immediately followed by a passage under the San Diego Freeway. (This also may be flooded during or after storms.) The trail has now entered Laguna Hills. There is a trail junction here; turn left. A quarter-mile pedal leads alongside the Alicia Parkway turnoff from the San Diego Freeway to the Laguna Hills Plaza.

Our route heads right and proceeds up a short grade past the commemorative Juan Avila Adobe marker, skirts below the local residences, then heads back down into a more open canyon area. The creek bottom supports natural growth in contrast to some of the concrete stretches to the north. Note the dirt trail across the creek; this is part of the equestrian trailway that will parallel the paved Aliso Creek Trail to its current terminus. In 0.3 mile is a four-way junction. Two legs travel a short distance and die out at local roadways. Take the middle route which has a trail marker for bikers coming from the opposite direction. This trail climbs just below the walls of nearby residences and heads south.

Shortly, bikers reach Paseo De Valencia and the bike trail leaves the creek (9.5). Turn left (south), staying on the east side of the street, and follow the signed Class I trail uphill past Kennington Drive and Beckenham Street to a crest near Stockport Street (10.2). Leave the Aliso Creek Trail and coast 0.3 mile downhill to Alicia Parkway, using either the Class II roadway or the Class I sidewalk, now on the street's west side; there is a shopping plaza at this intersection.

The Southern Section. Turn right (southeast) on Alicia Parkway and take the Class I path down into the drainage of an alternate Aliso Creek branch. Follow this wide trail downhill in the broad canyon area 0.7 mile to Moulton Parkway. Cross at the intersection and follow that street southeast. This Class II roadway heads uphill through a relatively new section of Mission Viejo. In another 0.6 mile is La Paz Road, the trip minimum elevation point, and just beyond is Oso Parkway (12.0).

Turn left (west) on Oso Parkway and either use the Class II roadway or join up with the Class I trail on the north side of the highway. Pass under the homes in the low hills in an area with limited tree cover near the path itself. Cross Nellie Gail Road and proceed through a small canyon. Pump uphill to a crest near Bridlewood Drive (13.3); at this point Oso Parkway heads downhill with the Class I bikeway parallel to and above the roadway. In 0.2 mile, cross Cabot Road and return to Mission Viejo.

The "Home Stretch." Transition to Class II roadway and cross a bridge over Oso Creek and the San Diego Freeway. In 0.3 mile, cut through the center of the Mission Viejo Golf Course, then head downhill past Montanoso Drive (14.3). Proceed uphill to a crest at Marguerite Parkway (14.7), turn left (north) and bike past the Mission Viejo Fire Station. There is a fine view of Mount Saddleback from this area (16.0). Begin a moderate upgrade which passes Estanciero Drive (15.3) and reach a crest near the trip origin at La Paz Road and Village Center (15.6).

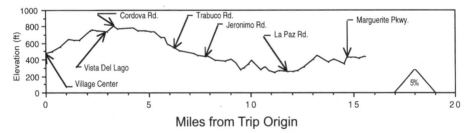

Miles from Trip Origin

CONNECTING TRIPS: 1) Connection with Aliso Creek Trail (Trip #29) - multiple connections by riding west from Los Alisos Boulevard (for example, Cordova Road, Trabuco Road, or Jeronimo Road) or by turning south onto La Paz at the Moulton Parkway intersection; 2) connection with Laguna Niguel Bikeway (Trip #11) - from the Oso Parkway intersection, continue 1.5 miles south on Marguerite Parkway to Crown Valley Parkway and turn right (west); 3) connection with the Oso Viejo ride (Trip #42) - bike east on La Paz Road at Marguerite Parkway; 4) connection with the Cities and Canyons ride (Trip #47) - at Marguerite Parkway and Cordova Road, continue north on the former street to Santa Margarita Parkway; 5) connection with the Arroyo Trabuco Loop (Trip #50) - on Alicia Parkway, turn east at either Oso Parkway, La Paz Road, Jeronimo Road, or Alicia Parkway, then bike to Felipe Road/Olympiad Road.

TRIP #31 - LAGUNA HILLS LOOP

GENERAL LOCATION: Laguna Hills, Irvine, Laguna Beach

LEVEL OF DIFFICULTY: Round trip - moderate to strenuous
Distance - 14.3 miles
Elevation gain - continuous steep grade on lower
   El Toro Road and moderate-to-steep grades on
   Laguna Canyon Road

HIGHLIGHTS: Relatively short, but with a wallop, this is a mixed canyon and flat-land adventure. The initial climb from Hummingbird Park is a short, steep, canyonlike workout to a super-scenic crest, followed by a refreshing coast to Moulton Parkway. That roadway is predominantly flat and Class II or III, but has heavy traffic and a short Class X stint. It is only for cyclists who are "traffic hardened." The loop transitions westward via Barranca Parkway on a Class II stretch through a modern commercial area. The finale is a rustic tour of upper Laguna Canyon and a return to the park via lower El Toro Road.

TRAILHEAD: From the San Joaquin Hills Transportation Corridor (State Highway 73), exit south at Laguna Canyon Road (State Highway 133); drive 0.75 mile to El Toro Road. Turn northeast, go 1.5 miles to Aliso Creek Road, turn (east) and proceed 0.1 mile to Hummingbird Lane. A right turn leads to the park. From the San Diego Freeway, exit south at Laguna Canyon Road and drive 5.5 miles to El Toro Road. Continue as described above. The park has a water fountain, tree cover, and a children's playground on the westside segment, and trees and a walking/biking path on the east side.

Bring one or two filled water bottles on hot days. The single public source is at the trip origin. However, there are commercial water sources at the many shopping plazas along the route.

TRIP DESCRIPTION: **Over the Top.** Backtrack to Class II El Toro Road and turn right. Cycle a workout upgrade in the lower tree-lined residential area past Calle Corta (0.3) and Canyon Wren Lane (0.8), reaching the crest in 0.1 mile. From the top is a panorama that includes El Toro, Irvine, Mount Saddleback, and an over-the-shoulder view of the undeveloped lower El Toro Road area. Glide past the shopping complexes on either side of the road at Calle Sonora (1.2) and continue coasting another 0.4 mile to a cluster of shopping centers at Moulton Parkway.

Northbound. Turn north onto this busy Class III thoroughfare and make a short climb to a crest at Gate #12, then cruise by Moulton Plaza to Santa Maria Avenue (2.3). Navigate a 0.3-mile Class X stretch between this street and Ridge Route Drive, then enjoy the transition to a Class II bikeway that extends all the way to Laguna Canyon Road. (An alternative after the turn onto Moulton Parkway is to bike the entire one-mile stretch on the westside sidewalk.) Cross over little Veeh Lake and pass Lake Forest Drive, where the road's name changes to Irvine Center Drive (3.1).

In this less-developed section, pass over San Diego Creek and meet Bake Parkway at (4.0). In 0.2 mile is Hubble/Lion Country, where a left turn leads to the Irvine Meadows

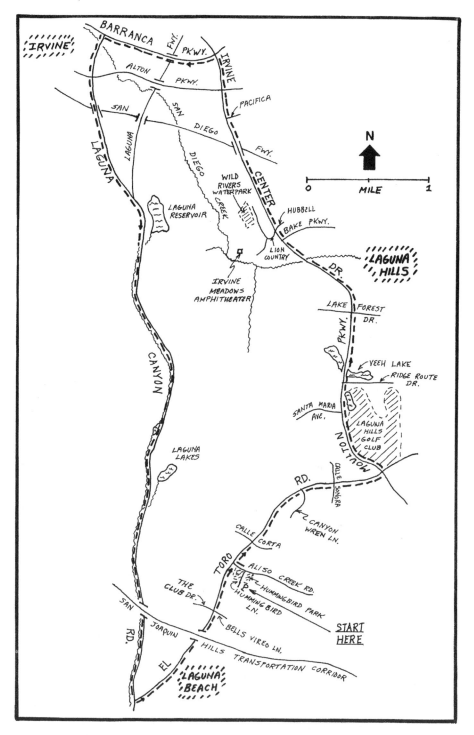

TRIP #31 - LAGUNA HILLS LOOP

Amphitheater and Wild Rivers Waterpark. Pedal over the San Diego Freeway (4.8) and bike past Pacifica, an entry to the Irvine Spectrum Center shopping area in 0.3 mile. Continue on the flat past Alton Parkway and reach Barranca Parkway at (5.7).

Westbound Connector. Turn left and cycle though a series of modern commercial sites on Class II roadway, passing over the Laguna Freeway at (6.0). The commercial development thins as the parkway heads west and meets Laguna Canyon Road (6.6).

Laguna Canyon Entry. Turn left onto Class II bikeway, which becomes Class X at Pasteur. Bicycle over the San Diego Freeway and cruise through agricultural environs. Laguna Canyon Road fuses with the Laguna Freeway outlet traffic in an area surrounded by open fields (8.1). In 0.1 mile, the bikepath starts heading into the canyon opening; the Laguna Reservoir is high on the hillside to the left. There are rolling hills and a small creek along the roadway as the route proceeds into the canyon proper. The roadway becomes a signed Class III at (8.4).

The Canyon Tour. Follow a moderate upgrade (9.0) and reach the top of the grade in an area with a few small shade trees (9.3). In another 0.4 mile, pass a small hamlet to the left (east); to the right are small tree stands and overgrowth. In about 1.3 miles of light rolling hills and nearly treeless roadway, cross over the outlet creek from North Laguna Lake (11.0). This creek has paralleled the road through much of the canyon.

Bike over the rolling hills within the canyon and head up a grade with a "Laguna Beach City Limit" sign near the summit (11.4). In 0.3 mile, pass under State Highway 73, then observe the interesting rock formations just beyond and to the right. In a short distance is El Toro Road (12.5).

The Return Segment. Turn northeast onto this Class II road which is sandwiched between undeveloped Aliso and Wood Canyons Regional Park (right) and the Laguna Coast Wilderness Park (left). Pass under Highway 73 again (13.5), enter the first housing developments, then continue climbing 0.2 mile past Bells Vireo Lane/The Club Drive. Groups of plush residences appear high on the hillside to the left. In another 0.4 mile of spirited uphill is Aliso Creek Road and a return to Hummingbird Park (14.3).

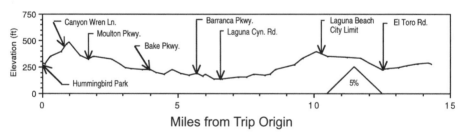

CONNECTING TRIPS: 1) Connection with the Laguna Canyon Road tour (Trip #9) - the trips share a common segment of northern Laguna Canyon Road; 2) connection with the San Diego Creek trip - at Barranca Parkway and Laguna Canyon Road, take the former road east to Jeffrey Road; 3) connection with the Aliso Viejo Figure "8" (Trip #46) - At El Toro Road and Aliso Creek Road, go east on the latter street to Glenwood Drive; 4) spur trips - at the trip origin, take hilly, Class II Aliso Creek Road eastbound - another neat option is to take Class II Moulton Parkway southeast at the El Toro Road intersection.

TRIP #32 - LAKE FOREST TOUR

GENERAL LOCATION: Lake Forest

LEVEL OF DIFFICULTY: Loop - easy

Distance - 5.3 miles

Elevation gain - periodic light grades

HIGHLIGHTS: The Lake Forest loop trip is entirely on Class I/II bikeways within this very pleasant community. The trip includes a tour along residential streets as well as a romp through Serrano Creek Community Park. The street route includes a pass-by of a lovely manmade lake community along Toledo Way. The park ride meanders through a major loop with several minor spurs and provides a very pleasant tree-sheltered environment. The park cruise might serve as a good family bike trip, while only more experienced riders should use the Class II roadways.

TRAILHEAD: From the San Diego Freeway, exit north on Lake Forest Drive and travel about two miles to Toledo Way. Turn left (northwest) and find parking within the local residential area. Check local parking signs and carefully avoid parking on any private streets, specifically those along Toledo Way. An option for low-use park days is to park alongside Serrano Creek Park.

Bring a moderate supply of water. The trip is short, but the only on-route public water source we found was at Serrano Creek Park.

TRIP DESCRIPTION: **Serrano Creek Community Park.** From the parking area, proceed in the direction away from Lake Forest Drive (northwest) on a Class II bikepath. Turn right at Serrano Road (0.3) and cycle along the north sidewalk to a downramp that leads to the Class I trail within Serrano Creek Community Park. Bike along the park's trail through lush tree-shaded surroundings to the picnic/playground area at the east end of the park (0.8). There is a water fountain here plus some unique kids' props such as a small "tire mountain" and a tree house.

The trail goes through a tight turn, crosses the creek and continues to parallel the creek. There are several small trail spurs off this section of path, and a horse trail as well. There are also a few short "ups and downs" on the route to give it some variety. The path reaches the west end of the loop, recrosses the creek and returns to the park starting point (1.1). Turn around and head back across the creek, but turn left at the next junction and cycle 0.2 mile to the trail exit near Serrano Drive and Lake Vista Drive.

The Industrial Loop and Toledo Way. Turn right on Serrano Road and return to Toledo Way, admiring the view of the residences surrounding the manmade lake. Turn right (northwest) on Toledo Way and proceed on the Class II bikeway across Bake Parkway (1.7). This begins a 2.9-mile loop through a modern, light industrial/high-tech area on a Class II bikeway. Bicycle 0.5 mile to Alton Parkway, turn left and pedal 0.6 mile to a bridge over a railroad. There is a fine view into the foothills to the southwest from this point (and a long-distance view of the Wild Rivers area).

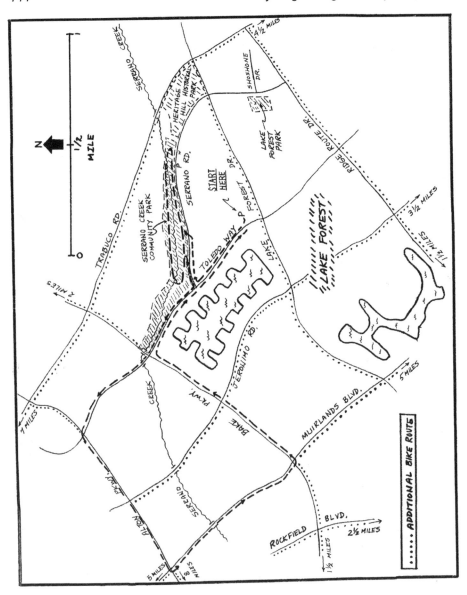

TRIP #32 - LAKE FOREST TOUR

Cruise 0.2 mile to Muirlands Boulevard and turn left. Next, ride another 0.8 mile to Bake Parkway and follow that roadway another 0.8 mile to complete the industrial loop (4.6). On the way is another panoramic vista from the bridge over the railroad tracks. Turn right at Toledo Way and continue 0.7 mile, admiring the waterfront Lake Forest community, and return to the starting point (5.3). Note that there are entries to the lake area at two points off of Toledo Way, one near Lost River Court on the lake's east side and the other near Quiet Oak Drive on the west side.

Optional Tours. There are many lengthy Class II roadways that pass through the Lake Forest area. A few of the longer routes are noted on the tour map. Exceptional examples are the Muirlands Boulevard/Barranca Parkway, Alton Parkway, and Trabuco Road/Irvine Boulevard bikeways.

CONNECTING TRIPS: 1) Connection with Aliso Creek Trail (Trip #29A) - take Bake Parkway northeast to Trabuco Road. Turn right and proceed about 2.5 miles across Lake Forest Drive, Ridge Route, and El Toro Road to the Aliso Creek Trail. Turn left to head northeast toward Santiago Canyon, and turn right to head southwest toward El Toro.

THE "BIG GUYS"

Santa Ana River near Ocean Outlet

TRIP #33 - WESTERN ORANGE COUNTY LOOP

<u>GENERAL LOCATION</u>: Strand Bike Trail - San Gabriel River - Coyote Creek - Fullerton - El Cajon Trail - Santa Ana River

<u>LEVEL OF DIFFICULTY</u>: Loop - strenuous
Distance - 63.5 miles
Elevation gain - periodic moderate grades in
Fullerton and El Cajon Trail areas

<u>HIGHLIGHTS</u>: This grand "looper" provides a testy mileage workout combined with a wide variety of bikeways and scenery. Well over half of the trip is on Class I bike trails. The tour begins at Huntington Beach State Park near the Santa Ana River outlet, proceeds along the coastal strand bikepath, then follows the San Gabriel River and Coyote Creek inland. The route meanders through Buena Park and Fullerton, joins up with the El Cajon Trail in Yorba Linda and follows a 21-mile runout down the Santa Ana River to the trip origin. The scenery along the coastline, the lower San Gabriel River, the El Cajon Trail, and selected Santa Ana River segments is exceptional. There are numerous top-of-the-line parks on or near this tour, including El Dorado Regional Park, Craig Park, Yorba Regional Park, Centennial Regional Park, Huntington Beach State Park, and Bolsa Chica Beach State Park.

A reduced-mileage trip option using Heil Avenue is also provided. This 25-mile alternative visits Huntington Beach State Park, Bolsa Chica Beach State Park, and Centennial Regional Park, and adds Mile Square Park to the itinerary.

<u>TRAILHEAD</u>: From the San Diego Freeway, exit south at Brookhurst Street. Continue about five miles to the road's end and turn right. Drive three quarters of a mile to Magnolia Street and turn left into the Huntington Beach State Park entrance. There is also free parking off of the inland residential streets.

From Pacific Coast Highway (PCH) southbound, continue four miles past the Huntington Beach Pier and turn right at Magnolia Street. For northbound traffic, drive 1.25 miles beyond the Santa Ana River and turn left at Magnolia Street.

Bring a couple of filled water bottles in order to minimize water stops. There are scattered water sources at the parks on the route. Bikers may have to buck the onshore late afternoon winds on the last leg of the Santa Ana River segment. If this is of concern, select an alternate starting point.

<u>TRIP DESCRIPTION</u>: **Huntington Beach State Park to the San Gabriel River.** The Trip #33 description discusses only new or potentially confusing portions of the ride. Refer to the individual trip writeups as identified below for details. The tour starts at Huntington Beach State Park and continues northwest on the coastal strand trail to the northern end of Sunset Beach (see Trip #4, Middle and Northern Segment Maps). Follow the Seal Beach/Sunset Beach Tour (Trip #1) through Seal Beach to the San Gabriel River (10.0).

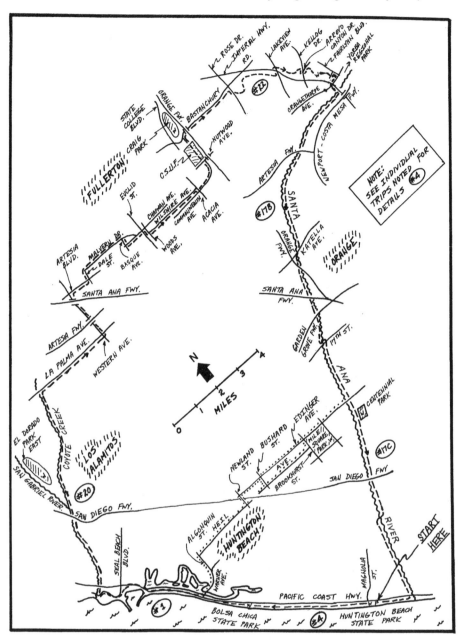

TRIP #33 - WESTERN ORANGE COUNTY LOOP

   San Gabriel River and Coyote Creek. Stay to the right at the junction and follow the Coyote Creek Trail (Trip #20), exiting at La Palma Avenue (19.0).

   The Inland Jigsaw (Buena Park to Fullerton). Turn right and bike 3.2 miles west on La Palma Avenue on mixed Class II and Class X path. At Western Avenue, directly under the Knott's Berry Farm parachute and "free-fall" rides, turn left (north) and ride 1.9 miles on Class III bikeway. Pass under the Artesia and Santa Ana Freeways, turn right at Artesia Boulevard, then left in 0.5 mile at Dale Street (25.2).

From here to Chapman Avenue, we found no single route with continuous bike route signs or unsigned roadway with continuous wide bike shoulder. One option is to bike a quarter of a mile to Malvern Avenue and turn right. After one mile of biking on narrow-shouldered Class X roadway, the street transitions to Class III beyond Gilbert Street. Cycle past Bastanchury Road and, in another 0.4 mile (two miles from Dale Street), turn right onto Basque Avenue (27.3) and then left at Chapman Avenue. The second option is to cycle one-eighth of a mile on Dale Avenue and turn right at Artesia Boulevard. Follow that lightly used Class X road alongside the Fullerton Municipal Airport and turn left (north) at Gilbert Street. Bike 0.3 mile on another Class X street to Malvern Avenue and continue as described above.

This is the beginning of a 4.5-mile Fullerton residential tour. Follow Chapman Avenue three quarters of a mile until it reaches Woods Avenue, turn right and bike to Wilshire Avenue, then turn left. Follow Wilshire Avenue 2.3 miles to Acacia Avenue and turn right. Soon turn left at Commonwealth Avenue until this roadway takes a long 90-degree curve northward and meets Nutwood Avenue (31.5).

California State University, Fullerton, to Yorba Linda. Cross Nutwood Avenue on the west side of the intersection. At the "can't miss" CSUF campus sign, turn right and bike on Class I trail through the campus to Associated Road at the north end. Follow this Class II road 0.3 mile to Bastanchury Road and turn right, pedaling uphill on the Class III street under the Orange Freeway. The route peaks in 0.3 mile and the ride flattens for the 2.0 miles to Rose Drive (35.0).

Santa Ana River near Ocean Outlet

El Cajon Trail. Turn right on Rose Drive; in 0.2 mile, cross the street to the east side at the Class I path entrance. Follow the El Cajon Trail (Trip #22) for 5.6 miles to the intersection of Fairlynn Boulevard and Esperanza Road. Turn right (this departs from the Trip #22 route) and bike 0.3 mile to Imperial Highway. Turn left and continue 0.7 mile to the bridge across the Santa Ana River (41.8).

Santa Ana River. Follow the Class I Santa Ana River Trail (Trips #17B and #17C) 21.4 miles to the ocean, then take a short cruise on the beach bikeway to the trip origin. The total trip mileage is 63.5.

Excursion: Shortcut Loop. Note that the loop can be altered by using the Heil Avenue segment in Huntington Beach. The Heil Avenue/Santa Ana River coastal loop is a nice 25-mile ride in itself. The route uses Class II Warner Avenue and Algonquin Street to get to the Class II main thoroughfare on Heil Avenue. Near the San Diego Freeway, a short Class X ride on Bushard Street leads to Class II Edinger Avenue which serves as the throughway to the Santa Ana River. At Edinger Avenue and Brookhurst Street, this shortcut route passes Mile Square Park, one of the premier parks in Orange County (see Trip #5).

CONNECTING TRIPS: 1) Connection with the Carbon Canyon Workout (Trip #23) - at Rose Drive and Bastanchury Road, bike north on Rose Drive; 2) connection with the Fullerton Tour/Craig Park ride (Trip #24) - at Malvern Avenue and Bastanchury Road, turn north onto the latter road. Also see individual trip writeups for the myriad of other connectors.

TRIP #34 - EASTERN ORANGE COUNTY LOOP (The "Granddaddy")

GENERAL LOCATION: Santiago Canyon - El Toro - Laguna Niguel - Laguna Beach - Newport Beach - Santa Ana River - Villa Park

LEVEL OF DIFFICULTY: Loop - very strenuous
Distance - 76.9 miles
Elevation gain - periodic moderate grades;
   frequent, long and steep grades in Santiago Canyon area

HIGHLIGHTS: The granddaddy of Orange County trips, this super 77-mile journey covers the southeastern half of the county and has the Santa Ana River as a common boundary with Trip #33. The variety in biking territory is mind boggling! The itinerary includes the rolling hills of Santiago Canyon, the mountains-to-sea ride down the Aliso Creek corridor, a 15-mile grand tour of the southern Orange County coastline, a pedal up the Santa Ana River, and a short return segment through the cities of Orange and Villa Park. Most of the trip is on Class I or Class II routes.

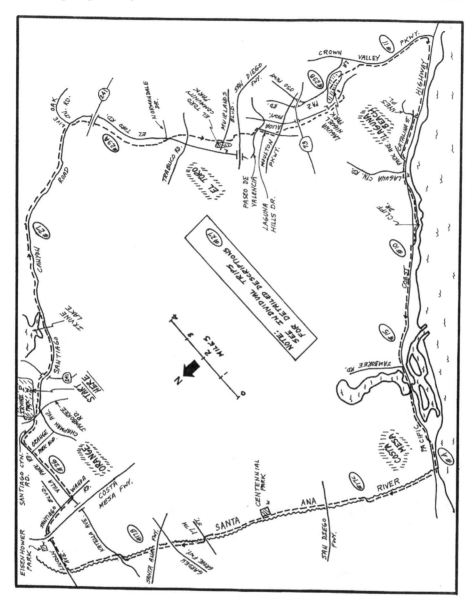

TRIP #34 - EASTERN ORANGE LOOP

With a modest Santa Ana River/Santa Ana Canyon Road extension, this trip can be turned into a "century" tour.

TRAILHEAD: From the Orange Freeway or Costa Mesa Freeway, take the Chapman Avenue turnoff east. The distances to the Jamboree Road intersection are 4.5 miles and 7.5 miles, respectively. Turn left (north), get into the right-hand lane and go one-third mile to the signed Irvine Regional Park entrance at Irvine Park Road. From the Eastern

Transportation Corridor (State Highway 241), exit at Chapman Avenue/Santiago Canyon Road and drive west one mile to Jamboree Road. Turn right and motor one-third mile to the park entrance.

Pay the entry fee and enjoy the park after the ride. (See the detailed map provided in Trip #26 for park facilities.) An alternative is to start at Santiago Hills Park off of Trail's End Lane and Chapman Avenue. The park has water, restrooms, walkway/bikeways, scattered tree cover, sheltered picnic/barbecue facilities, and a children's playground.

Bring a couple of filled water bottles in order to minimize water stops. There are scattered water sources along the route as noted in the individual trip writeups. The hilly and exposed 12.2-mile Santiago Canyon segment is essentially waterless.

TRIP DESCRIPTION: Santiago Canyon and Aliso Creek Corridor. The Trip #33 description discusses only new or potentially confusing portions of the ride. Refer to the individual trip writeups as identified below for details. Bike back to Santiago Canyon Road, turn left and follow the Santiago Canyon Road tour (Trip #27) (12.0). From the road's end at Cook's Corner, pedal about one-fourth mile south on El Toro Road and pick up the origin of the Aliso Creek Trail (Trip #29). Follow that route to Crown Valley Community Park in Laguna Niguel (27.6).

Laguna Niguel Bikeway. Follow the southern segment of the Laguna Niguel Bikeway (Trip #11) from the Crown Valley Community Park to the trip's end at Pacific Coast Highway (PCH) (30.8).

Cook's Corner

Coastal Segment. Turn right at PCH and bike 2.3 miles on Class X roadway through rolling coastal hills to Aliso Beach County Park. From this point, bike the Laguna Beach Tour (Trip #10) in reverse to Seaward Road in Newport Beach (42.2). Bike PCH to Tustin Avenue or follow one of the paths shown for the Newport Beach/ Corona Del Mar Tour (Trip #15). The former option is more direct but is on some narrow and heavily trafficked roads (47.2).

Bike one mile further on PCH to Balboa Boulevard/Superior Avenue and turn left. Turn right at 46th Street and pedal 0.2 mile to Seashore Drive. Follow the Sunset Beach to Newport Beach Strand (Trip #4) back to the Santa Ana River (49.4). On the north side of the river, look for a path that drops below road level, makes a tight turn to the north and goes under PCH. Note that there is a faster pace option to stay on PCH in this stretch on good biking road. For the PCH alternative, stay on PCH to Orange Street, turn left at the signal and bike to Seashore Drive, then cycle to the north side of the Santa Ana River.

Santa Ana River. Follow the Santa Ana River Rides #17C and #17B in the northerly direction in that order. Exit the river east at Lincoln Avenue (67.8).

The Return Segment. Follow Class X Lincoln Avenue 1.5 miles on a steady workout upgrade to Tustin Avenue; Eisenhower Park is just north of the intersection. Cruise under the Orange Freeway, turn right onto Class II Santiago Boulevard and follow that road 2.0 miles. Continue straight ahead on Wanda Road at the point where Santiago Boulevard veers sharply eastward; in 0.3 mile turn left at Katella Avenue/ Villa Park Road (71.6). Follow the eastbound segment of the Orange/Irvine Park Loop (Trip #26) to the trip origin at Irvine Park (76.9).

"Century Trip." A modest trip extension can easily turn this into a hundred-miler. A recommended option is to continue north on the Santa Ana River to Green River Road (Trips #17A and #17B). For variety on the return leg of this extension, continue south on Santa Ana Canyon Road beyond Weir Canyon Road and return to Lincoln Avenue via that roadway (Trip #25). Follow **The Return Segment** described above beyond this point.

<u>**CONNECTING TRIPS**</u>: Certainly you are kidding! See the individual trip writeups.

TRIP #35 - ORANGE COUNTY "CENTURY"

GENERAL LOCATION: Santiago Canyon - Laguna Niguel - Laguna Beach - Huntington Beach - Coyote Creek - Fullerton - Villa Park

LEVEL OF DIFFICULTY: Loop - very strenuous
Distance - 105.3 miles
Elevation gain - frequent, long and steep grades
    in Santiago Canyon; frequent moderate-to-steep
    grades in Laguna Beach area

HIGHLIGHTS: Yes Martha, you can build a "century" trip by riding the periphery of the Eastern and Western County Loops (Trips #34 and #33, respectively). This adventure from early morning to afternoon provides a bike tour of the best that Orange County has to offer: Santiago Canyon, the Aliso Creek Corridor, nearly 20 miles of scenic coastline, the San Gabriel River and Coyote Creek, and the El Cajon Trail. Go for it!! If this is your first "century," however, bring some phone change.

TRAILHEAD: Start at Irvine Park (see Trip #34) in order to complete most of the toughest trip segments in the first 40 miles. The 4.7-mile return segment from Villa Park Road/Santiago Canyon Road to Irvine Park is also a hilly workout. If your persuasion is to end the trip on an easier, more laid-back note, start it at Eisenhower Park near Lincoln Avenue and Tustin Avenue (see Trip #25).

TRIP DESCRIPTION: The route starts from Irvine Park and follows the Eastern Orange County Loop for the 49.4 miles to the Santa Ana River. Cross the river and bike along the coast, following the Western Orange County Loop. Bike the latter loop 46.8 miles to the Santa Ana River exit at Lincoln Avenue. From this intersection, follow **The Return Segment** described in Trip #34 an additional 9.1 miles back to Irvine Park.

CONNECTING TRIPS: See Trips #33 and #34. Also refer to the maps for those trips.

ADDITIONAL TRIPS

Jeronimo Greenbelt Park in Mission Viejo

TRIP #36 - TURTLE ROCK ROAD

<u>GENERAL LOCATION</u>: Irvine

<u>LEVEL OF DIFFICULTY</u>: Loop - moderate
                         Distance - 4.3 miles
                         Elevation gain - two moderate grades

<u>HIGHLIGHTS</u>: This low-mileage loop on Class II roadway surveys the upscale Turtle Rock neighborhood with its classy residences and grand landscaping. After leaving well-stocked Turtle Rock Community Park, cyclists follow a short climb to Ridgeline Drive, coast past Campus Drive, then pump a 1.5-mile moderate upgrade before coasting back to the park. There is also a fun Class I spur trip which originates near the park, wanders through the well-maintained neighborhood, crosses Turtle Rock Road near Campus Drive and ends in the eastern grounds of William R. Mason Regional Park.

<u>TRAILHEAD</u>: From the San Diego Freeway, exit south at Culver Drive, drive 1.5 miles to Campus Drive and turn left. In a quarter of a mile, go right at Turtle Rock Drive and motor two miles to Sunnyhill, then turn right to reach the Turtle Rock Community Park entry. From the San Joaquin Hills Transportation Corridor (State Highway 73), exit northbound at Bonita Canyon Drive. Drive two miles to Campus Drive, turn right and continue as described above.

Bring a light water supply for this short trip. There is water at the trip origin and at the water fountain near the Campus Drive intersection. Turtle Rock Community Park is a large well-stocked base of operations. It has a visitor center, nature center, water, restrooms, abundant tree cover, walkway/bikeways throughout, picnic areas and shelters, tennis courts, athletic fields, and hiking trails.

<u>TRIP DESCRIPTION</u>: **Turtle Rock Community Park to Campus Drive.** Exit the park on Sunnyhill and turn right on Class II Turtle Rock Road. The surrounding well-manicured grounds and stately residences are typical of those found throughout the tour. Pedal past Silkwood (0.4) and start a mild climb just beyond. In 0.2 mile on the right is one of the few undeveloped local hillsides (the frontal San Joaquin Hills).

Reach a crest near Highland View, then pass Ridgeline Drive, a scenic Class II ride in itself (0.8). Enjoy the quickie view of Irvine below and the estates high on the ridge to the left, and coast past Canyon Park (grassy knolls, limited shade, children's playground). Pass Hillsborough with some more barren hillsides to the right (1.3), then continue downhill to West Concordia, an entry to Concordia University (1.8). The road opens to a four-lane nearby and cyclists reach the trip low point at Campus Drive in 0.2 mile.

The Uphill Return. Cycle uphill on Class II roadway past Paseo Segovia, beyond which Turtle Rock Road skinnies back down to two lanes. At Amalfi is a short

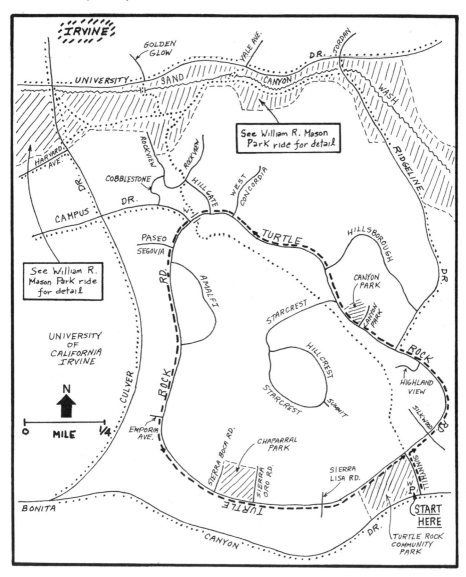

TRIP #36 - TURTLE ROCK ROAD

flat, then bikers continue the climb through a heavily tree-lined section to Emporia Avenue (2.8). Near Briarcrest is an open grassy area between residences, one of many open spaces planned into this purely residential community. At Sierra Boca (3.4) is the western edge of Chaparral Park, which provides trees, grassy knolls, a children's play area, and picnic benches. Just beyond is the crest, and cyclists are treated to a mild downgrade, passing Sierra Lisa Road at (3.7) and returning to Sunnyhill. A short ride to the park entrance completes the loop (4.3).

Excursion: Spur Trip. There is a fine Class I bikepath that starts across Turtle Rock Road at Sunnyhill and snakes its way between the classy local residences, letting out just across the street at Campus Drive (1.4 miles). By taking the tunnel under Turtle Rock Road, bikers can connect with the northern path section which meanders 0.5 mile further into the eastern grounds of William R. Mason Regional Park. The path reaches "The Triangle Junction" with park benches and an information kiosk within the triangle and merges with the major eastern grounds trail. There is a water fountain near the origin of the northern path section at Turtle Rock Road. The return ride to Turtle Rock Community Park from the tunnel area is a climb similar to that on the eastern half of the Turtle Rock Road loop.

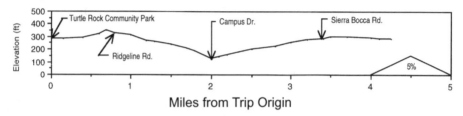

CONNECTING TRIPS: 1) Connection with the Irvine Bikeway (Trip #8) - take the spur trail into William R. Mason Regional Park to "The Triangle Junction," bike east to the Yale Avenue entry and follow that road to a bikeway/walkway over the San Diego Freeway; 2) connection with the San Diego Creek ride (Trip #18) - at Campus Drive, bike west to the creek; 3) connection with the William R. Mason Regional Park tour (Trip #37) - take the spur trail into William R. Mason Regional Park to its end, turning either east or west at "The Triangle Junction."

TRIP #37 - WILLIAM R. MASON REGIONAL PARK

GENERAL LOCATION: Irvine

LEVEL OF DIFFICULTY: Loop - easy (sample western grounds peripheral tour)
          Distance - 1.9 miles
          Elevation gain - essentially flat
          Up and back - easy (eastern grounds tour)
          Distance - 2.4 miles
          Elevation gain - essentially flat

HIGHLIGHTS: We've biked quite a few, but William R. Mason Regional Park has got to be one of the premier parks for family bike rides, along with others such as O'Neill Regional Park, Irvine Regional Park, Mile Square Park, and El Dorado Park (eastern Los Angeles County). Besides the miles of excellent bikeways/walkways, the western grounds have a lake, tree cover, well-located restrooms, picnic and barbecue facilities, athletic fields, playgrounds, picnic shelters, an amphitheater, and the Sand Canyon Wash. The eastern grounds are relatively undeveloped other than the clearings

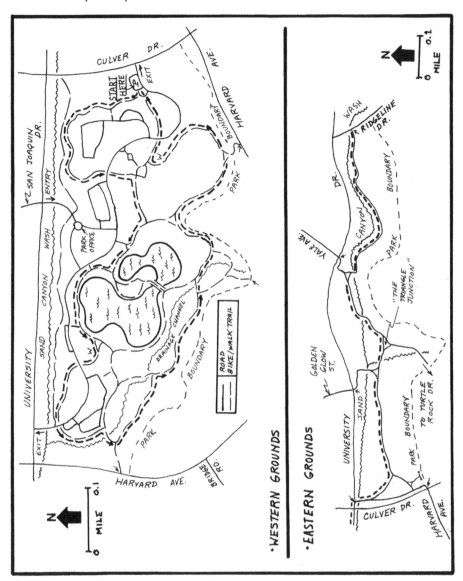

TRIP #37 - WILLIAM R. MASON REGIONAL PARK

for an excellent Class I bikeway which has numerous access points. (There are precautionary warnings on this side for both poison oak and wildlife.)

TRAILHEAD: From the San Diego Freeway, exit south at Culver Drive and proceed one mile to University Drive. Turn right and go 0.2 mile to the main entrance (across from San Joaquin) which is on the park's western grounds. From the San Joaquin Hills Transportation Corridor (State Highway 73), take the Bonita Canyon Drive off-ramp north and drive 1.75 miles (the street becomes Culver Drive) to University Drive. Turn left and follow the directions above from this junction.

Bring a light water supply for a tour of the western and/or eastern grounds. There are numerous public sources on the western side of the park. There are no sources of water on the relatively undeveloped eastern grounds, however tour mileage is short.

TRIP DESCRIPTION: **Western Grounds.** Pay the fee at the gate (weekdays are far less expensive than weekends) and find parking. There are an unlimited number of ways to connect walkway/bikeways, streets, and parking area, and we provide the peripheral route below only as an example.

From the parking area nearest Culver Boulevard, head north and make a semicircle around the easternmost parking group, cross the main park roadway and keep making right turns (ignoring all accesses back to the main park roadway). This will take bikers around the lake and across a drainage channel. At the first exit bikeway to Harvard Avenue, turn left, then continue the pattern of right turns, making a semicircle around the southern end of the lake on the outermost path.

Ignore the right turn along the drainage channel's origin, then continue the right turns, bypassing the second exit route to Harvard Avenue. Recross the main park roadway and continue the right-hand pattern back to the parking area. The total peripheral loop distance is 1.9 miles.

The inner loop around the lake is about 0.7 mile. On this route, there is also an option to cross the lake on a narrow bridge for walkers and bikers. (If the bridge is occupied, walk your bike across.) The inner loop will treat cyclists with a bevy of geese and ducks which permanently inhabit the park.

Eastern Grounds. Going from the eastern to western grounds requires crossing Culver Drive at University Drive or Harvard Avenue. In either case, the path entries are

Western Grounds: Bridge over Lake

near the intersections on the east side of Culver Drive. There are also walking/biking entries on University Drive across from the Golden Glow Street and Yale Avenue intersections, on the west side of Ridgeline Drive just south of the Sand Canyon Wash, and from the intersection of Campus Drive and Turtle Rock Road. (See Trip #36 under **Spur Trip** for a description of the latter.)

From the Culver Drive/University Drive intersection, bike along University Drive and turn right at the path entry (0.0). In about a hundred yards, veer left at the intersection with the bikeway coming from Culver Drive/Harvard Avenue. At the second intersection with the bikeway from Culver Drive/Harvard Avenue (another 200 yards), turn left again and join the main west-east route. Though near to the traffic sounds of University Drive, the area is relatively undeveloped, having large swaths of trees and brush; this look is typical of the eastern grounds.

The Class I bikeway, which is centered within a wide clear-cut swath, heads east through wildlife-filled environs, meeting the entries from Golden Glow Street (0.4), Campus Drive ("The Triangle Junction") (0.45), and Yale Avenue (0.65), and ends at Ridgeline Drive (1.05). There are benches scattered along the path, but no water. The eastern edge is particularly natural, with the path sandwiched between the low-lying greenery of Sand Canyon Wash and the steep hillsides below Concordia University. The total mileage from the Culver Drive/Harvard entry to Ridgeline Drive and back is 2.1 miles; add another 0.3 mile if starting from the westside grounds main entrance.

CONNECTING TRIPS: 1) Connection with the Upper Newport Bay ride (Trip #6) and Newport Beach/Irvine Tour (Trip #7) - from the main entrance, bike west on University Drive 1.5 miles to Jamboree Road - for Trip #6, continue across Jamboree Road to a street now named Eastbluff Drive; 2) connection with the Irvine Bikeway (Trip #8) - from the park's eastern ground, follow the Yale Avenue exit, cross University Drive and follow Yale Avenue to the pedestrian/bicycle path over the San Diego Freeway; 3) connection with the San Diego Creek tour (Trip #18) - from the main entrance, go 0.5 mile on University Drive to the Campus Drive intersection/entry; 4) connection with the Turtle Rock Road tour (Trip #36) - bike to the "triangle" junction on the eastern grounds of the park and turn south.

TRIP #38 - SIGNAL PEAK AND PELICAN HILL

GENERAL LOCATION: Orange County/Newport Coast

LEVEL OF DIFFICULTY: Loop - strenuous
Distance - 8.1 miles
Elevation gain - steep-to-sheer grade on Ridge Park Road; moderate-to-steep grade on Newport Coast Drive

HIGHLIGHTS: This is a ride for serious "hillies." The steep-to-sheer climb on Ridge Park Road is early in the ride, but it is a "doozie," with an average 8-plus percent incline. The return up Newport Coast Drive, though more moderate, will also keep

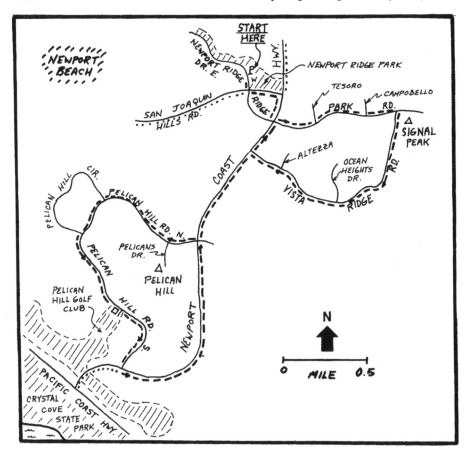

TRIP #38 - SIGNAL PEAK AND PELICAN HILL

your blood moving. The payoff for the hard work includes fabulous views of the Pacific Ocean, Catalina Island, Newport Bay, and the city of Irvine scattered over the Signal Peak and Pelican Hill areas. Both sections are on wide-shouldered Class X roadways, while Newport Coast Drive is Class II.

TRAILHEAD: From the San Joaquin Hills Transportation Corridor (State Highway 73), take the Newport Coast off-ramp southbound and go about one mile to San Joaquin Hills Road. Turn right and drive a quarter of a mile to Newport Ridge Drive East, then turn right to reach Newport Ridge Community Park. From Pacific Coast Highway (PCH), turn north at Newport Coast Drive and motor 2.5 miles to San Joaquin Hills Road. Turn left and continue as described above.

Bring at least a quart of water as there are no public water sources once you leave Newport Ridge Community Park. That park has limited shade, water, restrooms, grass, athletic fields, and a children's playground.

TRIP DESCRIPTION: Signal Peak. Leave the park and bike east to Newport Coast Road (0.3), turn right and pedal another 0.2 mile to Ridge Park Road. Almost immediately, begin a steep upgrade that becomes sheer for the remaining 0.8 mile of the pumpathon to the crest. Established residences give way to newer developments as the road passes Tesoro (0.8) and Campobello (1.1).

In another 0.3 mile, turn right onto Vista Ridge Road, enjoying a moderating upgrade and a joyful crest at (1.5). In the early portion of the downgrade on the south flank below Signal Peak, the Pacific Ocean and Catalina views appear. Near Ocean Heights Drive (2.2) are similar vistas plus drop-dead gorgeous looks into Newport Bay and the city of Irvine. Continue gliding past Altezza Drive (2.5) and reach road's end at Newport Coast Drive in 0.3 mile.

Pelican Hill. Turn left and bike south to Pelican Hill North (3.5), passing patchy hillside residences along the way. Turn right and climb to Pelican Crest in 0.2 mile, taking in the ocean views that open just beyond. As the road curves to the south beyond the first Pelican Hill Circle junction (4.2), scope out the hillside estates, particularly the palatial digs on the ridge to the west. There are more Pacific Ocean vistas in this area. (While taking them in, the road name has changed to Pelican Hill Road South.)

While circumnavigating Pelican Hill on the south side, the Pelican Hill Golf Club comes into view below. Further downhill is the entry to the pleasing-to-the-eye club itself (5.1). Continue mostly downhill another half mile to Newport Coast Drive.

The Return. This is the low point of the tour, which can only mean one thing! Time to cycle in earnest on a moderate-to-steep 1.5-mile climb which crests just south of Vista Ridge Road (6.9). A mix of flats and downhill lead back to San Joaquin Hills Road and a return to Newport Ridge Regional Park (8.1).

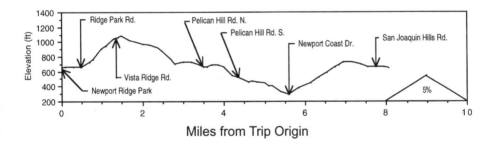

Miles from Trip Origin

Excursion: Continuation Option. Bikers seeking additional mileage and elevation change can coast south beyond Pelican Hill Drive South to PCH and return. This adds about 120 feet of elevation gain and an up-and-back mileage of 0.7 mile.

CONNECTING TRIPS: Connection with the Laguna Beach Tour (Trip #10) - take the **Continuation Option** described above to PCH.

TRIP #39 - WESTSIDE LAGUNA NIGUEL

GENERAL LOCATION: Laguna Niguel

LEVEL OF DIFFICULTY: Loop - strenuous
Distance - 8.4 miles
Elevation gain - two steep grades; moderate elsewhere

HIGHLIGHTS: This 100 percent Class II ride plies the westside hillsides of Laguna Niguel, primarily on Highlands Avenue and Pacific Island Drive. The upgrades on those two roadways are short but very steep. There are grand local and distant vistas near the Highlands Avenue summit and almost all the way up and down Pacific Island Drive. Another prime vista point is just below Niguel Hill on Talavera Drive at Seaview Park. The return segment on Crown Valley Parkway is a pleasant warmdown before completing the loop at the South Coast Regional Civic Center.

TRAILHEAD: From the San Joaquin Hills Transportation Corridor, exit south at Aliso Creek Road and motor 2.25 miles to Alicia Parkway. Turn right and go another 2.25 miles, passing Niguel Road. In one-third mile, turn right into the South Coast Regional Civic Center. Park as directed by the signs. From the San Diego Freeway, exit south at Crown Valley Parkway. Drive 3.75 miles to Alicia Parkway and turn right. In 0.1 mile, turn left at the Civic Center.

Bring a filled water bottle, as there are no on-route public sources on the loop. If you plan to roam the side streets off Highlands Avenue or Pacific Island Drive, it might be wise to bring a detailed street map in addition to the tour map provided here.

TRIP DESCRIPTION: **Highlands Avenue.** Exit the Civic Center and turn left on Class II Alicia Parkway, cycling by Ivy Glenn Drive/Pacific Island Drive in about 0.1 mile. Pass a small shopping center just beyond, then cross Niguel Road (0.4) and pedal under the rows of trees. In 1.4 miles of easygoing biking in a nicely landscaped residential neighborhood, reach Highlands Avenue and turn left.

Immediately start a steep 0.8-mile climb with over-the-shoulder vistas that improve with each pedal. (Consider a diversion to Ridgeview Park for a grand look at the Aliso Creek Drainage and Wood Canyon.) Near the Niguel Road summit, an impressive Laguna Niguel panorama opens to the left (east). A modest downhill leads past Tamarron (2.5) and goes to Pacific Island Drive in another half mile.

Pacific Island Drive. Turn right and start an equally steep 1.1-mile climb below the hillside homes to the right. Pass Club House Drive (3.4) and take in the ever-improving sweeping vista to the left. At Belle Maison (3.7), the view is nothing short of tremendous! Pump another 0.3 mile to a crest and turn right at Talavera Drive. A short, mild pedal leads to Seaview Park, a grassy overlook with benches, following the curving road just below the Niguel Hill summit. While going from one end of the park to the other, the panorama shifts from northward to the Sheep Hills to westward into the Aliso Creek drainage and the ocean.

Return to Pacific Island Drive (4.6) and prepare for a swift coast on grades ranging from 7 to 10 percent. Glide between the hills on the downgrade in an area with

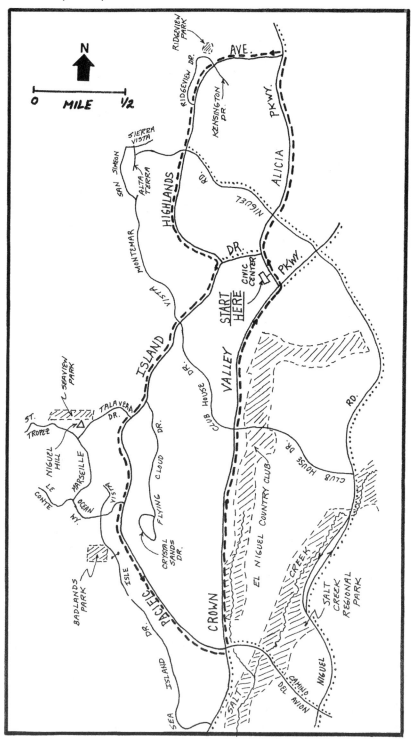

TRIP #39 - WESTSIDE LAGUNA NIGUEL

Seaview Park Looking East

relatively undeveloped hillsides, save for the scattered ridgetop homes on both sides. Pass Ocean Way (5.1) and reach a road segment where there are hillside-framed views while bicycling into Dana Point. Continue downhill through this lightly developed terrain, then pass a cluster of residences near Highcrest Road, just before reaching Crown Valley Parkway (6.2).

The Return Segment. Turn left (north) and bike a mild uphill in a well-manicured neighborhood with an abundance of trees. Pass West Nine Drive in 0.9 mile, then reach a crest 0.7 mile further near Paseo Del Niguel (7.8). Coast past Hill-hurst Drive before reaching Alicia Parkway at (8.3). Turn left and cycle 0.1 mile to the Civic Center.

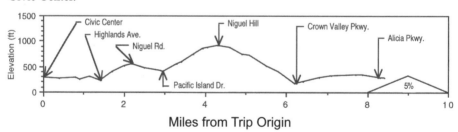

Miles from Trip Origin

Ride Extensions: There are several scenic diversions off the described route, in-cluding the Flying Cloud Drive, Isle Vista, and Vista Miramar areas in the hills. An-other option, which is more to extend trip mileage, is to add Niguel Road to the tour.

CONNECTING TRIPS: 1) Connection with the Laguna Niguel Bikeway (Trip #11) - the two trips share a common segment on Crown Valley Parkway; 2) connection with the Aliso Viejo Figure "8" (Trip #46) - at Highlands Avenue and Alicia Parkway, con-tinue north on the latter street.

TRIP #40 - HILLSIDE SAN CLEMENTE

GENERAL LOCATION: Capistrano Beach, San Clemente

LEVEL OF DIFFICULTY: **Northern Loop** - moderate
Distance - 9.7 miles
Elevation gain - periodic moderate grades; single steep
grade
Southern Loop - strenuous
Elevation gain - periodic moderate to very steep grades
Distance - 15.1 miles

HIGHLIGHTS: This San Clemente adventure plies two different parts of the city (on predominantly Class II roads). The two loops have been connected via Camino Vera Cruz since the original tour was designed.
Northern Loop. The loop heads inland using Avenida Vaquero and Camino De Los Mares and has a testy workout spur on Camino Vera Cruz. The area east of the freeway is hilly and particularly scenic, with the best views found at the current Camino Vera Cruz terminus. The return segment beyond Camino De Estrella is a pleasant down-hill with a nice coastal stretch along Camino Capistrano.
Southern Loop. This loop starts near the ocean at Ole Hanson Beach Club and heads north on Avenida Pico, the route's main thoroughfare. A steady 3.5-mile moderate climb is followed by a 0.9-mile coast to road's end at a private test facility. Next is a backtrack to Avenida La Pata and a scenic workout to Steed's Park at the San Diego County border. The next delight is a strenuous loop off of Avenida La Pata on Calle Del Cerro and Avenida Vista Montana. On the loop there are varied local hillside vistas and a single area with a long-distance view of Dana Point. The return from Avenida La Pata to the trip origin is a refreshing 3.4-mile downhill.

TRAILHEAD: **Northern Loop.** From the San Diego Freeway, exit south at Camino De Estrella and drive 0.5 mile to its terminus. Turn left (southeast) on Camino Capistrano and go 1.25 miles to Avenida Vaquero. Park in the shopping center on the latter street.
Southern Loop. Follow the "option" directions above, but continue past Avenida Vaquero on Camino Capistrano to El Camino Real. Turn left (southeast) and go one mile to Avenida Pico. Park at Ole Hanson Beach Club, which has limited tree shade, the club, and some nearby commercial refreshment stops.
Bring a couple of water bottles if doing both loops. We found no on-route public water sources on either loop. In a pinch, there are scattered commercial water sources on both loops.

TRIP DESCRIPTION: **Northern Loop.** From the shopping center, bike north on Class II Avenida Vaquero through a residential area. Cross the lower portion of the Shorecliffs Golf Course, pass Avenida San Gorgonio (a steep upgrade on this road leads to the like-named park, which has water, numerous facilities, and a great view) and go under the San Diego Freeway at (0.9). Continue on the long, mild upgrade and

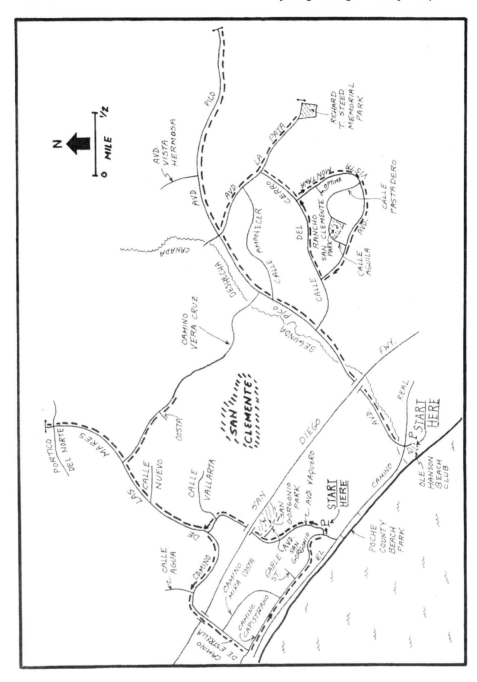

TRIP #40 - HILLSIDE SAN CLEMENTE

follow a sharp road curve left past Calle Vallarta while staring into the hills directly ahead. Cross the middle portion of the golf course just before reaching a "T"-junction at Camino De Los Mares (1.4).

Turn right (northeast) onto that Class II street and bike in residential environs while craning to view the hillside estates above and to the left. Just beyond Calle Nuevo (1.9) there is a Class I path on the east (right) side which transits a grassy tree-laden area with scattered benches, picnic areas, and sheltering pagodas. Pass Camino Vera Cruz (2.4) and cycle to the end of Camino De Los Mares (3.2).

Coast back to Camino Vera Cruz and turn right (southeast). (Skipping this segment turns the trip into an easy 7.6-mile ride.) Start climbing immediately and pass Costa at (4.6); in this area, the grade steepens dramatically. The good news is that the views also improve with each pump of the pedals. At the crest are excellent vistas of the city of San Clemente and the coast (5.1). From here, cyclists can continue southeast to Avenida Pico. However, for our tour, reverse the incoming route and enjoy the refreshing downhill back to Camino De Los Mares (6.1).

Turn left and cruise back to the intersection with Avenida Vaquero (7.1), then continue on the now-Class X roadway. Climb past Calle Agua and a shopping complex in half a mile, reaching a crest near Camino El Molino (7.9). Follow a sharp bend left toward the ocean, where the road becomes Camino De Estrella, then cross over the San Diego Freeway.

Coast half a mile to Camino Capistrano and turn left. This road parallels El Camino Real but is on the bluffs above. Glide through a residential neighborhood with scattered peeks at the ocean between the bluffside homes. Beyond Gable Street, the road veers left and heads more steeply downhill to Avenida Vaquero and the trip start point (9.7).

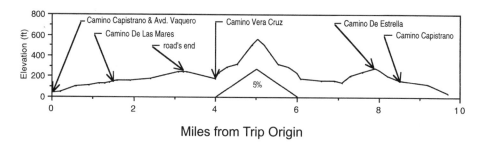

Miles from Trip Origin

Southern Loop. From Ole Hanson Beach Club, bike inland on Class III Avenida Pico and pass under the San Diego Freeway (0.7). Follow a short Class X section, then pass San Clemente High School and return to Class II roadway. Continue the modest climb and cross Calle Frontera/Avenida Presidio (1.1), Camino Vera Cruz (2.0), Avenida La Pata (2.5), and Avenida Vista Hermosa (3.0) in an area of rolling hills and numerous new housing developments. In another half mile there is a crest followed by a refreshing coast to the end of Avenida Pico at the Capistrano Test Site entrance (private) (4.4).

Backtrack to Avenida La Pata and turn east onto that Class II street. Pump steeply uphill past several high-tech businesses, enjoying a sweeping vista that improves with elevation. Pass Calle Del Cerro (6.9) and reach a crest in about a tenth of a mile. There is a manicured grassy area on the north side that is worth visiting just to take in the scenic panorama. Next enjoy a 0.7-mile mild coast to road's end at austere Richard T. Steed Memorial Park (7.7).

Repeat the incoming route to Calle Del Cerro (8.5) and turn uphill, climbing half a mile to Avenida Vista Montana. Head left and pump another 0.3 mile to a crest. From here are views to the surrounding electronics-bedecked hilltops and a breathtaking long-distance look into Dana Point and the harbor. Fly by Calle Pastadero (9.6), then make a decision near Calle Aguila (10.4). Uphill in a couple of hundred yards is San Clemente Park (water, restrooms, picnic areas, pagodas, children's playgrounds, basketball courts). If a rest stop is not in order, continue cruising down to Calle Del Cerro (10.7).

Another decision point! Make a left and coast down to Avenida Pico if "enough is enough!" (This cuts out the loop's most rugged hill climb and reduces total trip length to 12.6 miles.) However, the reference tour goes to the right and follows a 0.8-mile sheer uphill through an upscale neighborhood to Avenida Vista Montana, then passes over a nearby crest.

From this point, "life is good!" Freewheel downhill to Avenida La Pata, turn left and coast all the way to Avenida Pico, the Southern Loop's main thoroughfare (12.6). Turn left again and repeat the incoming route, returning to Ole Hanson Beach Club at (15.1).

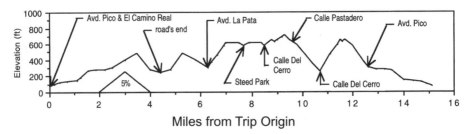

Miles from Trip Origin

CONNECTING TRIPS: Connection with the Doheny/San Clemente Bike Route (Trip #14) - from the origin of either the Northern Loop or Southern Loop, bike to El Camino Real.

TRIP #41 - TUSTIN RANCH LOOP

GENERAL LOCATION: Tustin

LEVEL OF DIFFICULTY: Loop - moderate
Distance - 8.0 miles
Elevation gain - steady moderate grades

HIGHLIGHTS: This is a moderate workout completely on Class II bikeway. Starting from Cedar Grove Park, cyclists climb to Jamboree Road, then enjoy a three-mile runout. The loop is closed with a flat segment on Alton Parkway and finishes with a steady climb on Tustin Ranch Road. Cyclists can link a 3.9-mile ride to the basic loop using the Class I Peters Canyon Bikeway.

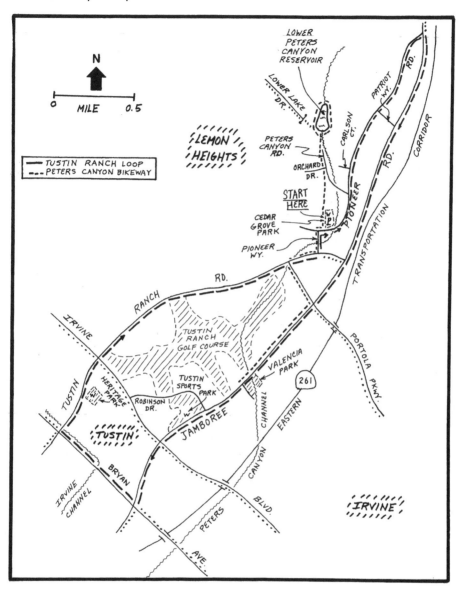

TRIP #41 - TUSTIN RANCH LOOP

TRAILHEAD: From the Santa Ana Freeway, exit northeast at Jamboree Road and drive 2.25 miles to Tustin Ranch Road. Turn left, go a quarter of a mile and turn right at Pioneer Way. In less than a quarter of a mile, turn right on Pioneer Road and proceed about 100 yards to the Cedar Grove Park entrance. From the Eastern Transportation Corridor (State Highway 261), take the Portola Parkway turnoff west and motor half a mile to Tustin Ranch Road. Turn right and go a quarter of a mile to Pioneer Way, then turn left. Proceed as described above.

Bring a light water supply, as there are two strategically located parks along the route. Cedar Grove Park, at the trip origin, has restrooms, water, limited tree shade, a children's playground, and bikeways/walkways. A section of Peters Canyon Bikeway is on the western perimeter, as described in the **Spur Trip Option** below.

TRIP DESCRIPTION: **Pioneer Road.** Leave the park and turn left on Pioneer Road, beginning a 1.4-mile moderate climb. This residence-lined Class II road passes Carlson Court (0.5) and Patriot Way (0.9) on the way up. The hills to the left separate the residential community from Peters Canyon, a superb off-road biker and hiker area. Turn right onto Class II Jamboree Road and observe State Highway 261 which is above and parallels this road to the left.

The Jamboree Road Downgrade. Enjoy the moderate three-mile downgrade that takes cyclists to the southern edge of the loop. Once on this main thoroughfare, there is a long series of walls which block off the nearby residential sections. Near (2.6), pockets of residences appear on the left as the freeway pulls away to the east.

Pass Tustin Ranch Road in 0.4 mile and Portola Parkway 0.3 mile beyond, taking in the bikeway and separate equestrian path to the right. The cycling path is part of the Peters Canyon Bikeway. At (3.9) is the Tustin Ranch Golf Course; the Tustin Sports Park (numerous athletic fields, water, restrooms) is reached at Robinson Drive (4.3). Pass Irvine Boulevard and the beginning of The Market Place, a very large shopping complex, before cruising to Bryan Avenue (5.0).

The Return Segment. Turn right on this Class II street and cross over the Irvine Channel, meeting Tustin Ranch Road in 0.6 mile. Turn right onto another Class II route, recross the Irvine Channel and begin climbing a steady moderate grade past Heritage Park (water, restrooms, limited tree cover, picnic/barbecue area, children's playground). Cross Irvine Boulevard (6.2) and continue the climb through residential environs, passing the Tustin Ranch Golf Club entry at (6.9). Cross Portola Parkway and parallel a stretch of the Peters Canyon Bikeway, continuing the sustained upgrade until (7.7). Reach a crest and turn left at Pioneer Way just beyond. A short flat pedal leads to a right turn at Pioneer Road and a nearby return to the Cedar Grove Park entry (8.0).

Excursion: Spur Trip Option. Bike to the west side of Cedar Grove park and take the wood-fenced Peters Canyon Bikeway northward (staying out of the paralleling dirt path which is reserved for equestrians). Follow the path as it comes along Peters Canyon Road, passes a small school, then ends in about 200 yards from the Orchard Drive crossing (about half a mile from Pioneer Road). Pedal or walk through a couple hundred feet of crushed gravel and head for the north side of the Peters Canyon Lower Reservoir. Bike around the paved head of the reservoir to a junction with the unpaved (dirt) Peters Canyon Bike Trail entry, where there is a porta-potty. Unless you have a fat-tire bike, return south via the paved trail on the east side of the reservoir, which outlets near the small school on Peters Canyon Road. Return south to Pioneer Road (1.1).

To continue on the bikeway's southern section, follow the bikeway and paralleling horse trail right at Pioneer Road, cross the street and follow Pioneer Way 200 yards to Tustin Ranch Road. Turn right and coast 0.2 mile to Portola Parkway, then go left. Pass along the Tustin Ranch Golf Course and continue 0.3 mile to Jamboree Road. Turn right and coast another 0.7 mile to Trevino Drive where the trail ends. The up-and-back on the southern section totals 2.6 miles and the total bikeway tour is 3.9 miles.

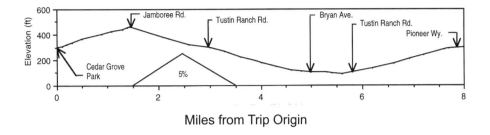

Miles from Trip Origin

CONNECTING TRIPS: 1) Connection with the Irvine Bikeway (Trip #8) - at Jamboree Road and Irvine Boulevard, cycle southeast 1.75 miles on State Highway 261 to Yale Avenue; 2) connection with the Lemon Heights Loop (Trip #45) - at the Peters Canyon Bikeway terminus on the reservoir's west side, veer left and pass through a locked gate, then bike on what is now (paved) Lower Lake Drive northwest to Lemon Heights Drive.

TRIP #42 - OSO VIEJO PARK

GENERAL LOCATION: Mission Viejo

LEVEL OF DIFFICULTY: Up and back - moderate
Distance - 4.4 miles
Elevation gain - periodic moderate grades

HIGHLIGHTS: This is actually a tour through a collection of side-by-side parks, of which Oso Viejo Park is the centerpiece. Most of the ride is on Class I trail through lush treed environs, and it passes through Pavion Park, Jeronimo Greenbelt Park, Oso Viejo Park, and World Cup Center Park. Our personal favorite segment is the "high road" through the greenbelt. Besides the pleasant park visits, there are numerous different looks at Oso Creek and its creekside attractions (such as the Butterfly Garden), as well as excellent distant views of Mount Saddleback.

TRAILHEAD: From the San Diego Freeway, exit east at La Paz Road and drive 2.5 miles to road's end at Olympiad Road. Turn left (north) and go one mile to Jeronimo Road, then turn left again. At the next road on the left (Pavion), turn left and find parking within Pavion Park. The park has water fountains, limited tree cover, athletic fields, a children's play area, benches, and a few barbecues.

From the Foothill Transportation Corridor (State Highway 241), exit west at Santa Margarita Parkway, then turn southwest in 1.25 miles on Alicia Parkway. Motor another 1.25 miles to Olympiad Road and turn right (south), then turn left at Pavion, the first street.

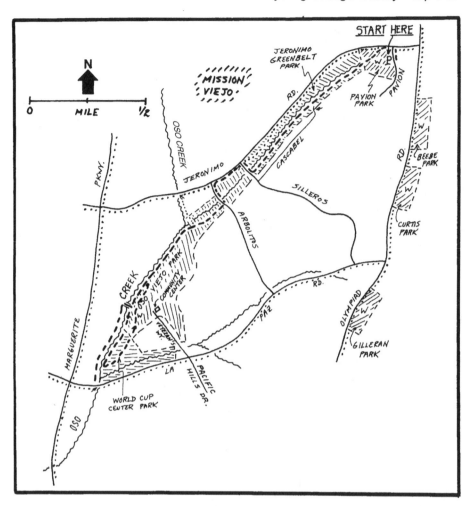

TRIP #42 - OSO VIEJO PARK

<u>**TRIP DESCRIPTION**</u>: **Outgoing Route.** Bike along the park periphery on Pavion to Jeronimo Road and turn left. In a short distance, take the Class I trail that leads away from the street. It passes along the park's northern edge and a fenced school playground. Follow an up-and-down path through this lovely treed section below the hillside residences and take in the lush creek drainage below. This is the Jeronimo Greenbelt Park. Pass the path entry from Cascabel (0.7) and follow the roller-coaster trail to a point where it crests, then continue as it descends steeply to Silleros (1.1).

Bike down to Jeronimo Road, turn left and parallel that street on a widened walkway which is a also a Class I path. Turn left on Arbolitos in 0.2 mile and follow the signed path through a residential area; here, the creek through the greenbelt merges with Oso Creek, and the route officially becomes the "Oso Creek Trail." An option is to continue on Jeronimo Road to Oso Creek and follow the signed path down to the creek. Turn left (south) and cross the bridge over the feeder creek to rejoin the Oso Creek Trail. (Due to construction, only the former option was available in the Winter of 2000.)

Follow this classy, wooden-fence-lined trail below the hillside residences above on the left and right. Note the many plantings which are part of a concerted effort to restore this creekside area to its former grandeur. Pass the walk/bike uphill entry to Oso Viejo Park and reach a small bridge over the creek just beyond (1.7). Continue on the creek's east side toward the marked World Cup Center Park entry and follow the signed bikeway/walkway as it switchbacks up to the grassy open fields of the park. Turn back north and cycle through Oso Viejo Park with porta-potties, a children's play area, benches, barbecue facilities, and the Norman P. Murray Community Center (2.0).

At this juncture there are two options to return to the bridge across Oso Creek. One is to retrace the incoming route, while another is to find the Oso Viejo Park walk/bike entry and take that trail back down to Oso Creek. Once there, cross over the bridge and turn left (southwest), cycle past the "Oso Creek Trail Butterfly Garden" and continue to the La Paz Road underpass (2.4). This is the nominal trip turnaround point, since the trail is packed dirt and gravel from La Paz Road to its end at Marguerite Parkway.

Return Route. Return along the Oso Creek Trail and Jeronimo Road to Silleros. Note that there are several excellent head-on views of Mount Saddleback when biking in this direction. The best workout is to retrace the incoming route on the "high road." Less-motivated souls can bike on the Class I "low road" which follows a short paved trail along the creek and then returns to the Class I sidewalk trail along Jeronimo Road for the trip's remainder. (Jeronimo Road also has a signed Class II bike route as yet another option.) The total trip mileage for all options is about 4.4 miles.

CONNECTING TRIPS: 1) Connection with the Mission Viejo Bikeway (Trip #30) - at trip's end at La Paz Road, bike west to Marguerite Parkway; 2) connection with the Arroyo Trabuco Loop (Trip # 50) - from Pavion Park, bike east on La Paz to Olympiad.

"High Road" in Jeronimo Greenbelt Park

TRIP #43 - YORBA LINDA BITS N' PIECES

GENERAL LOCATION: Yorba Linda

LEVEL OF DIFFICULTY: Loop - very strenuous
Distance - 23.6 miles
Elevation gain - periodic sheer grades

HIGHLIGHTS: Why "Bits and Pieces?" Because we pieced together three different and separate climbs, in the hills north of Yorba Linda, into a single ride. (It is a "bit" of a quadriceps burner besides!) The full ride is only for serious "hillies" in excellent shape or "advanced poke-alongs" like us who gut it out but always eventually get there. (Besides, we book authors need to stop frequently for elevation readings!) The rewards are an excellent aerobic workout and some serious panoramic views spread throughout the ride.

The tour is a mix of Class I, Class II, and Class X, although most of the latter sections are on lightly traveled roadway. There are options to do a single climb on Fairmont Boulevard, two climbs including Hidden Hill Road, or the full three-climb ride which adds Camino de Bryant. The key decision points for these options are noted in the detailed trip writeup.

TRAILHEAD: From the Riverside Freeway, exit north at Weir Canyon Road and drive into Yorba Linda, where the street becomes Yorba Linda Boulevard. In 3.5 miles from the freeway exit, turn right (north) on Fairmont Boulevard, then left on Cordova Lane in half a mile to reach the Fairmont Knolls Park access. The park has scattered benches under light tree cover, grassy knolls, and tennis courts. Another option is to park in the small shopping center on the northwest corner of Yorba Linda Boulevard and Fairmont Boulevard.

Bring a couple of quarts of water, particularly on hot days. Beyond San Antonio Park, easily accessible public sources were nonexistent on the eastern portion of the tour.

TRIP DESCRIPTION: **Fairmont Road Climb.** Leave the park, head left (northeast) and begin an immediate climb, with residences to the right and open hillsides to the left. The Class II roadway disappears, although the horse trails which pervade this general territory continue. There are over-the-shoulder views into Santa Ana Canyon and across to the Anaheim Hills area. The residences increase in both size and grandeur on the way up to the local summit; this is a general characteristic of the entire tour.

In 1.1 miles near Rim Crest Drive, the upgrade gives way to a flat and subsequent downhill. This brief respite gives way to a steeper 0.9-mile climb to a crest just before reaching San Antonio Road (2.3). Coast downhill and enjoy the view of the Santa Ana River floodplain, reaching View Park Drive and San Antonio Park at (3.0). The park has water, restrooms, limited shade, recreation fields, an equestrian staging area and peripheral trail, modest picnic/barbecue facilities, and a children's playground.

Continue the downhill to Yorba Linda Boulevard and turn left on that busy Class X (with wide shoulder) road (3.75). A more-moderate downgrade leads past Via de La

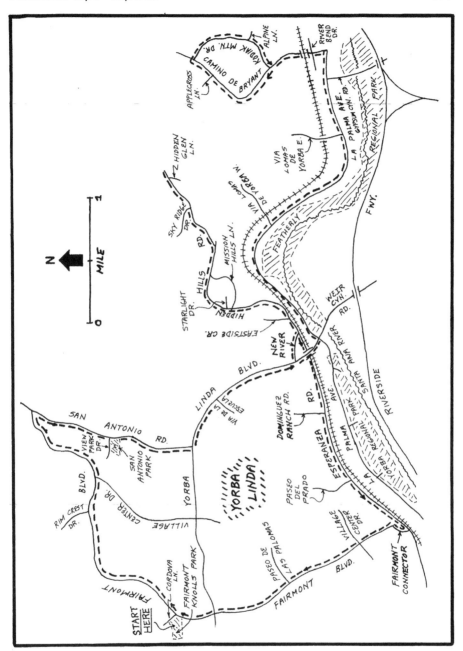

TRIP #43 - YORBA LINDA BITS N' PIECES

Escuela (4.2) to New River in another 0.7 mile. Turn left and take that curving street 0.3 mile to Esperanza Road; there is a shopping center across the street. By turning left at this junction, cyclists can return to Fairmont Knolls Park as described in **The Return Leg** below. The single-climb option is a total of 9.2 miles.

Hidden Hills Road Climb. Turn left and take a short easy pedal alongside railroad tracks and above the Santa Ana River floodplain, passing scattered commercial complexes. Just beyond Eastside Circle (5.4) the road bends left and becomes Hidden Hills Road. The grade steepens, starting the 1.9-mile, toughest climb of the full tour. Grind upward past Starlight Drive (6.0), then make a hard left in 0.5 mile at a short flat to stay on Hidden Hills Road (staying straight leads to a visible dead-end).

While sucking air, take in the impressive well-spaced residences to the right and less-developed hillsides to the left. At 7.0 is Sky Ridge Drive where sweeping southerly views of Santa Ana Canyon and its hillside backdrop open majestically. In another 0.4 sweaty mile is Hidden Glen Lane and the current road's end. (The road may be extended eastward to connect with Camino de Bryant in the future.) Enjoy the magnificent panoramic vista for a spell, then spin down the road and retrace the incoming route to Esperanza Road and New River (9.8). If you opt out of the final climb, continue west on Esperanza Drive. The double-climb option is a total of 13.8 miles.

Camino de Bryant Climb. Turn right on New River and make the short climb to Yorba Linda Boulevard. Turn left and pedal 0.3 mile to La Palma Avenue, then make another left. An easy 2.1-mile cruise on a Class I bikeway alongside the Santa Ana River floodplain leads to a sharp left turn, where the street name changes to Camino de Bryant. On the La Palma Avenue segment is Via Lomas de Yorba West (11.2), Via Lomas de Yorba East, a small shopping complex, and Gypsum Canyon Road (12.8). Cyclists must exit the Class I path to follow Camino de Bryant.

Pass Riverbend Drive, then bike under the railroad overpass (13.4) and follow a steepening upgrade. Pump past Kodiak Mountain Drive in another 0.3 mile and note the large plush residences scattered alongside the road. There are excellent vistas in this sheer-climb area and opportunities to take "Lookie Lou" breaks. Reach a heaven-sent flat near Applecross Lane and cycle a short distance to Kodiak Mountain Drive (14.6). A steep 0.5-mile coast leads past Alpine Lane, and this area has a particularly clear look at the Eastern Transportation Corridor across the canyon.

At the intersection with Camino de Bryant (15.5), turn left and coast back to La Palma Avenue, then retrace the incoming route to Yorba Linda Boulevard (19.1). Go right, then right again at New River, returning to Esperanza Road (19.6).

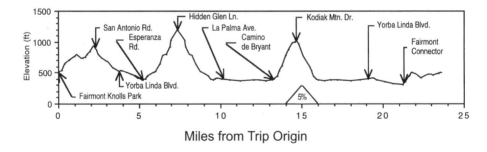

Miles from Trip Origin

The Return Leg. Pedal under Yorba Linda Boulevard and continue west on the Class I bikeway on the street's north side. Pass Dominguez Ranch Road (20.1) and Paseo Del Prado (20.6) before reaching Fairmont Connector at (21.2). Turn right and climb to road's end at Fairmont Boulevard in 0.2 mile. Turn left and continue the climb on the Class X road with paralleling horse trails.

Pass by Paseo de Las Palomas at (22.8) and the Class I trail to the right which plies Kingsbriar Park just beyond (see Trip #22). Enjoy a short downhill on a suddenly emerging Class II roadway, then cross Yorba Linda Boulevard at (23.1). A modest uphill leads back to Cordova Lane and Fairmont Knolls Park (23.6).

CONNECTING TRIPS: 1) Connection with the Santa Ana River Trail (Trip # 17A) - at La Palma Avenue and Yorba Linda Boulevard, go west on the former street and enter Yorba Regional Park, then bike toward the river; 2) connection with the El Cajon Trail (Trip #22) - the trips share a common segment on Esperanza Road east of Fairmont Connector; 3) connection with the Santa Ana Canyon Road ride (Trip #25) - bike south across the Santa Ana River on either Yorba Linda Boulevard (becomes Weir Canyon Road) or Gypsum Canyon Road.

TRIP #44 - ANAHEIM HILLS

GENERAL LOCATION: Anaheim Hills, Orange

LEVEL OF DIFFICULTY: Loop - strenuous
Distance - 14.2 miles
Elevation gain - periodic steep-to-sheer grades

HIGHLIGHTS: This roller-coaster ride in the Peralta Hills is essentially a tour of the plush Anaheim Hills residential area. The tour is primarily on Class X roadway and has several hearty well-spaced climbs reserving it for well-experienced in-traffic cyclists in good condition. The payoffs are the healthy workout itself, the grand scenic panoramas scattered through the trip, and the pleasant residential surroundings. Traffic is relatively light during non-rush-hour weekday periods and weekends.

TRAILHEAD: From the Costa Mesa Freeway southbound, use the Lincoln Avenue/ Nohl Ranch Road exit which lets out at Tustin Boulevard across from Eisenhower Park/The Brickyard. Go south, cross Lincoln Avenue and turn right into the Park and Ride area just beyond. Northbound traffic should use the same exit, which puts traffic onto Santiago Boulevard. Go north a few hundred feet and turn left onto Lincoln Avenue, then turn left onto Tustin Avenue and enter the Park and Ride area.

Another option is to start the ride from Eisenhower Park. There is parking to the west (Lincoln Avenue to Ocean View Avenue and right on Main Street) and north (Lincoln Avenue to Ocean View Avenue and right on Bixby Avenue). This is a pleasant, shaded little park with a small lake, picnic benches, play areas, a mini-barnyard, and a bikepath to boot! The park sits right next to The Brickyard, a shopping plaza. There is a fine restaurant with a verandah area that looks out over the lake; it's a great place to end the trip.

Bring a filled water bottle to see you through the hardest hill climbs. There is easily accessible water at Imperial Park, Oak Park, and Canyon Rim Park. Those parks are strategically placed along the route.

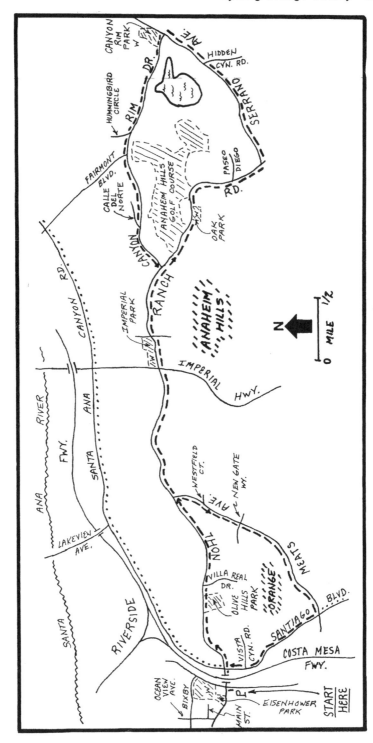

TRIP #44 - ANAHEIM HILLS

TRIP DESCRIPTION: **Nohl Ranch Road.** Bike east under the Costa Mesa Free-way where Lincoln Avenue becomes Nohl Ranch Road. Almost immediately there is a steep one-mile climb through well-manicured residential environs on Class X roadway with little or no shoulder. These local features are characteristic of those found on most of the ride. On the way up is Olive Hills Park off of Nohl Canyon Road (tennis courts, porta-potties, no water), then Villa Real Drive (0.9). The first of many views into the Santa Ana River floodplain, Yorba Linda, and the frontal Chino Hills opens up in this area. A nice coast takes cyclists past Meats Avenue (1.8) which will be part of the trip's second major loop.

An extended downhill with a couple of small rises leads to Imperial Highway and Imperial Park (3.0) which has water, a porta-potty, trees, grassy grounds, recreation fields, a children's playground, and a scenic northward vista. More of the same terrain takes cyclists past Anaheim Hills Road and a small shopping center at (3.8), and a local low elevation point at Canyon Rim Road in 0.1 mile.

The Eastside Loop. The eastside loop is essentially a ride on the Anaheim Hills Golf Course periphery. Climb past the western edge of those grounds, the Ana-heim Hills Saddle Club, and tiny Oak Park with its magnificent old oaks, water foun-tain, and benches. Then begin a 0.4-mile sheer pumpathon to a much flatter uphill near Paseo Diego (5.2). In 0.2 mile is Serrano Avenue.

Turn left and mostly climb through additional well-maintained residential areas, enjoying the views which reopen to the Santa Ana River, Yorba Linda, and the hills beyond. In 1.6 miles is Canyon Rim Road (7.0) and a turn left, unless a stop at Canyon Rim Park is needed. (The entry to the park, which has a restroom, limited shade, benches, barbecues, sports fields, and a children's play area, is accessed a little further north on Serrano Avenue.)

Now begins the start of a well-deserved downgrade. The scenic northward vistas are frequent on this road. Pass the Walnut Canyon Reservoir and revel in a particularly steep drop which starts near the Hummingbird Circle area. Pass under the mammoth power towers and power lines near Fremont Boulevard, then continue the glide past Calle Del Norte (8.7) back to Nohl Ranch Road.

The Westside Loop. Turn right and retrace the incoming route back to Meats Avenue (11.3). Turn left and pump a steep grade below the hillside homes in this nicely landscaped neighborhood. Near Westfield Court and beyond are sweeping vistas south to Orange, Villa Park, and Lemon Heights. Reach a summit near Newgate Way (11.9), then coast to Featherhill Drive, passing near some power towers and a seemingly out-of-place truck farm. In half a mile is Santiago Boulevard (13.0). Cycle on a flat Class II street, pass a small shopping center at Vista Canyon Road and reach Nohl Ranch Road at (14.0). Turn left and return to the Park and Ride zone in 0.2 mile.

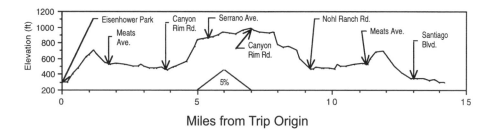

Miles from Trip Origin

West Side of Walnut Canyon Reservoir

Excursions: Weir Canyon Area Spur Trip. Cyclists can connect the trip with Weir Canyon Road by staying on Class II Serrano Avenue, bypassing Canyon Rim Road and turning right in 1.2 miles onto Class II Oak Canyon Drive. In another 0.6 mile is Weir Canyon Road. This leg has a drop in elevation of about 450 feet.

Walnut Canyon Reservoir Loop. There is a two-mile Class I trail which circumnavigates the reservoir. The circuit has several modest ups and downs plus a myriad of vistas of Anaheim Hills and distant places along the way. The bike and foot traffic is light and there is no access for motorized vehicles.

CONNECTING TRIPS: 1) Continuation with the Santa Ana Canyon Road ride (Trip #25) - at Nohl Ranch Road and Santiago Boulevard, go north on the latter street; 2) continuation with the Orange/Irvine Park tour (Trip # 26) - at Nohl Ranch Road and Santiago Boulevard, bike south on the latter street; 3) connection with the Santa Ana River Trail (Trip # 17B) - at Tustin Avenue and Lincoln Avenue, cycle west on the latter road across the Santa Ana River.

TRIP #45 - LEMON HEIGHTS SIGHTS

<u>GENERAL LOCATION</u>: Lemon Heights

<u>LEVEL OF DIFFICULTY</u>: Loop - moderate to strenuous
Distance - 6.1 miles
Elevation gain - two short, strenuous grades

<u>HIGHLIGHTS</u>: Though short on distance, this route is reserved for veteran bikers who are comfortable sharing narrow roadways with traffic and who like a challenging climb. The rewards for doing the winding Class X portion of the tour are the excellent vistas provided on both Skyline Drive and Foothill Boulevard. There is an extended stretch of roadway with views of Tustin and Irvine, Mount Saddleback, and Peters Canyon. A bonus is the myriad of upscale hillside homes that surround the route on its higher elevation segment.

<u>TRAILHEAD</u>: From the Santa Ana Freeway, exit northeast on Red Hill Avenue and drive 1.5 miles to Skyline Drive. Park under the trees to the south of the intersection, subject to posted laws. From the Eastern Transportation Corridor (State Highway 261), exit northwest on Irvine Boulevard, motor 1.5 miles to Red Hill Avenue and turn right. In half a mile is Skyline Drive.

Bring a quart of water on hot days. The single easily accessible source on the route is Bent Tree Park which has a water fountain, walkway/bikeway, tree shade, a children's play area, and a volleyball court.

<u>TRIP DESCRIPTION</u>: **The Workout.** Bike southeast through an upscale rural tree-lined neighborhood on Class X roadway. In half a mile, the straight-line street follows a curve to the left. The grade changes dramatically in another 0.2 mile just beyond Beverly Glen Drive, and bikers begin a strenuous 0.6-mile winding uphill to a summit near Foothill Boulevard. The shoulder is narrow and cyclists will have to work with the limited auto traffic on the climb. (Note that, at Beverly Glen Drive, a turn left is required to remain on Skyline Drive.)

At Wilding Road there is a three-way intersection where the reference route goes right on Foothill Boulevard/Skyline Drive (1.2). In a couple of hundred yards, Skyline Drive splits off to the left and we head right on Foothill Boulevard, reaching a crest just beyond. Cruise the next 1.5 miles on a sinuous roadway, mildly downhill, admiring the hillside estates and the panoramic vista that has Tustin and Irvine laid out below and Mount Saddleback in the distance. Foothill Boulevard becomes Lemon Heights Drive just beyond La Cuesta Drive (2.0). In the latter portion of this downhill stretch are scenic views into Peters Canyon and its upper reservoir.

At 0.2 mile beyond Sharon Lane (2.6) is a steep 0.4-mile climb. In this stretch, a left turn at Lower Lake Drive is required to stay on Lemon Heights Drive (2.9). A right turn leads to nearby Bent Tree Park. The road ends at a crest where cyclists turn right, rejoining Skyline Drive and enjoying an expanded road shoulder.

The Downhill Return. Enjoy additional looks at Peters Canyon and then coast by additional plush hillside residences before reaching Newport Avenue/Newport

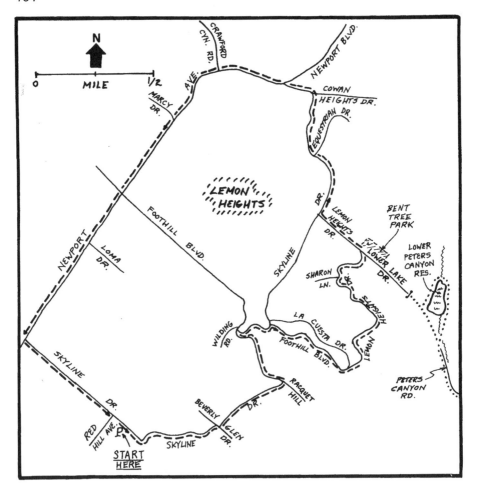

TRIP #45 - LEMON HEIGHTS SIGHTS

Boulevard (3.8). Turn left onto this busy Class X street and continue gliding the mild downhill through a pleasant (but less opulent) neighborhood. On this straight-line road, a marked Class II section appears near Marcy Drive (4.4).

Keep coasting past Foothill Boulevard (4.8) and reach Skyline Drive at (5.6). Turn left, returning to a smaller and tree-lined roadway on the flat. In half a mile after the turn is Red Hill Avenue.

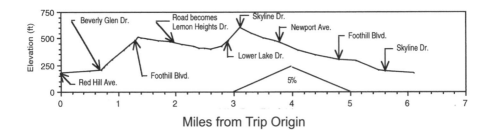

Lemon Heights Drive near Skyline Drive

CONNECTING TRIPS: Connection with the Tustin Ranch Loop (Trip #41) - at Lower Lake Drive, turn right and coast 0.9 mile to pavement's end. Pass through the locked gate, cross a short section of crushed rock, then bike south on Peters Canyon Road to the Class I Peters Canyon Bikeway on the west (right) side of the road.

TRIP #46 - ALISO VIEJO FIGURE "8"

GENERAL LOCATION: Aliso Viejo

LEVEL OF DIFFICULTY: Dual loop - moderate
Distance - 8.2 miles
Elevation gain - steady moderate grade on Pacific
Park Drive

HIGHLIGHTS: This 100 percent Class II ride wanders in the form of a double loop through the heart of Aliso Viejo. From a low point near the Aliso Creek drainage, cyclists work over to Pacific Park Drive and tackle a testy but scenic upgrade to a panoramic crest. Not long after crossing State Highway 73 on a portion of the long and vista-laden downhill, bikers meet Aliso Creek Road and follow it on a broad turn from north to east to return to the trip start point. A fun spur trip on Wood Canyon Road is also provided.

TRAILHEAD: From the San Joaquin Hills Transportation Corridor (State Highway 73), exit south at La Paz Road and drive 1.25 miles to Aliso Creek Road. Turn right and

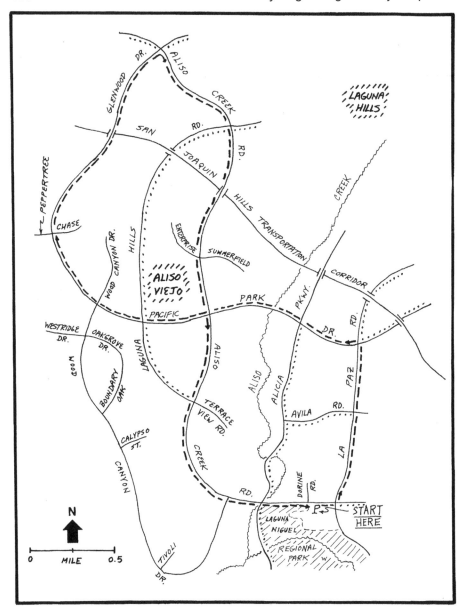

TRIP #46 - ALISO VIEJO FIGURE "8"

go a couple hundred yards to the Aliso Village shopping center entrance on the south side of the street. From the San Diego Freeway, go west at Oso Parkway, pass under State Highway 73 (the street becomes Pacific Park Drive) and continue a quarter of a mile to La Paz Road. Proceed left (south) one mile and turn right at Aliso Creek Road.

An alternate is to start from Laguna Niguel Regional Park. Bike north on the park path leading to the intersection of Aliso Creek Road and La Paz Road, then turn north on the latter street. (Refer to the Trip #29B detail map.)

Bring a light water supply. There are shopping plazas and centers scattered throughout the route; however, we did not find any convenient on-route public water sources.

TRIP DESCRIPTION: **Outwardbound and Upward.** Leave the shopping center and bike 0.2 mile to La Paz Road. Turn left (north) and bike past an interesting collection of commercial centers, residential sections, and modern industrial complexes. Pass Avila Road at (0.7) and proceed to Pacific Park Road in 0.4 mile.

Turn left, cycle past the large Plaza De La Paz shopping complex and cross Alicia Parkway at (1.5). Pass over the Aliso Creek watershed and bike through a residential development, reaching Aliso Creek Road in half a mile from Alicia Parkway. Start a steady mild climb past Wood Canyon Drive (2.75) and take in the over-the-shoulder views of Aliso Creek and the surrounding metropolis. Also notice the line of large residences on the ridge to the left and above. The vista only improves for the next three quarters of a mile of steady pumping on the trip's steepest grade. The road swings gradually north and reaches a crest near Chase/Peppertree (3.3).

Closing the Figure "8." Coast past a large residential complex below and to the right, taking the time to enjoy the panoramic views on the downgrade. Pass over State Highway 73 (the road is now named Glenwood Drive) and seemingly reenter the world of light industrial and commercial enterprises. At (4.6) is Aliso Creek Road and a turn right. The remainder of the tour will be on this street.

The downhill steepens and the views to the Aliso Creek drainage and surrounding cities continue. Pass the Laguna Hills Drive northern segment (5.3) and yet another shopping center, then recross State Highway 73 and pedal on flattening terrain past the mammoth Aliso Viejo Town Center. Cross Pacific Park Drive and make a short climb, reaching a crest at Laguna Hills Road South/Terrace View Road (7.0). Coast over Aliso Creek and reach Alicia Parkway at (7.9). In another 0.3 mile is the entry to Aliso Village shopping center.

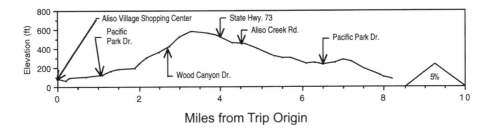

Miles from Trip Origin

Excursion: **Wood Canyon Road Spur Trip.** Wood Canyon Road is a Class X ride and is off the beaten track, below the Sheep Hills and above Wood Canyon. The most interesting segment is the predominantly residential 2.3-mile stretch south of Pacific Park Drive. Just south there are sweeping views of lower Aliso Viejo and Laguna Niguel. A short climb to Westridge Drive/Oak Grove Drive gives way to a brief coast to Boundary Oak. There are superb views to the nearby hillside homes, Wood Canyon, and the Sheep Hills, the latter two being within the Aliso and Wood Canyons Regional Park area. On the last downhill mile to Aliso Creek Road are the most impressive looks into Wood Canyon.

CONNECTING TRIPS: 1) Connection with the Laguna Niguel Bikeway (Trip #11) - at Aliso Creek Road and La Paz Road, take the former street south to Crown Valley Parkway; 2) connection with the O'Neill Regional Park tour (Trip #28) - turn into the park entrance on Trabuco Canyon Road; 3) connection with the southern segment of the Aliso Creek Trail (Trip #29B) - at Aliso Creek Road and Alicia Parkway, go west on the former road to the Aliso Creek Trail entry; 4) connection with the Laguna Hills Loop (Trip #31) - at Aliso Creek Road and Glenwood Drive, bike west on the former road to El Toro Road; 5) connection with the Westside Laguna Niguel tour (Trip #39) - at Aliso Creek Road and Alicia Parkway, bike south one mile on the latter street.

TRIP #47 - CITIES AND CANYONS

GENERAL LOCATION: Mission Viejo, Rancho Santa Margarita,
                                     Trabuco Canyon, Live Oak Canyon

LEVEL OF DIFFICULTY: Loop - strenuous
                                      Distance - 13.2 miles
                                      Elevation gain - periodic moderate grades;
                                          steep grade in Live Oak Canyon

HIGHLIGHTS: This is a trip reserved for cyclists with the strong legs and experience riding narrow roads shared with auto traffic. It plies the cities of Mission Viejo and Rancho Santa Margarita, then dives into Trabuco Canyon and climbs steeply out of Live Oak Canyon. The return leg beyond the trip summit at Old Stage Road is essentially a four-mile runout back to the start point at Pinecrest Park. The canyons segment is especially scenic, with cyclists riding for miles under the oak-dominated tree cover.

TRAILHEAD: From the San Diego Freeway, exit north on El Toro Road and proceed five miles to Santa Margarita Parkway. Turn right (southeast) and drive half a mile to the Pinecrest Park entry at Pinecrest. From the Foothill Transportation Corridor (State Highway 241), exit south at Santa Margarita Parkway and go 1.5 miles to Pinecrest. The grassy park lies within the Oso Creek floodplain just to the east and below Pinecrest. It has water, tree shade, bikeways/walkways, recreation fields, and a children's play area, but no restrooms.

Though a relatively short ride, bring at least a quart of water to see you through the climbs. Within O'Neill Park there are restrooms and water which are available to cyclists without an entry fee, but few other convenient public sources.

TRIP DESCRIPTION: **City Ride.** Join Class II Santa Margarita Parkway heading eastbound and climb to a crest in a residential zone at Promenade (0.8). A 0.9-mile coast leads past Alicia Parkway to a nearby low point and a passage over the Arroyo Trabuco, initiating a modest climb of three miles to Antonio Parkway. Proceed by the first of Santa Margarita Parkway's plethora of shopping centers and pass over State Highway 241 at (2.8).

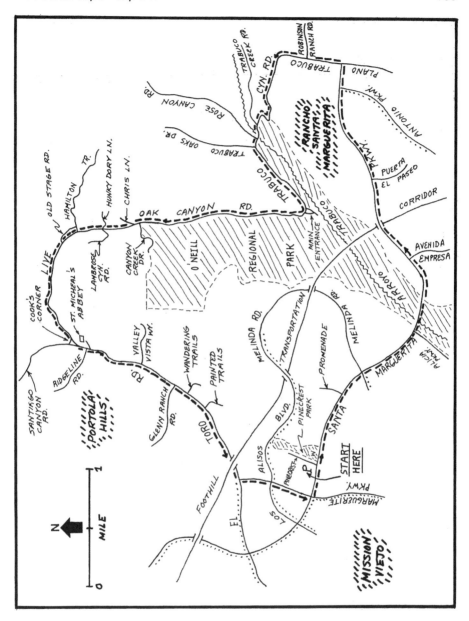

TRIP #47 - CITIES AND CANYONS

Pedal closer to the base of Mount Saddleback and reach Antonio Parkway at (4.1). Bike across that street and turn left in 0.2 mile at road's end onto Plano Trabuco. A mild 0.6-mile climb through a mix of residential properties and commercial complexes on this northbound stretch leads to a sharp left. At this local crest, the street name changes to Trabuco Canyon Road while the road remains Class X.

The Canyon Tour. Begin a winding dive toward Trabuco Creek (below and to the right) while stealing a glance at the dense stand of oaks to the left. Further down the narrow serpentine road, the tree cover begins to surround it. Shortly, the road straightens again and flattens in a more open area which holds Trabuco Creek. Nearby is unpaved Trabuco Creek Road (5.7).

After a short climb through a continuous tree canopy, begin a one-mile coast on continued narrow roadway alongside the eastern reaches of O'Neill Park and come to the main entrance at (8.6). (See Trip #28 for the park's features.) On what is now Live Oak Canyon Road, start the tough four-mile climb out of the canyon, probably working with an impatient driver or two on the way up. Pump up the wiggly route past the western park edge and through the sometimes dense and overhanging tree cover, passing scattered residences offset from the road.

Climb past Canyon Creek Drive (10.3) and note the thinning tree line just before reaching Hamilton Trail in 0.9 mile. Cyclists gain the summit in another 0.2 mile at Old Stage Road, where the road is now sun-exposed. In the distant hillsides ahead, the dense Portola Hills developments can be seen. A 0.9-mile runout through scattered residences and small farms follows, mostly on a more open and exposed roadway. At road's end is El Toro Road and Cook's Corner with its rustic bar/restaurant.

City Return. Turn left and take the Class I Aliso Trail described in Trip #29 or coast down Class II El Toro Road. Pass Ridgeline Road followed by the entry to Saint Michael's Abbey, bike a short uphill, then continue coasting below the Portola Hills homes on the ridge to the right. Aliso Creek is below and to the near right.

Glide past Valley Vista Way (10.7), Glenn Ranch Road (11.1), Wandering Trails (11.3), and Painted Trails (11.5), through this open territory before passing under State Highway 241 (12.0). Pass a shopping center, then turn left at Class II Marguerite Parkway at (12.2), reentering residential environs and continuing downhill. Bike left at Santa Margarita Parkway in 0.8 mile near a shopping complex, then coast to the Pinecrest Park entry at (13.2).

Live Oak Canyon Road near O'Neill Park

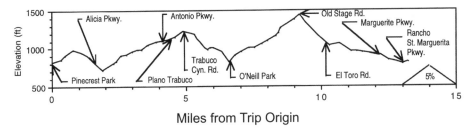

Miles from Trip Origin

Excursions: Rose Canyon Road and Trabuco Oaks Drive Spurs. An interesting spur just north of the Trabuco Creek crossing is Rose Canyon Drive. It climbs modestly uphill on a narrow roadway alongside Rose Canyon Creek, passing through a collection of rustic abodes in a rural setting. Tree cover is plentiful on this mile-plus side road. The accessible upper portion is signed private property.

A second and similar spur is Trabuco Oaks Road. Once past the Feed, Tackle and General Store and the venerable Trabuco Oaks Steak House (don't wear a tie to this excellent eatery unless you want to have it "modified"), this slim road climbs for just less than a mile to a gated and locked entry to private grounds. It follows the course of Hickey Canyon Creek through sections of dense, overhanging tree cover.

CONNECTING TRIPS: 1) Connection with the Santiago Canyon Road tour (Trip # 27) - the trips share a common segment on El Toro Road below Cook's Corner; 2) connection with the O'Neill Regional Park ride - turn into the park at the main entrance at the junction of Trabuco Canyon Road and Live Oak Canyon Road; 3) connection with the Aliso Creek Trail (Trip #29A) - take the Class I path on the west side of El Toro Road at Cook's Corner; 4) connection with the Mission Viejo Bikeway (Trip #30) - at Marguerite Parkway and Santa Margarita Parkway, continue south on the former street; 5) connection with the Arroyo Trabuco Loop (Trip #50) - the tours share a common segment on Santa Margarita Parkway between Alicia Parkway and Antonio Parkway.

TRIP #48 - SILVERADO CANYON

GENERAL LOCATION: Silverado Canyon (Cleveland National Forest)

LEVEL OF DIFFICULTY: Up and back - moderate to strenuous
Distance - 11.3 miles
Elevation gain - steady moderate grade beyond
Ladd Canyon Road

HIGHLIGHTS: This superb canyon ride is for experienced cyclists who are comfortable biking on Class X roadways with little or no shoulder. Note that traffic is light and the speed limit in most stretches is below 25 mph. The tour starts at the Silverado

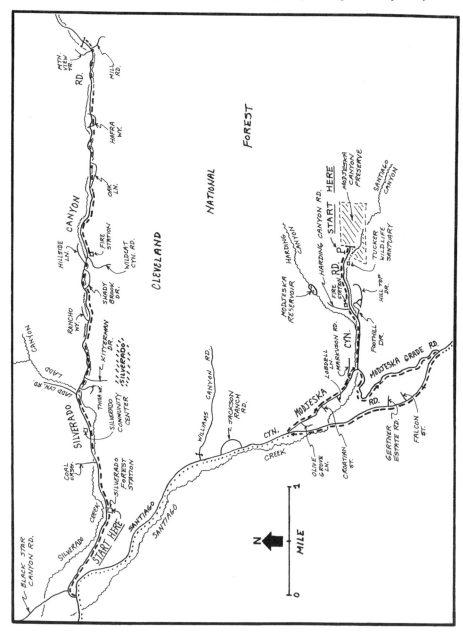

TRIP #48 - SILVERADO CANYON & TRIP #49 - MODJESKA CANYON

Forest Station and winds its way modestly up an ever-narrowing canyon about four miles to road's end. Residential pockets line the road, squeezed so tight to the canyon walls in the upper stretches that some homes are built directly over Silverado Creek. Interesting scenery and scattered overhanging tree cover are along the way, as well as cafés and a country store that are available for a pleasant rest stop.

TRAILHEAD: From Santiago Canyon Road, turn north on Silverado Canyon Road and go three quarters of a mile to the Silverado Forest Station. Bring a light water supply. There is a water fountain at the trip origin. Cafés, markets, and taverns are located along the road.

TRIP DESCRIPTION: Leave the parking area and turn right while noting the Silverado Creek floodplain to the left. Coast by the elegant Calvary Chapel of the Canyons and take in the nearby scrub-filled hillsides. Make the first of many creek crossings, then pass Ladd Canyon Road (1.1) on the beginning of a four-mile upgrade to road's end. The canyon walls begin to narrow and a mixed residential/commercial pocket opens beyond Thisa Way (love that name!). This area includes a restaurant with patio dining, a post office, and a second café (1.5).

The canyon narrows further and the road follows suit. Take note of the homes built with sections lying directly over the creek, and the scattered auto and walking bridges interspersed along Silverado Canyon Road. Pass beneath the overhanging tree cover near Shady Brook Drive (2.7) and reach the Silverado Fire Station just beyond. Then work the pedals past the Shady Brook Country Store and more scattered canyon-squeezed residences in the Hazel Bell Drive area.

Continue pedaling past scattered pockets of homes in the narrow canyon, reaching Belha Way (3.8) and cycling under another overhanging tree stand. Pass through a short undeveloped zone and cross Silverado Creek once again, where it shifts from the north to south side of the road. Drop slightly into a last residential pocket with a "Flooded during storm" sign and pass Mountain View Trail (4.7). In another 0.2 mile there is a metal gate where travel beyond is restricted to authorized vehicles. There is parking here for hikers and mountain bikers who have National Forest Adventure Passes and are planning to go further into the Cleveland National Forest.

Coast all the way back to the start point (9.7), then bike a relatively flat but winding stretch 0.8 mile to Santiago Canyon Road. A turnaround and return to the Silverado Forest Station makes cyclists veterans of the full canyon road (11.3).

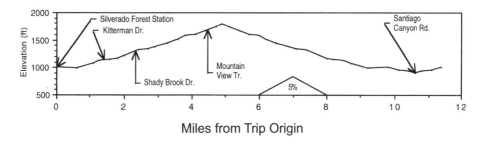

Miles from Trip Origin

Excursions: Additional Options. Cruise some of the side streets to get a better feel for the canyon area and lifestyle. There are particularly interesting areas off of Kitterman Drive and near Hazel Bell Drive.

CONNECTING TRIPS: Connection with the Santiago Canyon Road tour (Trip #27) - turn in either direction at the Silverado Canyon Road/Santiago Canyon Road intersection.

TRIP #49 - MODJESKA CANYON

GENERAL LOCATION: Modjeska Canyon (Cleveland National Forest)

LEVEL OF DIFFICULTY: Loop - moderate to strenuous; up and back on
                                      Modjeska Canyon Road - moderate
                          Distance - 6.2 miles (loop)
                          Elevation gain - single steep-to-sheer grade on
                                      Modjeska Grade Road (loop)

HIGHLIGHTS: This ride starts at Tucker Wildlife Sanctuary parking lot and cruises under the overhanging trees of the rural canyon environs to Modjeska Grade Road. A steep-to-sheer 0.8 mile climb on that street leads to a couple of excellent vantage points, then rockets down to Santiago Canyon Road. A short climb and refreshing downhill on that street leads to Santiago Canyon Road. Next is a short pedal through the treed lower Santiago Canyon Road residential area, a return to the Modjeska Grade Road intersection, and a backtrack to the start point.

The canyon and grade areas are Class X on narrow roadways with limited shoulder. However, because the road is somewhat winding and narrow, autos travel at slow speeds. (The locals are also very courteous.)

TRAILHEAD: From Santiago Road, exit at Modjeska Canyon Road and drive one mile to the Modjeska Grade Road junction. Turn left and go another mile to road's end at the Tucker Wildlife Sanctuary parking lot.

Bring a filled water bottle for Modjeska Grade Road on hot days. There is a single source of water at the store near Markuson Road.

TRIP DESCRIPTION: **Outgoing on Modjeska Grade Road.** Glide back down Modjeska Canyon Road on a mildly winding road that is 1.5 to 2 lanes wide. Santiago Creek is to the left and rural residences are scattered within the broad canyon. Pass Harding Canyon Road and veer left, then cross Santiago Creek (0.5). Continue through light residential environs and cycle under a light tree canopy before reaching a four-way junction: Modjeska Grade Road is left, the Modjeska Canyon Road continuation is right, and Shadowland Circle is sandwiched in-between (1.1).

Turn left and start an immediate steep climb on a winding road which turns west and reaches Canyon Heights Drive at (1.4). There is an impressive vista here that includes the Santiago Canyon Road area. The road switches sharply southward, the grade steepens, and cyclists pass alongside several ridgetop homes. Near Oriole Street and a set of power-line towers there is a crest with a commanding view southward to the Portola Hills area (1.9). Soar down the winding roadway another half mile to its terminus at Santiago Canyon Road.

Return on Modjeska Canyon Road. Turn right and bike a modest upgrade to Santiago Canyon Road's highest point, then coast below the ridgeline residences near Falcon Street and Gertner Estate Road (3.2). Pass a nursery/plant farm and recross Santiago Creek in another 0.6 mile. The wide floodplain of this creek emanating from

Modjeska Canyon is impressive. In another 0.4 mile is Modjeska Canyon Road and a turn to the right (4.2).

Start a modest climb through overhanging tree cover in a scattered residential area, mostly concentrated to the right. Pass Croatian Street in half a mile and stare ahead and above to the ridgeline estates that you passed on the Modjeska Grade portion of the tour. Enter a short, sun-exposed valley area, pass the Modjeska Country Store and recross Santiago Creek near Markuson Road (5.0). In another 0.1 mile is the junction with Modjeska Grade Road. Turn left and retrace the outgoing route back to Tucker Wildlife Sanctuary parking lot (6.2).

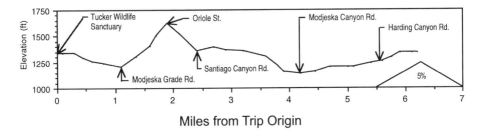

Miles from Trip Origin

Excursions: Additional Options. Cruise some of the side streets to get a better feel for this peaceful sylvan area. Best bets are in the Hill Top Drive and Harding Canyon Road areas.

CONNECTING TRIPS: Connection with the Santiago Canyon Road tour (Trip #27) - turn in either direction at the Modjeska Canyon Road/Santiago Canyon Road or Modjeska Grade Road/Santiago Canyon Road intersections.

TRIP #50 - ARROYO TRABUCO LOOP

GENERAL LOCATION: Mission Viejo, Rancho Santa Margarita,
                   San Juan Capistrano

LEVEL OF DIFFICULTY: Loop - strenuous
                      Distance - 27.1 miles
                      Elevation gain - periodic moderate-to-steep grades

HIGHLIGHTS: This predominantly Class II loop takes bikers around the lower reaches of Arroyo Trabuco before it fuses with Oso Creek in Mission Viejo. The route passes over the arroyo in the county area between Mission Viejo and Rancho Santa Margarita and in San Juan Capistrano. Antonio Parkway parallels its floodplain above Oso Parkway. The general tour includes three cities, the relatively undeveloped southern section of Antonio Parkway, a brief stretch of Ortega Highway, and a passage over San Juan

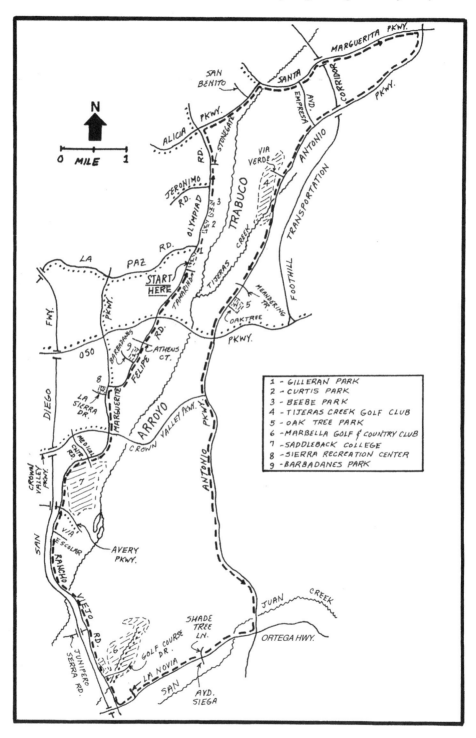

TRIP #50 - ARROYO TRABUCO LOOP

Creek. There are excellent vista points in both the cities and outland areas. There are no terrifying grades on this tour, but the 1600-plus feet of elevation gain will wear at your legs with time. There is an option to cut the mileage roughly in half using Oso Parkway as a connector.

TRAILHEAD: From the San Diego Freeway, go east at Oso Parkway and drive 1.75 miles to Felipe Road. Turn left and motor one mile to Gilleran Park entrance just north of Tamarind. From the Foothill Transportation Corridor (State Highway 241), exit west at Oso Parkway and proceed 2.25 miles to Felipe Road. Turn right and continue as described above. The park has water, restrooms, an awning-covered area for shade, and several athletic fields.

Bring a couple of quarts of water for hot days. There was one public park with water and restrooms (Oak Tree Park) directly on-route on the eastern half of the loop. Though commercial centers are plentiful on much of the ride, there were almost no "pit-stops" on Antonio Parkway below Oso Parkway or on most of the eastern section of Ortega Highway.

TRIP DESCRIPTION: **Gilleran Park to Antonio Parkway.** From the park exit, turn right and bike 0.2 mile to La Paz Road, where Class II Felipe Road becomes Olympiad Road. Pass Curtis and Beebe Parks, which are similar in design to Gilleran Park, then climb to a crest at Stonegate, enjoying the excellent panorama north and east (1.9). In another 0.4 mile is Alicia Parkway and a turn right (northeast).

Bike to a nearby crest, then cruise downhill on this Class II road, enjoying one of the many views of the Santa Ana Mountains and Mount Saddleback (the popular name for the combination of side-by-side Santiago and Modjeska Peaks). The terrain flattens at San Benito and cyclists reach Class II Santa Margarita Parkway at (3.5). Turn right, pass over the Arroyo Trabuco and continue the climb to Antonio Parkway. Proceed by the first of this street's shopping centers and pass over State Highway 241 at (4.6). Cycle closer to the base of Mount Saddleback and reach Antonio Parkway (5.9), making a right turn.

Antonio Parkway to Rancho Viejo Road. Surprisingly, this downhill-dominated segment starts with a short climb to the trip's summit. In the 5.6-mile section north of Oso Parkway, cyclists start through dense mixed residential/commercial development, then glide past mixed patches of development and open space. Pass over State Highway 241 again (7.6) and stare down into little Tijeras Canyon on the left.

Avenida Empresa comes up at (8.0), followed by the first peeks at the Tijeras Creek Golf Course and a transit over Tijeras Creek (9.6). In 1.3 miles is Meandering Trail; Oaktree, the entrance to Oak Tree Park, is 0.3 mile further. This was the single easy-access public park with water on the eastern half of the loop when we passed through. (It also has restrooms, athletic fields, and a covered patio area.) Oso Parkway follows in another 0.4 mile, best recognized by the sudden appearance of residential pockets and shopping complexes (11.7).

Antonio Parkway changes complexion beyond this cross-street, remaining Class II but passing through environs that are even more lightly developed, with Arroyo Trabuco paralleling to the right. There is a pocket of development near Crown Valley Parkway (12.8), then Arroyo Trabuco pulls away to the west and cyclists enter open spaces on a Class X roadway with wide shoulder. Near (14.3), Antonio Parkway follows a ridgeline,

Tijeras Canyon Crossing at Antonio Parkway

where there are open views of a successive line of hills, then the first looks at Ortega Highway below. The hillside residences of San Juan Capistrano come into sight and bikers pass over San Juan Creek at (15.7). In another half mile is Ortega Highway.

Turn right and cruise on this flatter Class X road, passing a nursery and recrossing San Juan Creek (15.7). As the shoulder narrows, cyclists have the option to bike on the wide walkway along the highway. (There are few stoplights and the intersections are lightly trafficked by cross traffic in this rural zone.) Pass a produce market at Shade Tree Lane/Avenida Siega (17.1), then enter a sparse rural residential area and cross La Novia Avenue (18.3). In 0.3 mile is Rancho Viejo Road at the lowest point of the tour.

Rancho Viejo Road to Gilleran Park. Turn right and climb uphill on a Class I path on the right side of the street, then pass the entry to the Marbella Golf and Country Club at Golf Club Drive (19.0). The road creeps next to the San Diego Freeway (as it will stay for the next three miles), passes through the first commercial area in a while and meets Junipero Serra Road at (19.9). In 0.6 mile, the Class I path leaves the roadside and passes over Arroyo Trabuco, then cyclists arrive at Via Escolar (21.6). (There is a Class I path that follows Arroyo Trabuco under the San Diego Freeway to the west side, as described in Trip #12.) This is the San Juan Capistrano/Mission Viejo boundary where there is a transition to Class II bikeway and the street name becomes Marguerite Parkway.

Cross Avery Parkway, climb past several shopping centers and bike alongside the Saddleback College campus, meeting College Drive/Medical Center Road at (23.0). In 0.1 mile is Hillcrest and an exceptional view northward to Mission Viejo. Coast to Crown Valley Parkway, then begin climbing again to La Sierra Drive (24.1). A turn left leads to the Sierra Recreation Center, which has public water and restrooms; however, other facilities are for members only. Another crest and pleasant downhill lead to Felipe Road where the route heads right.

Pass Barbadanes (left is Barbadanes Park with water, limited shade, grass, and a children's playground) (25.1) and pump uphill once again to a crest just beyond Athens Court in half a mile. Here is another broad vista point. Glide past Oso Parkway, start pumping uphill past Tamarind and return to the park entrance at (27.1).

Excursions: **Mini-Tour of the Arroyo Trabuco.** The northern and southern segments can be ridden separately using Class II Oso Parkway as the shortcut connector. The northern and southern loops are 14.6 miles and 12.5 miles in length, respectively. The southern loop requires a more skilled rider, as it passes through somewhat desolate surroundings having some Class X sections.

Horno Creek Trail. At the Marbella Golf and Country Club entrance at (19.0), the Class I path along Golf Club Drive follows the rough contour of Horno Creek. The one-way distance is 1.2 miles. Admittance is a courtesy. Cyclists are expected to respect bicycling rules of good conduct.

Trabuco Creek Trail. There is a Class I trail at the northern end of Antonio Parkway. Pass the trailside kiosk and bike north and west 0.25 mile, then follow El Camino Montana or enter O'Neill Regional Park's Mesa area at one of the fence entries. (See the Trip #28 Map for detail.) With the former option, the trail continues southwest under State Highway 241, on a bike/walk bridge. (It is two miles, one way.)

CONNECTING TRIPS: 1) Connection with the Laguna Niguel Bikeway (Trip #11) - at College Drive/Medical Center Road, bike northwest on the latter road to Crown Valley Parkway; 2) connection with the Doheny Bikeway (Trip #12) - at Junipero Serra Road, cycle west under the San Diego Freeway to Camino Capistrano; 3) connection with the Del Obispo Bikeway (Trip #13) - at Ortega Highway and La Novia Avenue, turn left (southeast) on the latter street to reach San Juan Creek or follow Ortega Highway under the San Diego Freeway to Camino Capistrano; 4) connection with the Aliso Creek Trail (Trip #29A) - at Santa Margarita Parkway and Alicia Parkway, go west on the former road to El Toro Road; 5) connection with the Mission Viejo Bikeway (Trip #30) - from Felipe Road and Oso Parkway, bike west on the latter street to Marguerite Parkway - from Olympiad Road and Alicia Parkway, bike west on the latter street to Marguerite Parkway; 6) connection with the Oso Viejo ride (Trip #42) - at Jeronimo Road and Olympiad Road, turn west on the former street; 7) connection with the Cities and Canyons ride (Trip #47) - the tours share a common segment on Santa Margarita Parkway between Alicia Parkway and Antonio Parkway.

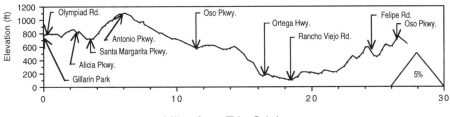

Miles from Trip Origin

TRIP #51 - COTO DE CAZA TOUR

GENERAL LOCATION: Coto De Caza

LEVEL OF DIFFICULTY: Loop - moderate
                        Distance - 11.2 miles
                        Elevation gain - long moderate grade on Coto
                            De Caza Drive

HIGHLIGHTS: **This tour is for Coto De Caza residents or guests only, as Coto De Caza is entirely private.** The route is 100 percent Class X with wide biking shoulder. The initial five-mile upgrade on Coto De Caza Drive is tedious but moderate; in addition, there are a few short climbs on the east side. The vistas include Mount Saddleback and Coto Valley with its surrounding hillsides. Slow down and admire the classy residences, the equestrian center, and the Golf and Racquet Club. Who knows? This tour may convince you to take a long look at living in this well-planned enclave.

TRAILHEAD: From the Foothill Transportation Corridor (State Highway 241), exit at Oso Parkway and continue two miles to its terminus at Coto De Caza Drive. Turn left, pass through the guard gate (a guest or resident pass is required), then turn right at Water Lily Way (the first street on the right). From the San Diego Freeway, exit east at Oso Parkway and go 6.25 miles to road's end. Continue as described above.

    The above trailhead starts near the trip's low point. An option (which leaves the hard climbing until the end of the trip) is to start at the Coto Sports and Recreation Park near Coto De Caza Drive and Vista Del Verde.

    Bring a filled water bottle. Though a reasonably short trip, there are no on-road (i.e., direct-access) water sources within Coto De Caza. A strategically located option is to divert to the Coto Sports and Recreation Park near the trip's midpoint.

TRIP DESCRIPTION: **Coto De Caza Drive and Plano Trabuco.** Return to Coto De Caza Drive and turn right (north). This segment has the heaviest (but still modest) traffic and the major amount of the trip's climb. Start uphill immediately and take in the stately residences scattered over the Coto Valley floor, on the nearby hillsides to the left, and on the more distant hillsides to the right. Pass Cantamar (0.2) and take in the head-on view of Mount Saddleback, which will remain in direct sight for over 1.5 miles.

    Follow a stair-step upgrade past Hilldale Way and the southern edge of the Coto De Caza Golf and Racquet Club (1.1). Pump past Shoal Creek in 0.4 mile, where the hills on the left squeeze toward Coto De Caza Drive. Cross San Miguel (2.0), the single road through the golf course, and reach a false crest at Calle Castile in another 1.3 miles. Enjoy a flat stretch for about 0.3 mile and pass Vista Del Verde, which has directional signs to such places as the CVCC Restaurant (right) and the Coto Sports and Recreation Park (left).

    Further climbing leads to Trigo Trail where there is an exceptionally revealing view southward that highlights the valley floor and the residence-pocketed hillsides

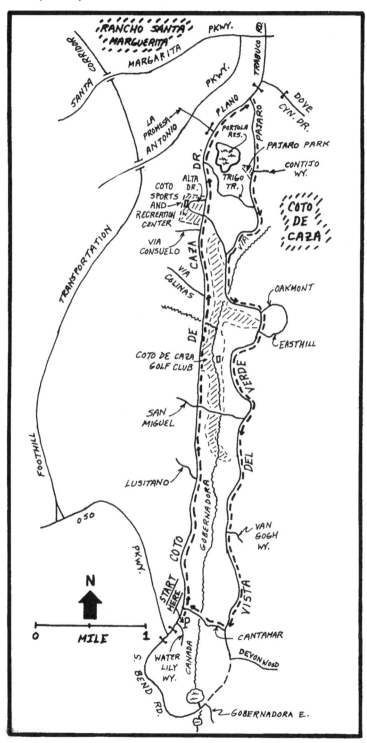

TRIP #51 - COTO DE CAZA

(4.1). In 200-300 yards, Coto De Caza Drive veers to the left and our reference route swings to the right on Plano Trabuco. Cycle another 0.6 mile in less-developed and more heavily treed environs and meet Via Pajaro at (4.8).

Via Pajaro and Vista Del Verde. Turn right, make a short climb to the trip's crest and coast past Vinedo Road (5.1), tiny Pajaro Park (5.7), and Trigo Trail (5.9). The lots are larger, the homes more stately, and there is an abundance of horses in this stretch. Also, the traffic from here to Cantamar is significantly lighter than on the west side (Coto De Caza Drive).

Pass a general store and the CVCC Restaurant, then turn left onto Vista Del Verde (6.5). Cross Cañada Gobernadora, which runs down the center of Coto Valley, and bike on a more winding road with its little ups and downs (generally downhill). The golf course comes into view again and the route hugs the course before taking a slow turn to the right past Oakmont (7.4). Continue between the course and the nearby residences, completing the turn near Cherry Hills Drive. Reach San Miguel and a nearby fire station, then coast past the entry to the Club House of the Golf and Racquet Club (8.8).

A mild 0.3-mile upgrade near Atherton Drive (9.8) interrupts the refreshing coast from the club house to Cantamar (10.5). There was no outlet by continuing south on Vista Del Verde (in early 2001), so our reference route turns east onto Cantamar, cruises to the second Cañada Gobernadora crossing and returns to Coto De Caza Drive in another 0.2 mile. From here, simply retrace the outgoing route to Water Lily Way (11.2).

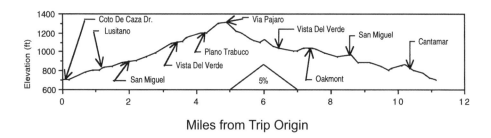

Miles from Trip Origin

CONNECTING TRIPS: REVISIT 1) Connection with the Mission Viejo Bikeway (Trip # 30) - at the northern gate at Coto De Caza Drive, continue on what is now La Promesa, turn right on Antonio Parkway, turn left on Santa Margarita Parkway, go four miles to Marguerite Parkway and turn left again; 2) connection with the Cities and Canyon ride (Trip #47) - at Via Pajaro and Plano Trabuco, stay north on the latter street; 3) connection with the Arroyo Trabuco Loop (Trip #50) - at La Promesa and Antonio Parkway, go in either direction on the latter road.

INDEX TO LANDMARKS AND ATTRACTIONS
BY TRIP NUMBER

(Bracketed Entries { } Denote Other Counties)

SUNBELT PUBLICATIONS

"Adventures in the Natural History and Cultural Heritage of the Californias"

Series Editor—Lowell Lindsay

SUNBELT'S OUTDOOR RECREATION BOOKLIST

Incorporated in 1988 with roots in publishing since 1973, **Sunbelt Publications** produces and distributes natural science and outdoor guidebooks, regional histories and reference books, plus pictorials and stories that celebrate the land and its people.

Our publishing program focuses on the Californias which are today three states in two nations sharing one Pacific shore. Sunbelt books help to discover and conserve the natural and historical heritage of unique regions on the frontiers of adventure and learning. Our books guide readers into distinctive communities and special places, both natural and man-made.

We carry hundreds of books on southern California!

Visit us online at:

www.sunbeltbooks.com